Dedicated to Duntov

"Harley Earl saw it all coming. He wanted an American sportscar and he wanted General Motors to build it. And today the Corvette is still America's only sportscar."

William L. Mitchell, 1979

Corvette!
SPORTS CAR OF AMERICA

Published by

Michael Bruce Associates, Inc.

Staff for this book

Publisher and President
M. B. Antonick

Executive Vice President
D. G. Sims

Design Director
R. J. Antonick

Graphics Director
J. F. Yaeger

Corvette! Sportscar of America is published by Michael Bruce Associates, Inc. Printing by West-Camp Press, Inc., Westerville, Ohio. Binding by the H & H Bookbinding Company, Indianapolis, Indiana. Color separations by Engraving Arts Inc., Dayton, Ohio. Typography by Dwight Yaeger, Typographer, Columbus, Ohio. Photo/text credits, page 236.

Direct correspondence to: Michael Bruce Associates, Inc., Post Office Box 396, Powell, Ohio. 43065.

1980 Annual

Limited Edition First Printing

ISBN: 0-933534-11-6

Contents

Collectors' Choices

Firestone
Firestone

The Collectors' Choice

XP-819

Ye shall not sell prototypes to the public

oops!

Dream cars have been a part of the American automobile industry for as long as most of us can remember. Harley Earl and his Motorama extravaganzas conjure up vivid memories of wild styling exercises, though a loose definition of "dream" cars could easily include thousands of engineering prototypes as well.

Through Harley Earl, and especially later through Bill Mitchell, the Corvette has a particularly rich history of one-off prototypes. From the first Motorama Corvette, to the modern derivatives of the Aero-Vette, there has hardly been a year that Chevrolet hasn't had some unique piece of Corvette machinery making the show circuit, and keeping everyone's expectations high. It might be a pure styling exercise that won't even run (though GM has generally preferred showing operable cars), an opinion sampler of something contemplated for production, or a prototype for a new chassis/engine configuration.

A question that often circulates among Corvette enthusiasts is whatever happens to these vehicles after they've served their purposes? Put more simply, how do you go about buying one of these things?

Unfortunately, the answer is that usually you don't. Though there is apparently nothing written in stone at GM proclaiming, "Ye shall not sell prototypes to the public," GM seldom does. And with the current battery of government qualification exams a car must pass, it isn't very likely that any future exotics from the GM stable will be sold to John Q, either.

That isn't to say that GM couldn't sell off some of the "used" dream cars tucked away in warehouses, or that it couldn't have done so in the past. Rumors of just such a sale, with the proceeds going to charity, make the rounds every year or two and stimulate the saliva glands of all Corvette enthusiasts in range. But it hasn't happened yet, and the smart money advises not holding your breath waiting. From GM's viewpoint, it's just a matter of nothing much to gain, maybe a lot to lose. The spectre of one of these one-off creations falling apart and resulting in a big bucks lawsuit has a definite lack of appeal for the folks at GM. Letters relieving GM of responsibility signed by the purchasers? Apparently not good enough. Legally, almost worthless, in fact.

So the great Corvette prototypes and dream cars—some of auto history's most significant vehicles—rest in museums, hide in warehouses, or have long since been chopped up for junk.

But wait. There is a bright spot in this otherwise bleak story. As long as there are enterprising individuals around who "have gasoline in their blood" as Harley Earl put it, some of these cars will escape the General's grasp. Which is as it should be. Surely, there must be sympathy for the GM end of this dilemma, but a more important issue is at stake. When a dream car has outlived its corporate usefulness, GM gets rid of it one way or another. By so doing, history is destroyed.

Our world is in a period of tremendous change. Plentiful fuel supplies are a thing of the past. In this context, so too are the cars of the fifties, sixties and even the seventies. And so too are its dream cars. A period of automotive history is vanishing right before our very eyes. Years from now, this period that we've been privileged to live through, will be written about in glorious terms by writers as the "golden age of performance," or similarly appropriate words. You can be sure enthusiasts will preserve the autos of the period, and that those cars will grow in value almost beyond imagination. So it is only right and just that at least a few of the one-off Corvettes of the period find their way to the garages of individual enthusiasts, to the people who will love, cherish, and nourish them as no museum or warehouse ever could. And so it is with XP-819.

What Is It?

You could say the saga of XP-819 has been a quiet one. Few enthusiasts have ever heard of it, let alone seen it. It was never tagged with a catchy name like Shark or Manta Ray. It didn't make the cover of all the magazines with the typical "Is this the new Corvette?" caption. In fact, you have to look very hard to find mention of it in any publication. Call General Motors' Public Relations and ask for information about the XP-819 experimental Corvette and they'll answer, "The what?"

The XP-819 didn't blaze its way across the race tracks of America. It didn't blaze its way across anything. Its most exciting moment on the track came at the GM proving grounds when it smacked a guard rail.

But semi-reliable sources (the best we could do) tell us that GM spent over a half-million dollars putting the XP-819 together. The car was a product of interdepartmental rivalry between Frank Winchell's Research and Development group, and Zora Duntov's Engineering group.

The XP-819 was designed and built in 1964 and running by 1965. Consider the history of that time. After a shaky start, the Corvair was off and running with its sporty Monza. Chevrolet had done some snazzy Monza show prototypes that were not only beautiful, but handled well. Based on what they'd learned from these rear engine cars, Winchell and his R&D people believed they could put together a Corvette with a V-8 mounted behind the rear axle, and make it handle properly.

Larry Shinoda, the stylist who figured so strongly in many Corvette designs, remembers the XP-819 well. In a meeting with Winchell, Duntov, and everybody else who counted, Shinoda recalls clearly a discussion of the XP-819 while it was still in the talking stage. Each person in the room was giving his thoughts about hanging a V-8 out the back of a Corvette, and the concensus seemed to be "no way." Duntov said it would be an "ugly duckling."

Page 8-9: *XP-819 in its restored glory. Photographed at the historical "rotating" jail in Gallatin, Missouri.* **Right above:** *A highly stylish door pillar flows nicely into the roof section. Note '68 production style backlight. XP-819 also has a removable roof section.* **Right below:** *Interior features automatic shift selector on console, forward of safety belt buckle storage device.*

Long since chopped up for junk

Finally, the floor went to Frank Winchell who said, "I don't think I'll comment until we hear from Larry Shinoda." Shinoda felt every eye in the room on him and said, "I think we can make it a beautiful car." To prove it, Shinoda led the group down to his studio to show them the drawings that he and John Schinella had worked up for the radical new Corvette. They all agreed it was beautiful, finding it hard to believe Shinoda and Schinella could take the weird configuration and make it look so good. "Where did you cheat?" asked Duntov.

What little has been written about the XP-819 maintained its handling was poor. If you believed all you read, you'd conclude the XP-819 wouldn't outhandle a Porsche, wouldn't outhandle Mercedes, would be hard pressed to outhandle a Renault Dauphine. In a word, its handling stunk.

Not so, says Shinoda. He drove the XP-819 a lot and says it handled great, but only if the special tires designed for it were used. Shinoda says the XP-819 was doing "evasive maneuvers" on the track when it hit the rail, and he's sure it was on regular street tires at the time. Shinoda remembers the XP-819 having side-guard beams in the doors, a removable roof, and some very slick styling touches. "Larry Nies was in charge of building it," says Shinoda, "and he did a tremendous job."

According to Karl Ludvigsen, who wrote one of the few accounts of the XP-819 in **Corvette — America's Star Spangled Sports Car,** the XP-819 was compactly designed with a short wheelbase made possible by the engine's rearward location, and a backbone-type frame down the center of the cockpit. Suspension was fully independent in the racing car manner, and the wheels were the same as later used on the Chaparral 2. Ludvigsen stated that a 327 cubic-inch Corvette engine was installed in the "duck-tailed bustle" at the rear of the car and connected to a modified transaxle unit from the 1963 Pontiac Tempest. The car weighed under 2,700 pounds, but fully seventy percent was on the rear wheels.

Ludvigsen continued, "Winchell's aim with this car had been to get acceptable handling with the

text continues on page 15

CAR # XP-819
MODEL FUTURE VETTE
OLOR BLUE
LANE
STALL
XP819

Left: *Original Chevy key on R&D tag, and windshield ID sticker contribute to authenticity of Tate's XP-819 dream car.* **Right:** *"In process" shots show XP-819's rough, but fairly complete condition shortly after Tate's purchase from Smokey Yunick.*

Left: *With orders from Semon Knudsen to "Chop it up and use what you can," Smokey Yunick did just that to the XP-819 chassis as these photos attest.* **Right above:** *Sophisticated components, including aluminum brake calipers, shown in their unrestored state.* **Right below:** *This shows the front and rear chassis components at the time of Tate's purchase of XP-819. The frame section between the front and rear chassis members was missing and had to be fabricated.*

extreme rearward weight bias by using front and rear tires of the same diameter but markedly different widths, much wider at the back." Former Chevrolet Research and Development engineer Paul Van Valkenburgh was quoted as saying, "The car could be set up to handle properly on a skid pad in steady-state cornering, but the transient or dynamic response was nearly uncontrollable at the limit."

Ludvigsen concluded the discussion of the XP-819 by indicating that the stability problem was never corrected satisfactorily, and that other problems, such as high cockpit temperatures, ruled out the XP-819 from consideration as a production vehicle. Larry Shinoda placed the blame more on the fact that the XP-819 couldn't accept the Chevrolet "big block" engine, and that was the coming trend at the time.

The XP-819 was apparently the first running prototype of a Corvette with aft engine placement, though Duntov's group was working somewhat in parallel on a proposal for a mid-engine Corvette during the same approximate time period. The XP-819 could also well be the first running Corvette with body-colored urethane bumpers. It had fixed seats with electrically adjustable pedals. It had a wild inner door panel, which actually formed part of the seat when the door was closed. The body and chassis were hand-made, though trim components were scavenged from the stock Corvette's parts bin when possible. From some angles, it's a strange looking thing, from others it is simply breathtaking.

But a number of factors ganged up on the XP-819 and forced its departure from grace. The Corvair, such a hit for a while, was suffering the effects of Ralph Nader and a raft of irate owners. Corvair lawsuits were piling up and threatening to cost GM a bundle. Speaking rear engine to a high GM executive being battered with the Corvair dilemma was next to suicide. And the finished version of the XP-819 wasn't loaded with advantages. As a production vehicle, it would have been expensive to build, yet would offer iffy handling, cooling and heating problems, and marginal passenger accommodation. With all this going against it, it was deemed the best thing to do was just roll it into a warehouse and forget it.

PEDALS

Left: *Detail shots of Tate's resurrected XP-819 show degree of quality GM originally put into this R&D vehicle. Note electric buttons for pedal adjustment (seats were fixed). All interior vinyl and virtually all other interior and exterior trim items are original.* **Right:** *It looks like something is missing, but Chevy engineers really "hung" the engine out back just as it appears.*

The Owner . . . and How He Got XP-819

XP-819 is now in a restored state, and in the possession of one Steve Tate, a private owner. How he got it is quite a story in itself.

The story starts in 1976, when Smokey Yunick ran an ad for "30 years of racing parts" to clean out his garage a bit. Smokey Yunick, if you didn't already know, is an extraordinary man. Born in Pennsylvania, Yunick moved to Daytona Beach, after deciding it "looked good" from the cockpits of B-17 bombers he test-piloted during the second world war. But flying was very definitely secondary to Smokey. He was first and foremost an engine man. His efforts certainly weren't confined to Chevrolet products—at one time or another, Smokey had worked with practically all American auto manufacturers—but it was with Chevrolet engines that Smokey seems to have most left his mark.

During his years of racing, and building racing engines, Smokey Yunick met and made friends with some top executives at General Motors, especially those who shared his love for racing. The list included Ed Cole, and Semon Knudsen. Knudsen headed both Pontiac and then Chevrolet, before leaving General Motors for the presidency of Ford. Henry Ford II later fired Knudsen and Knudsen became the president of White Motors. Throughout the years, many "deals" were struck behind the scenes between Yunick and his influential friends at GM to circumvent the official corporate no-racing policy of General Motors. This often included shipping components to Yunick undercover, and providing all sorts of assistance. Smokey Yunick was a man who could be trusted.

A Kansas City Corvette enthusiast, Dick Walker, saw Smokey's "30 years of parts" ad and responded. Walker, knowing something of Smokey's special relationship with Chevrolet over the years, thought there might be a chance that Smokey would have some Corvette fuel injection parts, which happened to be Walker's specific area of interest. A phone call to Smokey's place brought the response that sure, there must be some FI parts laying around somewhere, and Walker should come on down to Florida for a look.

Dick Walker found what he was looking for and more. While he was looking around, he noticed three very exotic semi-hemispherical head 302 CID Chevy racing engines with aluminum blocks. When he inquired if they could be purchased, Smokey said, "Naw, I don't think so."

Regardless, Walker was very pleased with what his trip to Florida produced and, after returning, sent a note of thanks to Smokey for his nice treatment during the visit, and for the opportunity to look around the shop and find the fuel injection parts. Smokey must have appreciated that gesture, because he let it be known later that maybe Walker could buy those aluminum engines afterall.

At this point, Dick Walker phoned his friend and fellow Corvette enthusiast, Steve Tate. He told Steve about the engines and suggested they go in together as partners to buy all three. Steve agreed, sight unseen.

A deal was struck over the phone with Smokey, and Steve and Dick hired a friend to go down with his van to Florida and pick up the engines and a few other things that Smokey was throwing in. But when the friend got there, he called back to Steve and Dick and told them there was too much to fit in the van. He needed help. That was as good an excuse as any to spend a few days in the sunshine state, so Steve and Dick hopped a plane to Daytona Beach. They figured they'd scope the situation out in person, then rent whatever vehicle they needed to get everything back home.

After arriving, Steve took advantage of Smokey's hospitality to look around a shop that was obviously filled with years of racing memories and history. After seeing about everything, or so he thought, Steve asked if he'd missed anything. One of Smokey's guys asked the boss if they should show them the experimental Corvette. Smokey said, "Sure, why not?"

In a remote paint booth that hadn't been used for years, rested the fairly complete remains of XP-819. Steve Tate couldn't believe his eyes, though he

text continues on page 22

Right: *The XP-819's unique "seat belt from door" concept is shown clearly in door panel photo. Note that under-hood photo indicated Chevy engineers borrowed from the stock Corvette parts bin when possible for items like the radiator surge tank and some brake components.*

Show 'em the experimental Corvette?

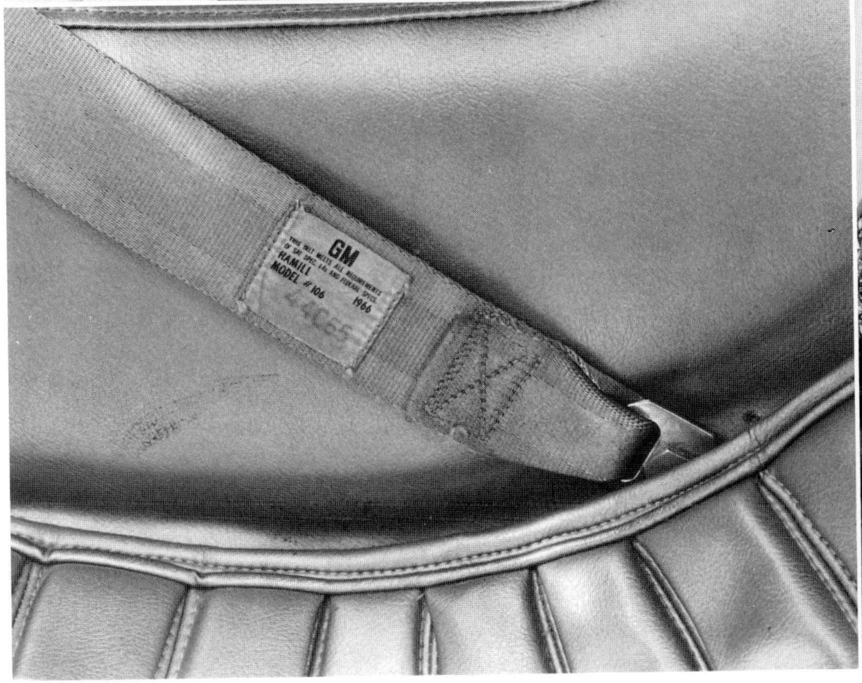
GM
HAMILL
MODEL #106
1966

Left: *XP-819 styling defies its age, especially in views showing its sleek front and side sculpturing.* **Right above:** *Larry Shinoda designed the special wheels as two-piece units that could be adjusted in rim width to accommodate different width tires. The same style later appeared on Jim Hall's Chaparrals.* **Right below:** *Note lower section of inner door panel which actually forms part of the seat when door is closed. Neato.*

wasn't exactly sure what it was his eyes were seeing. Whatever it was, it sure as hell had to be one rare Corvette. And whatever it was, he sure wanted it.

While Steve poked around the XP-819 in awe, Smokey was called away to the phone. Steve walked into the office while Smokey was still on the line and, pointing in the direction of the paint booth, mouthed, "How much?" Smokey kept right on talking on the phone, but flashed a price with his fingers. Steve said, "SOLD!" Soon, the XP-819 and crates of parts were loaded into a rented U-Haul for the trip back to Missouri.

How did the XP-819 wind up in an obscure paint booth in Daytona Beach? Well, it seems that Semon (Bunkie) Knudsen had it shipped down to his good friend in Florida. Knudsen was head of Chevrolet at the time and knew that Smokey was dabbling with rear-engine Indy cars. Knudsen also knew that Chevy had spent a bundle on the XP-819 and there were some sophisticated components in that machine. He shipped it to Smokey with instructions to chop it up and salvage anything from it he could for his racing project.

Smokey did just that. After lifting the body off intact, he hacked the chassis in two, then built a racer around the front and rear suspension components. But unfortunately, the racer had some of the original XP-819's ill-handling characteristics, so the project was scrubbed. But Smokey wisely gathered everything together and shoved it into the booth.

Rebirth Of A Dream

When Steve Tate arrived home with his new acquisition, he immediately surveyed what he had purchased. He discovered a curious assortment of stock Corvette parts, but also lots of things that were obviously hand-made just for the XP-819. Trim items like window moldings, front turn signals, rear taillights, door handles, wiper arms, and some controls, were pure Corvette. Even the grills on the rear deck were taken from the '65 stock Corvette big block hood. But a lot of the parts looked strange to him. Aluminum brake calipers. Funny two-speed automatic transaxle (it turned out to be Pontiac's).

GM wished Tate and his car would just go away

Fixed seats with a specially made, adjustable pedal setup.

The good news was that almost everything was there. The original wheels, tires, engine, upholstery, and most chassis parts. The bad news was that it was in a zillion pieces.

The XP came into Steve Tate's life at a time when, for personal reasons, he couldn't tackle the restoration by himself. He entrusted the bulk of the work to Delmar Hines, a former drag racer, Corvette enthusiast, and general Mr. Fix-anything type of guy. Hines did what you'd expect. He spent long hours studying the whole mess, reasoned as best he could how it all went back together, then put it back together. In this regard, General Motors was of little help. Chuck Jordan in Styling came through with some color glossies of the XP-819. But the engineering file, which Tate and Hines desperately needed for a 100% accurate restoration, was at first "lost" then "unavailable." Whatever transpired behind the scenes at General Motors regarding the XP-819 and Tate's acquisition of it isn't known. Officially, the Corporation appeared to just wish Tate and his car would go away. Certainly no assistance was forthcoming. However, certain individuals within GM were delighted that the car had miraculously survived and was being resurrected. Count Duntov among them.

Because of the lack of success in getting adequate information from GM, Tate and Hines had to guess about some things. The exhaust system is, for instance, their own creation and surely different from that designed for the XP-819 by R&D. That bothers Tate, though nobody is likely to point to it and say it's wrong. Who's to know? But authenticity is a big deal to people like Tate. The same line of thinking has resulted in a restoration that is not top show quality. Most of the components of the XP-819, especially body and interior, were in good enough condition to recognize the degree of quality originally attained by Chevrolet. This car was designed as an engineering test-bed, not a glittering show piece. Tate and Hines tried to restore the car to its original condition, no better, no worse.

The XP-819, as photographed today, still wears its original wheels, tires, and upholstery. Some chassis pieces had to be fabricated, but nearly everything visible is original. In some ways, Chevrolet never finished the job. Headlights, for instance, were never fitted to the pop-up mountings, nor are they now.

The public unveiling of XP-819 in its re-born state came at the big 1978 Bloomington Corvette Corral in Bloomington, Illinois. Did it draw a gigantic crowd of enthusiastic admirers? No. According to Tate, most spectators thought it was a Volkswagen kit car. (Come to think of it, it does sort of look like one.) This is a car that, for the most part, was unknown. It didn't get the magazine bally-hoo. At Bloomington, thousands of people walked by one of the few dream Corvettes ever to escape the grasp of General Motors. . . and kept on walking. You can't blame them. It took a very astute Corvette enthusiast to realize what he was viewing.

It was at the 25th anniversary meet staged in Flint by the National Corvette Restorers Society that Duntov saw Tate's XP-819. Tate allowed it to be displayed for one week at GM's Sloan museum, and witnesses said sight of the XP-819 nearly brought tears to Zora's eyes. He said something like, "I was told it had been destroyed. . . how can this be?"

Later Steve Tate got together with Zora Duntov to talk about the XP-819. Though it wasn't one of his personal pet projects, Zora remembered it well. It is probably safe to say that not much happened around Chevrolet related to the Corvette that Zora didn't get into sooner or later. He remembered driving the XP-819, and he remembered its problems. He also remembered that the XP-819 was in a sense the lead off of a number of fierce mid-engined Corvettes that Duntov put his heart and soul into. At some point in his twenty-two year Corvette career, Duntov came to the realization that his cherished dream of building the ultimate Corvette, the Corvette that would out-perform every other production sports car in the world, would never be. Viewing a car like the XP-819 has to be a mixture of pain and pleasure. Pain in the knowledge of what could have been, but was not to be. Pleasure in the knowledge that enthusiasts like Steve Tate, and thousands of others, understand.

The Collectors Choice

1975 Convertible

You probably should call it a convertible, not a roadster. Convertible doesn't sound as classy, but at least you'll be in the majority.

There are three schools of thought on this crucial matter. The first says that you can only call a car a roadster if it seats two, has a trunk / rumbleseat, and has side curtains in place of roll-up side windows. If you buy that, Chevrolet hasn't made a Corvette roadster since 1955.

The second school of thought is the most common and is supported by most dictionary definitions of "roadster" which leave out the business of side curtains. If you take the part about trunk or rumble seat as meaning something accessible from the rear, the conclusion is that the last true Corvette roadster was the 1962 model. This was the last with an externally opening trunk.

However, if you really want to call all open Corvettes roadsters, it's not too difficult to find reference sources that make no mention of how access to trunk is made. Just open your Webster's and point to "roadster" and say, "Show me where it says you have to get to the trunk from the outside." Just don't bother to look up trunk.

Whatever you call it, Chevrolet built Corvettes with tops that folded down through the 1975 model year. Then, during the last week of July, 1975, they stopped. They stopped because convertibles didn't sell well and there might be problems with safety standards. Because convertibles were more expensive to make, and they leaked more, and they rattled more, and the soft tops deteriorated. They stopped because, thanks to the fouling of our environment, windows-up air conditioned driving became more popular. Oh yes, there were lots of good reasons.

The only problem is, there have always been people willing to pay the price, regardless of what it might be, to enjoy the unique experience of open-top motoring. It is hard to imagine, but many young people now growing up will never have the opportunity to ride in an open car. The closest they'll be able to come will be to power-down a window and hang their head out in the wind. That won't quite do it. The true sensation will become something romantics write about. Horse-drawn sleigh rides at Christmas through freshly fallen snow. Breezing down a country lane at dusk in a convertible.

It comes as no surprise then when Chevrolet announced that 1975 would see the last Corvette convertible built, speculation started as to the future value of these models. By comparison to previous years, convertible production in 1975 was low, just 4,629 units. In the first years of coupe and convertible availability, the mix was fairly even and usually favored the convertible slightly. The real decline of the Corvette convertible started in 1968 when the T-top was introduced. The partially open roof with

Stingray
GOODYEAR
STEELGARD
CORVETTE

hard filler panels was a compromise that suited many people. The die-hards kept buying convertibles, but those on the fence fell to the T-top side.

By 1975, Chevrolet just decided to let the Corvette join the bulk of its other lines that were phasing out convertibles that year. This created a minor spurt of demand, but most people, including many dealers, either weren't aware or didn't care that the convertible Corvette's days were limited.

Bob Kaiser, a Chevrolet dealer across the street from the St. Louis Corvette plant, was an exception. He requested the last Corvette convertible built, the very last one. He was allowed to buy it and the last Chevrolet Caprice convertible, too. Apparently no one else was smart enough to ask. By the way, the Caprice was immediately sold to a customer, but Mr. Kaiser put the Corvette away for himself. Kaiser made his first Corvette sale in 1953 to the late Gil Newsome, a well known radio personality, and he ordered his '75 in white with red interior to match.

1975: Much More Than Just The Last Convertible

It used to be that someone who knew cars could spot a model year from two blocks away. That's no longer the case for the Corvette or any other car. But it is unfair to lump the 1975 Corvette in with all the other Corvettes that look similar, because it is a year unto itself with many unique characteristics.

In the year preceding the 1975, a body-color rear bumper system was introduced on the Corvette as part of evolving technology to meet Federal impact standards. Most Corvette buffs know that this 1974 rear system for the Corvette had a two-piece outer shell with the dividing line running vertically down the center. And they know that subsequent Corvettes had a one-piece rear cap. In fact, a rumor used to circulate at Corvette meets to the effect that

An opening at Chevy Engineering

Some ditched the entire system

the engineer who designed the two-piece system had flatly stated it simply couldn't be made one-piece. So the following year there was an opening at Chevrolet Engineering!

What many don't realize is that the 1975 rear Corvette bumper is completely different from the '74. Not only does the '75 have a new shock-absorbing system inside, it is different outside also. "Pads" painted to look like rubber were added at the corners and the sides were reshaped and tapered. The result is a much slimmer appearance, though you have to see both years together to appreciate the degree of improvement. The pads were added to the front bumper also, and it received an inner core of honeycomb plastic to better absorb impact.

Though it might not be considered an improvement by most, 1975 was the year for introduction of the catalytic converter on Corvettes. By cleaning the exhaust in the exhaust system, Chevrolet engineers were able to re-calibrate the engine for slight improvements in performance and economy. However, the Corvette's dual engine exhausts were piped into a single converter, located under the floor on the passenger's side which then split again into dual exhaust exits. This had the effect of strangling the engine to a degree with increased back-pressure. Some owners responded by ditching the entire system and putting on '69 straight-through side exhausts.

Addition of the catalytic converter also meant that the 1975 Corvette was the first that required use of non-leaded fuel and the special sized fuel filler opening.

Emission control considerations led Chevrolet to introduce its HEI (High Energy Ignition) system on the '75 model Corvette. This replaced the breakpoint distributor with an electronic unit that (hopefully) requires no maintenance. The plug non-fouling characteristics of unleaded fuel combined with the carefully controlled spark distribution of the breakerless ignition meant that periods between tune-ups were stretched dramatically. The deletion of a standard distributor also dictated that the Corvette's tach drive had to become electronic. The earlier manual drive was geared to the center shaft of the distributor. Thanks to emission certification grief, fuel economy emphasis, and a general wave of anti-performance sentiment, the optional engines available for 1975 was down to one, the L-82. And even it wasn't used for a time because of problems passing emission tests. This meant that the previous year was the last for the famed "big block" Corvettes. 1975 was the first year since 1966 that a Corvette buyer didn't have a choice of engine displacement. The choice of only two horsepower engines hadn't been so slim since 1955. As compensation for all this, the buyer of a '75 L-82 did get a special hood emblem. And all '75 Corvettes have a kilometer per hour subface on the speedometer. Look, 50 mph equals 80 kilometers per hour. Some joker could say he was doing 80 when he shifted. Big deal. All in all, it wasn't a good time for performance addicts.

For looks, the '75 is a tough one to beat. Factors may have ganged up to put the Corvette's performance into a stall, but there was no reason it still couldn't look great. Ten beautiful exterior colors could be mixed with seven interiors, five in leather, to produce stunning combinations. And the hardtop for the convertible was still available in both painted and vinyl-covered surfaces. The regular hardtop went for $267, while the vinyl job set you back $350.

The Owner: Corvette Passion Almost Cost Him His College Degree

When Marc Erwin was thirteen years old, he went to the 1966 **Cavalcade Of Wheels** in nearby South Bend, Indiana. There he saw and fell head over heels in love with the Mako Shark II. Remember now, this was 1966. The original Sting Ray body series still had a year to run. The Mako Shark was being used by GM Design to prepare the public for the next generation of Corvettes starting with the 1968.

Needless to say, when the 1968 model did come out, Marc Erwin decided he'd have to have one. He surely didn't know how, but he'd have it someway. In

1969, he got up the nerve to actually sit in a yellow Corvette on the showroom floor of his local Chevy dealership. That just made matters worse.

In 1970, Marc went off to college. First things first, after all, and the Corvette would just have to wait. But in 1972, Marc began hearing rumors. He heard that GM was thinking of dropping the Corvette, rather than spend the money to make it comply with federal bumper standards, emission standards, crashworthiness, and the like. Then he heard the rumor that makes the rounds about every three or four years . . . the rumor of the Corvette body going to metal. Linked with the need to meet all this government business, the metal body possibility started to take on a more plausible ring.

One way or the other, it began to look like the Corvette that Marc loved wouldn't be around much longer. He decided to quit college, go to work, and order his new Corvette while he still could. He'd decided long ago, after looking at numerous second-hand Corvettes, that only a new one would do for him. This was not to be a casual purchase. This was to be a car that Marc would keep for a lifetime.

Most parents would have some difficulty understanding a scheme requiring quitting college midway through to buy a car. Marc's parents, sure enough, didn't understand. Fortunately the rumors

text continues on page 32

A car for a lifetime

Corvettes from the post '68 period have become so commonplace, one can almost forget how beautifully the side contours are styled.

1975 Corvette Options And Retail Prices

Number	Suggested Retail	Description
1YZ37	6810.10	Base Corvette Sport Coupe
1YZ67	6550.10	Base Corvette Convertible
—	154.00	Custom Interior Trim
A31	93.00	Electric Power Windows
A85	41.00	Custom Shoulder Belts
C07	267.00	Auxiliary Hardtop (for convertibles)
C08	350.00	Vinyl Covered Auxiliary Hardtop
C50	46.00	Rear Window Defroster
C60	490.00	Air Conditioning
FE7	7.00	Gymkhana Suspension
—	12.00	Positraction Axle, Optional Ratio
J50	50.00	Power Brakes
L82	336.00	Optional 205 HP, 350 CI Engine
M21	nc	4-Speed Close Ratio Transmission
M40	nc	Turbo Hydramatic Automatic Transmission
N37	82.00	Tilt-Telescopic Steering Column
N41	129.00	Power Steering
QRM	35.00	White Stripe SBR Tires, GR70 x 15
QRZ	48.00	White Letter SBR Tires, GR70 x 15
U05	4.00	Dual Horns
U58	284.00	AM-FM Stereo Radio
U69	178.00	AM-FM Radio
UA1	15.00	Heavy Duty Battery
UF1	5.00	Map Light
Z07	400.00	Off Road Suspension and Brake Package

Note: The cost of the M-40 Automatic Transmission with the L-82 engine option was $120.00.

Interior And Exterior Colors

Exterior Body	Wheels	Interior (Recommended by GM)
Bright Blue	Silver	Black, Dark Blue, Silver
Steel Blue	Silver	Black, Dark Blue, Silver
Bright Green	Silver	Black, Neutral, Medium Saddle, Silver
Orange Flame	Silver	Black Neutral, Medium Saddle
Dark Red	Silver	Black, Neutral, Dark Red, Medium Saddle, Silver
Mille Miglia Red	Silver	Black, Neutral, Dark Red, Medium Saddle, Silver
Medium Saddle	Silver	Black, Neutral, Medium Saddle
Silver	Silver	Black, Dark Blue, Dark Red, Medium Saddle, Silver
Classic White	Silver	Black, Dark Blue, Neutral, Dark Red, Medium Saddle, Silver
Bright Yellow	Silver	Black, Neutral, Medium Saddle

Note: Black, Dark Blue, Red, Saddle and Silver were available in leather.

CORVETTE

died down. Chevrolet would indeed keep building Corvettes, for a while at least. Peace and tranquility returned to the Erwin household.

Marc graduated from college with a degree in education and promptly set out to find a teaching position. He soon signed a contract for a total of $8800 for the following school year. He then went about the task of ordering his new Corvette. Tallying up the options he wanted, his new Corvette would list for $8749.10. Which didn't exactly leave much money to live on. Thank God for lending institutions.

The time was late summer. Marc shopped the local dealers and couldn't wrangle much of a deal. It was all talk of list price or even a few hundred over. So he tried one of those computer ordering firms. One of those deals that advertise, "Any new car for $50 over dealer's cost." Except for Corvettes and other "special" cars. However, the computer did promise "substantial" savings even on those.

The first response from the computer priced a '74 model. Marc figured he might as well have a new model, and requested that Mr. Computer try again. It did, and came back with a quote of $8185 for the '75 listing for a retail price of $8749.10. One thing complicating this whole matter was that the price of Corvettes had shot up dramatically. General Motors blamed the new bumper systems and catalytic converter. Whatever the reasons, the base price of the Corvette convertible had jumped from $5765.50 in 1974, to $6537.10 (later $6550.10) for a '75. Maybe quitting school two years earlier wasn't such a dumb idea afterall.

At this time, Marc had no idea that the '75 would be the last Corvette convertible. He'd never owned anything but convertibles, and never considered ordering his Corvette any other way. One thing was particularly distressing though. Marc had intended to order the biggest engine possible and he thought that would be a 454. Deletion of the big blocks in 1975 was a blow from GM that Marc hadn't expected.

Marc took his computer deal to his local Chevy man and handed it to him. "Match this, and I'll order the car from you." The salesman and sales manager went off to a corner for what seemed like

STEELGARD
GOOD/YEAR

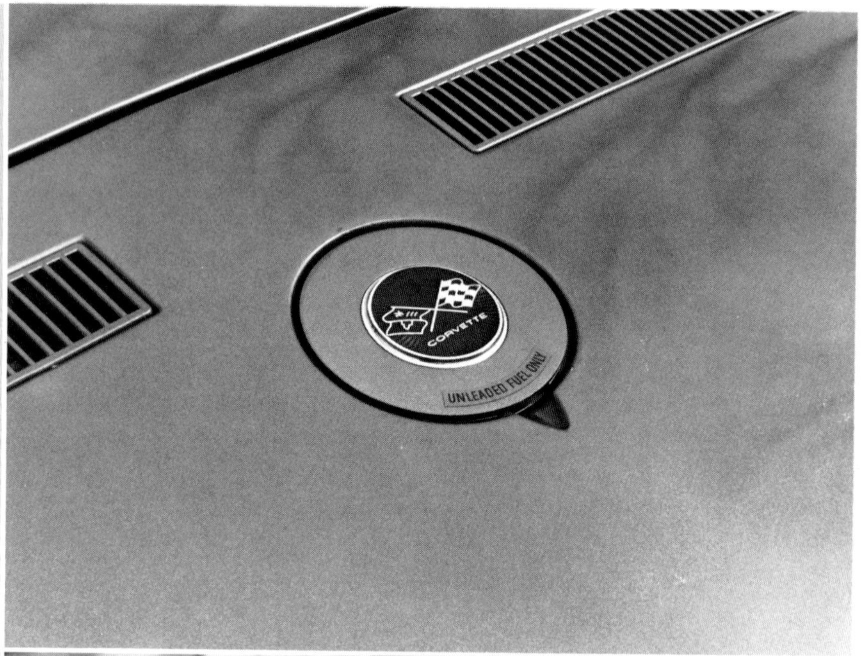
CORVETTE
UNLEADED FUEL ONLY

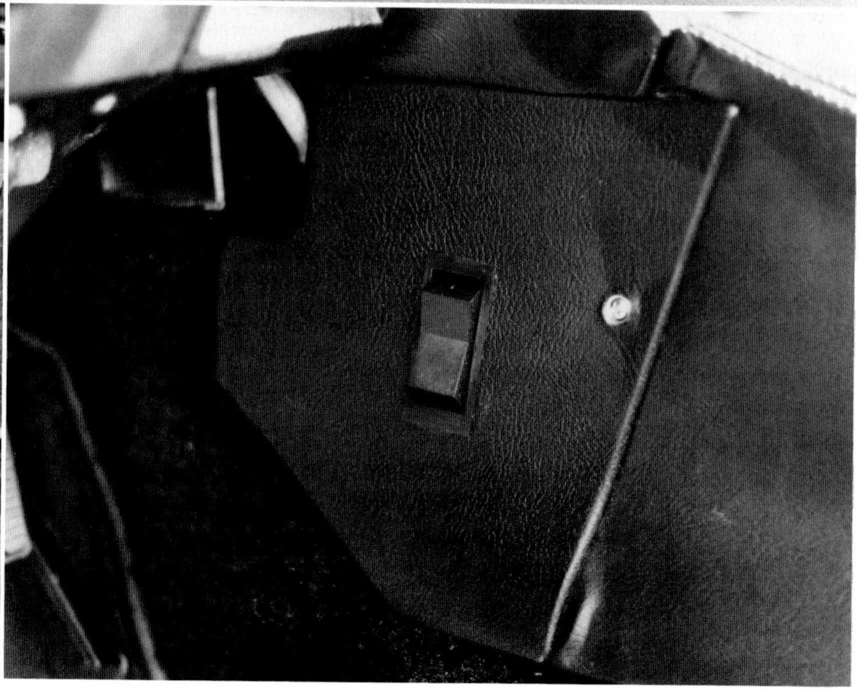

hours. Marc says he felt like he was getting the "Wheels" treatment.

Finally the salesman returned. With an expression indicating that this deal would probably bankrupt the dealership, he said they'd be willing to order the car for $8100. Take it or leave it. Marc told him to order it. The date was November 4, 1974.

Big deal

The convertible Corvette Marc ordered was equipped as follows:

A31 Power Windows	93.00
C08 Auxiliary Black Vinyl Hardtop	350.00
C50 Rear Window Defogger	46.00
C60 Four-Season Air Conditioning	490.00
J50 Power Brakes	55.00
L82 Special 350-4 BBL V-8 Engine	336.00
M40 Turbo-Hydra-Matic Transmission	120.00
N37 Tilt-Telescopic Steering Wheel	82.00
N41 Power Steering	129.00
UF1 Map Light	5.00
U05 Dual Horns	4.00
U58 AM/FM Stereo Radio	248.00
QRZ GR70-15/B Stl Belted Radial W/L	48.00
192 LBB2 Black Custom Interior	154.00

Marc considers himself a patient fellow. He only called the dealer once a month for a status report on his car. He doesn't remember exactly what he was told, but something about the engine being on hold rings a bell. At the five month point, Marc Erwin remembers that he was about ready to "chew holes in the dealer's brochures."

On the last day of April, 1975, the salesman called in a panic. "Your car is in, but something's wrong. You've got to get down here right away." Marc had visions of his new Corvette laying in a heap, having been dropped from the car hauler.

Things weren't so bad. The salesman had made two mistakes in ordering the car. First he specified the black vinyl roof as CO7 with a side note about vinyl. He should have marked CO8, a separate order code for black vinyl. Next, he forgot to figure in the extra $120 for the heavy-duty automatic required with the L-82 engine option when he figured the original deal. The real problem was that this was the last day of the month, and the salesman was afraid that Marc would refuse to complete the deal. Refusing meant that the salesman would miss his quota.

The dealer offered to forget about the lost $120 in profit if Marc would forget about the top mixup. To seal the deal, a set of FREE floor mats were even thrown in. Such generosity combined with the excitement of finally getting his dream car was enough. Mr. Erwin drove out in his new Corvette.

Which brings up an interesting point. Prior to driving home from the dealership that evening, Marc Erwin had never even driven a Corvette. Talk about looks selling a car.

Driving home was uneventful, except that it was rush hour and Marc remembers feeling that everyone on the road was out to get him and his new Corvette. In a great display of Indiana defensive driving, the Corvette made it home safe and sound.

Close inspection of the new pride of the neighborhood by all of the neighborhood residents revealed that this was indeed something worth waiting for. Except for little details of workmanship like an upside down gas cap emblem and a crooked "E" in the C-O-R-V-E-T-T-E lettering on the rear deck, St. Louis did itself proud on this one. Marc corrected the gas cap, but kept the "E" the way it was. Even though it is his first and only Corvette, Marc is an appreciator of only factory original cars and plans to keep his just that way. Today, with just over 4,500 miles, it looks like it was just driven off the assembly line.

Notes on the windshield

The purchase of a new Corvette has met every expectation of Marc Erwin. He delights in driving it, though it sees only limited service. Since the day it was new, this Corvette has never spent one night outside. Neat trick since Marc lives in an apartment complex. Fortunately, this complex has garages available, and Marc has a double unit for his Corvette and '64 GTO convert, his "driver."

Marc says he'd never sell his Corvette for any price. He waited too long for it and now it just can't be replaced. Besides, it's just too much fun. It's the center of attention wherever he goes. It never leaves his sight for more than a few moments when out of the garage. But when it does, there is invariably a "if you'd like to sell this Corvette . . ." note left on the windshield. Ah, how sweet it is.

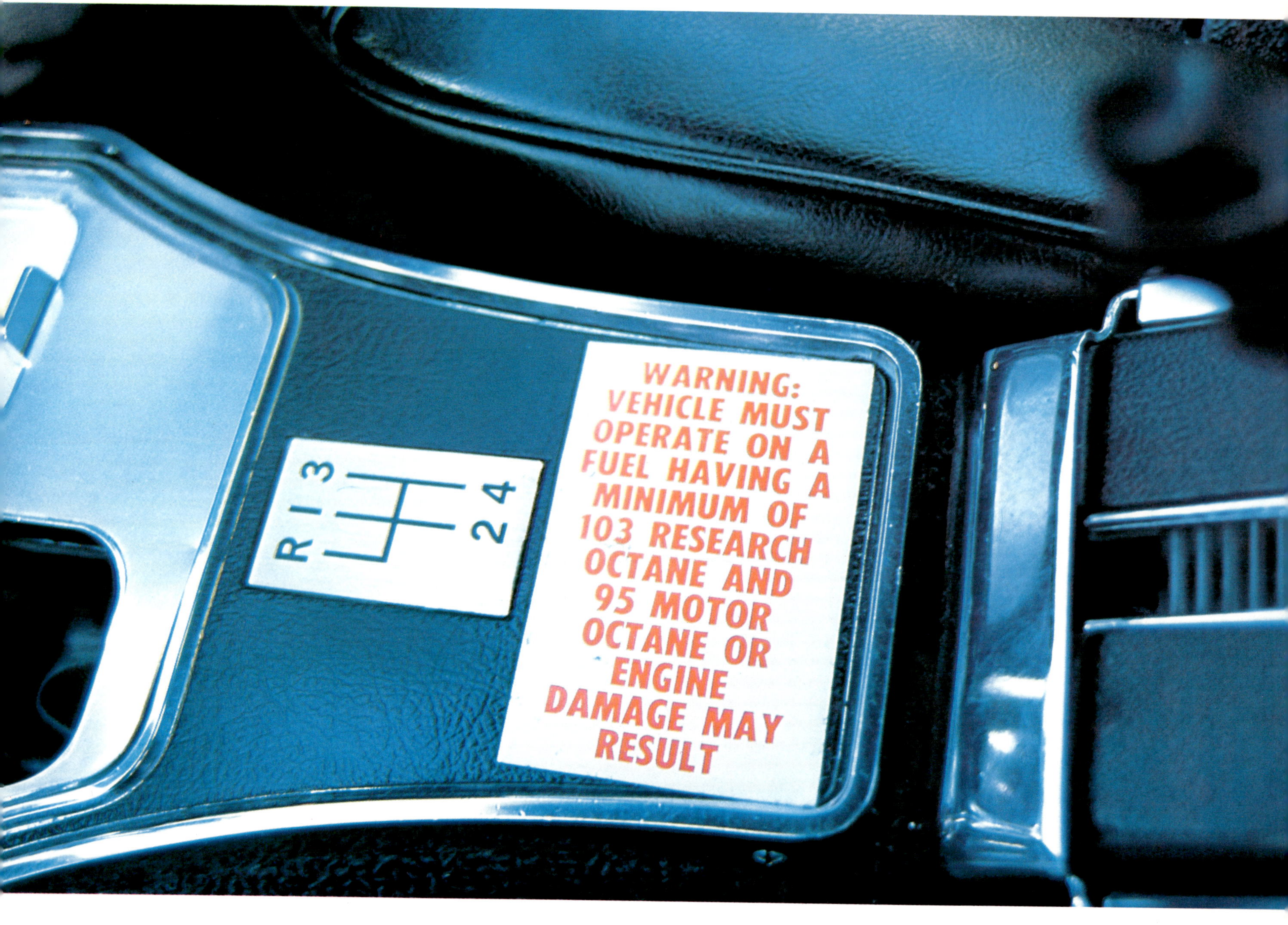
R 1 3
2 4
WARNING:
VEHICLE MUST
OPERATE ON A
FUEL HAVING A
MINIMUM OF
103 RESEARCH
OCTANE AND
95 MOTOR
OCTANE OR
ENGINE
DAMAGE MAY
RESULT

L-88

The Collectors' Choice

1967 Coupe

It's amazing how people adapt. Not too many years ago, sports car buffs got really upset if a model hung around for more than three or four years without a major body change. Consider the 1967 Corvette, for instance. It was the fifth year for the Sting Ray shape introduced in 1963. Heavens. And, it was supposed to be an all-new body, styled after the Mako Shark dream car. Corvette enthusiasts were so mad they responded by ignoring the '67 to the extent that it became the first Corvette model to not outsell the previous year (except for 1955, which is another story altogether). Production in 1967 reached only 22,940, lowest since 1964. And only 8,504 of those were coupes.

Maybe it's no wonder Chevrolet had trouble selling '67 Corvettes, considering how Chevy went about it. Rather than proclaim the '67 model a proud continuation of the fabulous Sting Ray introduced in 1963 (notice how easy it is to scope this out a dozen years later?), ad writers felt hell-bent to proclaim the "all new" aspects of the '67. Which is understandable, since that's what everybody was conditioned to expect. But with the '67 Corvette, that presented some problems.

Consider the task of writing the dealer brochure for the Sting Ray introduction in 1963. Easy. "Graceful body panels and compound-curved side windows emphasize the miles-ahead aerodynamic design. Power-operated, retractable headlamps rotate out of sight to blend into the unobstructed hood line. Doors extend upward into the roof, adding armchair ease and comfort to sliding in and out . . . Corvette's new frame is stronger and more torsionally rigid than in past models. The new four-wheel independent suspension irons out even the rutted trails, keeps handling steady and sure . . . the new Corvette's weight is distributed in a different way. More than half the weight now rests on the rear wheels — a first among modern American front-engine cars . . . The rear suspension features a three-link independent system at each wheel. A radius arm running from the frame to the rear spindle support, a control rod attached to the differential and wheel spindle, and the double universal-jointed tubular axle shaft combine to provide nearly vertical wheel movement. One multi-leaf transverse spring (bolted to the differential carrier) extends from rear wheel to rear wheel and takes only vertical suspension loads. Braking, acceleration, and lateral forces are transmitted by the radius arms, axles, and control rods to the differential and the frame. The differential assembly is attached to the frame by a bolted-in crossmember; large rubber cups serve to dampen driveline vibrations. Small movements of the differential are taken up by universal joints on the one-piece propeller shaft."

It goes on and on. But now listen to what the writer had to resort to for the "new" '67, "the newly designed parking brake lever stands ready at hand on the center console. And overhead, there's a new vinyl-covered foam-and-fiber-cushioned headlining with special niches for the padded sun visors. More features worth mentioning: newly designed gas filler door and door sill moldings."

The point is that the '67 Corvette was not an all new car. But it was the ultimate refinement of one of the finest series of automobiles ever produced. It is no secret now that the '67 Corvette is one of the all-time favorites. Many people who know Corvettes flatly state that it is the best Corvette ever made . . . period. From the status of a model about which ad writers had to scrape hard for something to say, to **THE** Corvette to have.

Why? Well, sometimes it takes the passage of a few years for all the facts to gel so that the reasons for emergence of a single model like the '67, a model that should have been just another Corvette, can be analyzed and explained.

In the case of the '67, the familiar name of Zora Arkus-Duntov again figures strongly. It was he who tipped the scales and put the kabash on the original plan to revise the '67 to strongly resemble the wild Mako Shark. As Duntov put it in a 1977 CSA interview, "The new model Corvette which appeared in 1968 was supposed to appear in 1967. Styling had completely finished the design of this production Corvette and the design was based very strongly on the Mako Shark dream car. The fender peaks on this car were so high that the visibility was very poor and there was a very confined feeling in the cockpit."

Duntov continued, "I took Pete Estes, then Chevrolet's general manager, for a ride in this car and explained to him that I believed it would be a mistake to sell it to the public. He agreed and the design was cancelled. Naturally, Styling was very upset. I understood, but what else could we do?"

Duntov's criticisms were not the only factors involved in postponing the introduction of a Mako Shark-inspired production Corvette. Federal regulations were starting to creep into car design, and the new Corvette coupes were to have removable roof panels which were causing severe design headaches. Everything considered, it just became obvious that the thing to do was to get one more year out of the Sting Ray body before the change.

That left designers with the last minute task of doing a few things to spruce up the '67 model and give it a little identity. Rather than "tack" things on the body, they did just the opposite. They removed trim from the body and created the least adorned Corvette ever. Many believe this is the key ingredient in the popularity of the '67 model now.

The sides of the '67 were devoid of any trim. Side fender flag emblems were gone, and the roof pillar of the coupe was perfectly smooth. There was still a nose emblem, but it was of a smaller design than previous years. Side fender engine air louvers were still present and functional, but changed in 1967 to a five vent design instead of the three used in 1965 and 1966.

The new "clean" look carried over to the wheels, also. The new Corvette body was slated for "rally" style wheels to replace conventional hubcaps. The logical thing for Chevrolet to do was to carry-over the standard hubcap from 1966, perhaps with a new paint scheme or spinner. But the government had come to the odd conclusion that spinning things on hubcaps were somehow a dangerous hazard, so they had to come off the '67. Chevrolet decided to go with the new rally style, but there was a problem with rim widths. The rage of the day was wide wheels, and the Mako-inspired production Corvette was designed with fender clearance to accept much fatter rubber. But the '67 couldn't comfortably accept a rim wider than six inches. So a six-inch rally wheel was designed exclusively for the '67. In 1968, when the Mako-based Corvette finally made it, the wheels were seven inch. Though the wheels are similar in appearance, the '67 wheel, trim ring, and center cone are all unique. If you exclude the "Bel Air" discs used on the first handful of '53 Corvettes built, and the small caps used on wide-rim optioned Corvettes for several years, these '67 rally wheels were the cleanest styled ever to appear on a Corvette. Chevrolet had planned to paint the steel section black to contrast with the bright trim ring and center cone, but changed to silver in keeping with the "toned down" look they were striving for. This switch has caused confusion, because many promotion photos (including the dealer brochure shots) show the '67 wheel accented in black.

The unexpected carrying-over of the Sting Ray body to 1967, and the government wheel spinner ban, combined to create another item unique to the '67 model; cast aluminum wheels that bolted on. Cast aluminum wheels first appeared in 1963 as an across-the-parts-counter dealer option. The wheels available for the 1963-1964, 1965, and 1966 Corvettes

Right: *Snazzy promotional photo highlights exquisitely clean body surfaces of '67 model Corvette. Tree dweller unidentified.*

Cleanest ever

had subtle differences, but all attached with knock-off spinners mated to adapting hubs. For 1967, the wheel was redesigned to bolt directly to the standard hub, then the bolts were covered with a snap-on trim cap. Where the earlier knock-off wheels have a gutsy, business-only look, the '67 wheels have a feel of detailed elegance, much in keeping with the '67's overall feel. All of the 1963 through 1967 aluminum wheels have 36 ribs, but the ribs of the '67 were designed thinner. This was done to present a more pleasing appearance where the ribs of the trim cap mesh into the ribs of the wheel. It is this minor difference in rib width that contributes to the finely detailed look of the '67 style.

Some aftermarket reproductions of the '67 bolt-on aluminum wheel do not have the same elegance because the ribs are thicker. While Chevrolet designed a completely new wheel for '67, the reproduction molds were made with a common rib section and interchangeable center sections for the two different styles. This resulted in a lower mold cost, but a '67 aluminum wheel which was really a hybrid. It had a '67 center section, with '63-'66 ribs.

The gas filler cap of each 1963 through 1967 model was unique, but the '67 is especially so because it is the only one painted to match the color of the car. The cap itself is metal and trimmed with a small crossed-flag emblem. Designers placed the backup lamp for the '67 above the license holder.

The interior of the 1967 was not drastically changed, but did see some refinements. The seat covering design was completely new. Seats were more highly styled, but actually offered slightly less "bucket" feel. For the first time on a Corvette, the seat back would not tilt forward for access to the rear without first releasing it with a handle located on the side of the seat. In previous Sting Rays, each seat was held in place with just two bolts at the front. This made for easy installation, as the rear portion of the seat simply slid into retaining clips. But the safety march was on in 1967, and this model Corvette's seats bolted in at all four corners. The fore and aft adjustment knob for the '67 seat was changed to a chrome, screw-on ball.

text continues on page 45

1967 CORVETTE PRODUCTION

RPO/CODE	DESCRIPTION	RETAIL COST	UNITS INSTALLED	%
19437	Base Corvette Sport Coupe	$4388.75	8,504	37.1
19467	Base Corvette Convertible	4240.75	14,436	62.9
A01	Tinted Glass—All Windows	15.80	11,331	49.4
A02	Tinted Glass—Windshield	10.55	6,558	28.6
A31	Windows—Electric Control	57.95	4,036	17.6
A82	Head Restraints	42.15	1,762	7.7
A85	Shoulder Harness	26.35	1,426	6.2
C07	Auxiliary Top	231.75	6,880	47.6
C08	Exterior Soft Trim Roof Cover	52.70	1,966	13.6
C48	Heater Deletion	−97.85	35	.2
C60	Air Conditioning	412.90	3,788	16.5
F41	Special Front and Rear Suspension	36.90	2,198	9.6
J50	Power Brakes	42.15	4,766	20.8
J56	Heavy Duty Brakes	342.30	267	1.2
K19	Air Injection Reactor	47.55	2,573	11.2
K66	Transistor Ignition	73.75	5,759	25.1
L36	Optional 390 HP, 427 CID Engine	200.15	5,933	25.9
L68	Optional 400 HP, 427 CID Engine	305.50	2,101	9.2
L71	Optional 435 HP, 427 CID Engine	437.10	3,754	16.4
L79	Optional 350 HP, 327 CID Engine	105.35	6,375	27.8
L88	Optional 430 HP, 427 CID Engine	947.90	20	.1
L89	Optional Aluminum Heads for L-71	368.65	16	.1
M20	Four Speed Transmission	184.35	9,157	39.9
M21	Four Speed Transmission, Close Ratio	184.35	11,015	48.0
M22	Four Speed Transmission, Heavy Duty	237.00	20	.1
M35	Powerglide Automatic Transmission	194.35	2,324	10.1
N03	36 Gallon Fuel Tank	198.05	2	—
N11	Off Road Service Exhaust	36.90	2,326	10.1
N14	Side Mount Exhaust System	131.65	4,209	18.3
N36	Telescopic Steering Column	42.15	2,415	10.5
N40	Power Steering	94.80	5,747	25.1
N89	Cast Aluminum Bolt-On Wheels	268.30	720	3.1
P92	Whitewall Tires, 7.75 x 15	31.35	13,445	58.6
QB1	Redline Tires, 7.75 x 15	46.65	4,230	18.4
U15	Speed Warning Indicator	10.55	2,108	9.2
U69	AM-FM Radio	172.75	22,193	96.7
—	Leather Seat Trim	79.00	1,601	7.0

Note: Percentages are based on total production of 22,940; except for option N03 (coupe only) is based on production of 8,504 coupes, and options C07 and C08 (convertibles only) are based on production of 14,436

Both the standard "rally" wheel and the optional "bolt on" typify the elegance strived for in the '67 model.

The hand brake location for the Mako-influenced production Corvettes was moved between the seats from its old location under the dash, and Chevrolet designers decided to move it in '67 too. A number of less noticeable items also changed. The dash control knobs were new, flatter and bigger. The turn signal lever looked different, and worked differently too. In the '67, it could be held down temporarily for lane changing. The door sill plates and seat belt buckles were changed. The grab bar above the glove box disappeared. The controls for fresh air were moved from beside the steering column to beside the radio console. Moving the parking brake to the area between the seats required that the retaining clips for seat belt buckles not in use be moved to the sides of the parking brake console. The twisting door lock button on the inner door panel was moved forward for better access.

General Motors went on a quality binge in 1967, and started placing "GM Mark of Excellence" mylar stickers on the inside door pillars of all its 1967 models, Corvettes included. They embarrassingly ceased this practice at the end of the model year after finding that many of the stickers fell off. It also didn't help that assembly workers delighted in putting the stickers on upside-down.

Air conditioning was ordered on 3,788 Corvettes in 1967, or 16.5% of total production. Contrary to previous practice, an air conditioned Corvette ceased to be identified by a window decal in 1967. Air conditioning could be ordered with any Corvette engine in 1967, except for the 435 bhp L-71/L-89 and, of course, the L-88, with which you couldn't even get a heater.

The '67 Corvette continued the four-wheel disc brake system introduced on the '65. The caliper design was modified slightly in '67 for better corrosion resistance, but the big improvement was a dual master cylinder. This provided two wheel stopping power in the event of hydraulic failure, and the driver was alerted to the malfunction by a warning light on the dash. This was the same warning light as used to warn of emergency brake engagement.

Color choice in 1967 was excellent. Seven different interiors could be matched to ten exterior acrylic lacquer finishes. Actually, there were eight interiors, because the white came with either blue or black carpeting and instrument panel. All standard interiors were vinyl, but genuine leather could be specified with any but the white or green seat interior. The real leather set you back a mere $79. In 1967, the optional hardtop for the convertible could be ordered covered in black vinyl, instead of painted body color. 1,966 of the 14,436 convertibles delivered in '67 were so equipped.

The standard steering wheel in the '67 looks like all other Sting Rays from 1964 on up, but it too was slightly modified. The rim is the same, but the horn button is slightly thinner and more rounded. The optional telescopic wheel adjusted with a lever over the button, rather than the special button used previously. A collapsible steering column became standard equipment. A four-way flasher was mounted to the right of the steering column, another Corvette first. While lap belts were standard, shoulder belts were optional in '67. But the shoulder belt anchoring device is on all Corvettes built in '67. Also optional were head restraints. Clearly, many of the changes and new options of the '67 were safety-inspired.

Throughout the production year, seven different engines were available in the Corvette. The standard engine remained the 327 cubic-inch, 300 horsepower unit that had served Corvette so well. It came equipped with a manual three-speed transmission, though all but a fraction were fitted with the optional four-speeds or automatics. These standard engines had painted steel valve covers and painted cast iron intake manifolds. The optional sister to this engine, and the only other "small block" for 1967, was the 327/350. This engine, used from 1965 through 1968, is one of the enthusiasts' all-time favorites. It combines incredible strength with light weight, quietness (hydraulic lifters), and reasonable smoothness. These were factory fitted with aluminum intake manifolds and cast aluminum valve covers. Both of the small blocks came with aluminum radiators and filler tanks. Carburetion for both was by Holley four-barrels.

Big block "427" engines dominated the power options for 1967. The least powerful 427 was the L-36 rated at 390 horsepower. It used a four-barrel

STING RAY
1967
CORVETTE

Holley carburetor and had stamped steel valve covers with a painted finish. Next came a 400 horsepower unit, the L-68. With its hydraulic valve lifters, this engine was a near twin to the L-36, except that it came with three two-barrel carbs. It also had the stamped, painted valve covers like the L-36, but the triple carb setup required a special, triangular air cleaner.

The strongest regular production engine was the L-71, rated at 435 horsepower. It also had the triple carburetion, combined with solid valve lifters and special camshaft. A special option, the L-89, fitted aluminum cylinder heads to the L-71. This engine had the same horsepower rating of 435 since it was essentially the same other than the heads (and chromed valve covers). All of these big blocks had conventional copper radiators, not aluminum. All 427 equipped Corvettes also came with a host of heavy duty equipment including stronger front springs, front and rear stabilizer bars, rear wheel

Triple carbs, solids, aluminum heads, 435 hp . . . gawd

spindle supports, clutch, starting motor, and much more. All things considered, the option cost of the big blocks, ranging from $200.15 for the L-36 to $805.75 for the L-71 with L-89 heads, was a heck of a bargain.

The engine that hasn't been mentioned yet is the L-88. Chevrolet didn't have much to say about it in 1967, either. It was one of those things that just appeared in some literature without much explanation. Chevy listed the horsepower at five less than the L-71 or L-89, yet the L-88 cost more. Just what did Duntov have up his sleeve this time?

The L-88: Duntov's Last Stand

Just a single decade before, Chevrolet shocked the motoring world with a new fuel-injected Corvette engine that pumped out 283 horsepower. It really put out a bit more, but Chevy ad men liked the ring of 283 horsepower from 283 cubic inches. Who would believe that less than ten years later you could walk into your Chevy salesroom and drive away in a bone-stock production 427 Corvette belching out 435 horses, again conservatively rated. In 1967, that's what you got with production option L-71. But an option many failed to take note of was called L-88. It never made it into dealer brochures. Dealers were notified directly. If it hadn't been for **Corvette News** telling us about it, hardly anybody would have noticed. At the time, not too many did anyway.

On the surface, the L-88 looked like a bum deal. It was the most expensive engine on the option sheet in 1967 at $947.90 That was just for openers, because you had to buy all sorts of heavy duty paraphernalia to go with it. To make matters worse, Chevrolet wouldn't even tell what the power of the mystery motor was. Studebaker tried to do that when they brought out the Avanti. The old Stude V-8 just couldn't be made to deliver the horses. The Avanti sliced the wind well, and the blown V-8 moved it along like gangbusters, but the horsepower numbers didn't impress anyone, so they just didn't publish them. Was this the case with the L-88?

Chevrolet finally did give in and release a 430 horsepower rating for the L-88. But wait a minute. This was the most expensive engine, yet it was not the most powerful. What's Chevrolet up to here? Maybe it's a slightly detuned engine for longer life and more pleasant street performance. Sure, that must be it.

Wrong. The L-88 was the most powerful engine ever available in a Sting Ray. Chevrolet wasn't exactly fibbing about the horsepower, but they weren't laying it on the line either. The catch was that they rated it at 5200 rpm. At the engine's true horsepower peak, somewhere around 6400 rpm, the horsepower was more like 530 . . . or maybe 620, depending on who tuned it and who was trying to read the dyno while the L-88 threatened to shake the building down. Oh, this was a fire-breather.

Why the games with the horsepower ratings? The simple truth is that Chevrolet didn't want to sell these brutes, at least not many of them. This engine was Duntov's last big shot at the Cobra, at Ferrari, at anybody else out there. It was absolutely a pure racing engine, completely unsuited for anything ever approaching street use. Then why offer it all? To qualify it as a "production" race car. Besides, GM was still officially out of racing. If Duntov started getting high level flak, he could always say, "It's just a little regular production engine that happens to do well on the race circuit." Ah, Zora, we love 'ya.

So the L-88 was not designed for the street. It was a factory-built racer, specially assembled on a separate line, extensively tested before delivery. It was a money-loser. It really boiled down to being a factory-subsidized race vehicle. But it created a problem for Chevrolet marketing. They knew from experience that when you offer something, somebody's going to buy it, no matter what it costs. In the case of horsepower especially, they knew that there is always that customer who walks into the dealership, runs his finger down the specs sheet to the highest horsepower figure, and says, "Order me this one." How do you accurately pass along Duntov's intentions for the L-88 to 6,000 Chevrolet dealers and who knows how many salespeople?

Small catch to the horsepower rating

The deflated horsepower figure was one of Chevy's ploys to ward off unwanted purchasers. And it worked. You can almost hear the salesman and his customer now.

"I believe I'll take that L-88 engine."

"No sir, I don't believe you'd want to order that."

"Why not?"

"Well, sir, you could order the L-71 and get five more horsepower. And, instead of paying $947.90 for the L-88, it'll only cost you $437.10."

"How come the L-88 costs more?"

"Well, sir, sometimes these things don't make sense to me either. But here it is in black and white. See here? The L-71 says 435 horsepower, but only 430 for the L-88."

"How come the L-88 costs more?"

"Well, the L-88 does have aluminum heads, sir."

"Is that good?"

"Well, sir, that saves about 75 pounds."

"Ah, so that's it. OK, order me the L-88."

"But sir, I can order you option L-89 aluminum heads with the L-71 motor. That will give you aluminum heads on the 435 horse, and still cost less than the L-88."

"Boy, I just don't know . . ."

"Do you want a heater with this car, sir?"

"You kidding? Of course I want a heater!"

"Not available with the L-88, sir."

"Darn, this is confusing. What would you do?"

"Frankly, sir, I'd get the smallest engine you could. And automatic transmission. Take it from me, these big motors and four speed transmissions will never hold their value . . ."

At least the salesman was right about the heater part. That was another ploy by Chevrolet to discourage sales or, to put it more correctly, to aim sales in the right direction. Also, you could not get an automatic transmission in the '67 L-88, nor air conditioning.

Chevrolet also used **Corvette News** to spread the word. In an article suitably called "Proceed With Caution" from the Volume 10, Number 3 issue, **CN** said about the L-88, "Designed only as an engine for use by qualified, competitive racing groups, a number of radically different features have been added to Corvette's already potent 427 cubic-inch

V8 to make it a "real swinger" for performance buffs."

Corvette News continued, "The L-88 is not an engine for ordinary everyday driving. It gives a rough idle, is not the easiest engine to start and was not designed with high fuel economy in mind. As a matter of fact, the L-88 requires higher octane gas than most stations carry. It is strictly a high-performance engine for competition use."

But at the end of the article, salesman turned editor Joe Pike couldn't resist adding, "Okay . . . now if we're still unsuccessful in talking you out of the L-88 option, how would you go about getting it? Just talk it over with your Chevrolet dealer . . . he may even special-order the Corvette of your dreams."

Just what was it, you may be wondering, about this L-88 that made it so beastly? For starters, it was built around the same block as the L-71. This was a four-bolt-main block with a casting number of 3904351 and engine boss suffix of "IT". (One wonders if the "IT" was an intentional pun on the part of Chevy's engineers?) The L-88 of 1967 had a special forged steel crankshaft which was crossdrilled and magnafluxed at the factory. It was also tuffrided and this, plus the crossdrilling, distinguished it from other heavy duty 427's.

Pistons were forged aluminum with floating pins. The combustion chamber volume of the L-88 was 4.64 inches compared to 4.92 for the L-71. This resulted in the L-88's incredible 12.5:1 compression ratio and **Corvette News'** warnings about fuel octane. The factory stuck a red and white warning label about the octane requirements on the center console of L-88s, and also hung a warning tag from the turn signal (or taped it somewhere easily visible) for transport people unloading an L-88. This tag said: **1. Engine must not be raced. 2. There is no operational choke. If difficult to start, pump gas pedal. 3. This unit operates only on Sunoco 260 or equivalent gas of very high octane. Under no circumstances should regular gasoline be used. 4. Suggest carriers have supervision during unloading and loading.**

text continues on page 54

Left: *You're seeing it correctly, there is no vacuum advance on an L-88 distributor.*
Right: *Unusual free-breathing air cleaner screen looks like it should stop most small rocks and medium-sized bugs. Look again, there's an air cleaner element fitted to the inner hood.*

The connecting rods of the '67 L-88 were shot-peened and heavy duty. They were held in by three-eighths inch rod bolts and these turned out to be the weak point of the engine. Switching to seven-sixteenths inch bolts in the '68 L-88 cured the shortcoming.

The special high-lift/duration cam shaft was chain-driven, and activated solid lifters. Push rods were a huge seven-sixteenths inch in diameter and had heat-treated ends. Likewise, the rocker arms were special and were heat-treated at high wear points. Dual springs acted on 2.195 inch inlet and 1.885 exhaust valves. The cylinder heads were aluminum, the same L-89 option units which could be ordered with the L-71, 427 engine.

The L-88 produced very little vacuum at low idle and for this reason, Holley had to specially calibrate the R3418 four-barrel used. The intake manifold was aluminum with an open plenum chamber. Exhaust manifolds were cast iron, though Chevrolet also had special headers available over the counter. The distributor, #1111240, had no vacuum advance and you were duly warned not to try to hook one up. RPO K-66, transistorized ignition, was required.

The L-88 also had a unique hood, though the modifications were on the inside, not the outside. A ducting arrangement was fixed to the inside surface of the hood which drew air from the rear of the hood to the Holley. The Holley itself was fitted with an unusual free-breathing screen arrangement.

While the rest of the 427 arsenal of 1967 came with copper/brass radiators, Chevy engineers opted for the weight savings of aluminum for the L-88. They also deleted the fan shroud. More weight saved, and cooling is actually better at high speed without it. That leaves the problem of low speed cooling, but who cared about that? This was not a hamburger-joint cruisin' Corvette.

But if you had one of these babies and did seek out a little after-hours road racing, chances are you'd have gained new respect from your peers. The L-88s were awesome, to put it mildly. They weren't as nimble as some of the competitors, but give them room and watch out! Nimbleness was never a big trait of Duntov-inspired cars anyway. Duntov liked cubes and go-power. At LeMans in 1967, an L-88 coupe entered by California's Dana Chevrolet dusted the track down at 171.5 mph. It weighed 300 pounds more than anything else there, including the eventual winning Ferrari. Nobody, including the Ferrari, came within even twenty miles per hour of the L-88's lap time. But alas, it let loose at just over eleven hours into the race.

It's easy to believe what we have experienced in our own times. 1967 is not yet the distant past, and most of us can remember what those high-performance days were like. We may not specifically remember an L-88. There were only 20 sold in 1967, and just 216 over the three year period they were produced. But we've all personally seen, and maybe owned, fast and exciting cars, especially Corvettes. A few years from now, fewer and fewer people will be able to say that. The cars of the future probably won't be as terribly dull as everyone fears, but we'll certainly never see anything like L-88s again. At least we had them for a while.

Track dusting at 171.5 mph

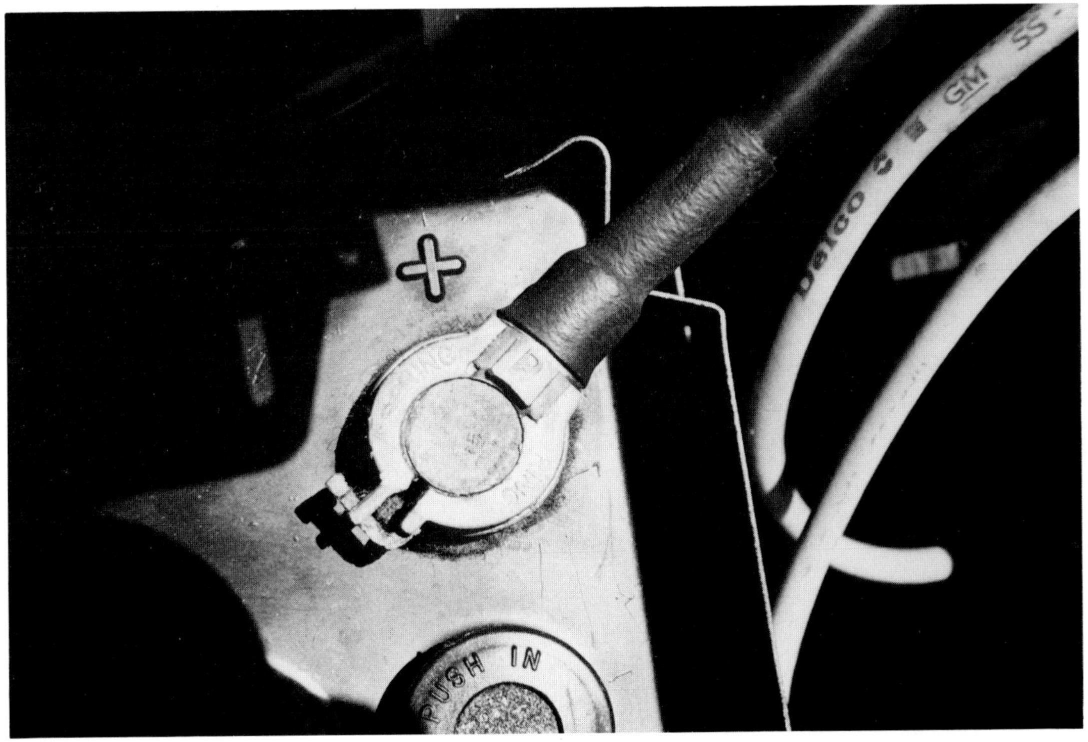

One of twenty

The Owner: It Started With A Model "A"

While he was still in high school, young Bill Miller completely restored a model "A" with his own hands. During the past two years, Bill Miller restored a 1967 Corvette coupe.

Any 1967 Corvette is sufficient to start the juices flowing in any automobile enthusiast, but Miller's also happens to be an extremely rare (one of just twenty built) L-88 optioned '67. And the L-88 just happens to be one of the fiercest, go-for-broke performance cars ever offered for public consumption.

Roughly twenty years elapsed between the "A" and the L-88. During that twenty year span, lots of things changed. Cars changed. Sports cars officially arrived, some flourishing and some departing. For a time, styling and performance reigned supreme as the prime criteria for building desirable automobiles. But by the end of the period, styling and performance took a back seat to more "practical" concerns imposed by our changing world.

Bill Miller changed too. From a teenager whose first love was tearing apart and rebuilding automobiles, his horizons broadened somewhat to include, among other things, the study of medicine. Bill Miller, the teenage auto restorer, is now Dr. William Miller, Director of the Missouri-Illinois Regional Red Cross Blood Services. But Dr. Miller is also still Bill Miller, grown-up auto restorer. See, some things change but others don't. Restoring automobiles provides as much enjoyment and excitement for Bill now, maybe more, as it ever has. There have been many cars between that backyard "A" and the L-88 screamer.

People who love cars, probably those who love Corvettes especially, tend to become rigidly opinionated. They stake out their field of interest, and they stay in it.

Some of these enthusiasts frown on restorations. To them, the "high dollar" cars must be factory original right down to hoses and clamps. This sort of person reasons that a restored car can never approach the value of an original, even if the restored model is cosmetically half again as good.

Bill Miller doesn't buy that. He prefers original parts and he'll salvage every piece possible during a restoration. But he gets his real pleasure, his real sense of satisfaction and accomplishment, from bringing the "basket cases" back to life. That's not to say he brings cars back to something they never were. He would not, for instance, restore a 300 HP '65 as a fuel injected car. But if he were restoring a fuel Corvette that had somehow become separated from the original injection unit, he'd feel no qualms about locating another unit, provided it's as close as possible to what was supposed to be installed.

By Dr. Miller's reasoning, every Corvette has merit, no matter what its condition. Just because it has parted company with some of its original parts is no reason to abandon it.

Take, for example, his '65 Rally Red fuel convertible. When he bought it, it had no interior, no instruments, no engine, and no wheels. The body was all right, provided you overlooked the hole poked in it by the police looking for serial numbers after it was recovered . . . after it was stolen. Bill paid $700 for that one. When finished, it was about as perfect, beautiful, and complete as an automobile could be. What he sold it for would buy a couple years of medical school, even at today's prices.

How did this all start? For Bill Miller, the craving for a Corvette was always present, but really surfaced in 1965 when a medical school classmate got a new Sting Ray for graduation. Residency, fellowship, and other medical school post-graduation activities prevented Bill from acquiring his own Corvette until 1973. That first was bought right off a used car lot, a '65 Milano Maroon FI coupe with knock-off wheels and saddle interior. There have been several Corvettes between that first coupe and the L-88, both classics and late models. But it is the story of the L-88 that deserves re-telling.

His first awareness that L-88 Corvettes actually existed came in 1975 as a result of reading Karl Ludvigsen's excellent Automobile Quarterly publication, **Corvette! America's Star Spangled Sports Car.** Ludvigsen said that Chevrolet hadn't released actual horsepower ratings for the L-88, but "a reliably-reported power figure for the L-88 was 560 bhp at 6,400 rpm on fuel of 103 research octane. It was as pure a racing engine as Chevrolet had ever supplied for the Corvette."

This sort of descriptive terminology led Dr. Miller to believe that an L-88 would be an incredible thrill to restore and own. But one doesn't simply start watching the Sunday ads in the local newspaper for cars of this scarcity. Only a few hundred L-88s were built, and if you limit your consideration to 1967, the year that particularly interested Dr. Miller, the number produced was only 20. Add to that the early L-88's tendency to self-destruct and it's almost universal application as a race vehicle, and the problem of locating one of these things becomes all too apparent.

The big break came late in 1976. While perusing the December issue of **Motor Trend** magazine, Dr. Miller caught an article titled, "Survivor Vette." With a sub-title of, "When it comes to L-88s, old doesn't necessarily mean feeble", the article went on to

relate the story of how a particular L-88 was located, and some of the owner's experiences with it. The article's description of L-88 performance rekindled Dr. Miller's interest.

Dr. Miller wondered if the L-88 described in the article could be purchased. Then he figured, "Aw, probably not." Forget it.

Except he couldn't forget it. Something inside kept telling him that this L-88 might just be the car. At least it was worth the price of a phone call. The article in **Motor Trend** had mentioned the owner's name and home town of Oklahoma City. Bill tried the information operator and bingo! The number was listed. And the owner answered the call with the news that the L-88 was indeed for sale. In fact, he had placed ads in both **Hemmings** and **Vette Vues** which would be out in a few days. The asking price was $9,000. The response from the good doctor was that if this was indeed a genuine L-88, and if this could be documented to his satisfaction, he would pay the asking price. It was what it was said to be, and the L-88 moved in with the Millers.

This '67 wasn't in the sad state of the '65 basket-case convertible Bill Miller had restored earlier, but neither was it any creampuff. As best could be determined, the '67 had been purchased new and drag raced in the Spokane area. By 1969, it was on a used car lot in Montana with a replacement short block. The gentleman who purchased it in Montana used it up until 1974 for drag racing. The Corvette was sold in 1974 and towed by its new owner to Kansas.

The brother of the man from whom Bill Miller purchased the L-88, saw it parked behind a gas station and tipped his brother off.

By the time the L-88 rolled off the trailer in Miller's driveway, it had seen more abuse, and probably smoked more competition in the process, than any fifty average Corvettes. During its first week of residency, it behaved very unpleasantly, spinning a main bearing while backing out of the garage. Oh well, it wasn't the original short block anyway. Besides, the ads that by then had appeared in **Hemmings** and **Vette Vues** resulted in two solid offers of $12,000 for the L-88, bad main bearing or no. Maybe this was a good buy afterall.

Note the heater control block-offs on the dash of Dr. Miller's L-88.

Even though the block was not original, all was not lost under the hood. The critical parts that make an L-88 an L-88 were mostly there. Still, Bill's "laundry" list of items he'd need, which he makes up before starting each restoration, was quite lengthy. He considers the tasks of first determining which parts are correct for a restoration, and then finding them, as the most challenging aspects of the project. Strangely, he also finds them the most interesting. That's because of the hundreds of people he meets while doing the research, and the knowledge he picks up personally.

As a matter of advice, the first thing Bill Miller does after making his list of needed parts is to head for the parts department of his local Chevrolet dealer. Despite limited usage and apparent rarity, many valuable parts are still lurking in the dark corners of Chevy warehouses. Sometimes part numbers change and sometimes GM substitutes a perfectly functional (but incorrect in the restorer's eye) replacement part. With the help of a knowledgeable and persistent friend behind the parts counter, many correct parts will trickle in.

To illustrate, consider the road draft tube (crankcase breather) for the L-88. These things vent crankcase fumes directly to the atmosphere and disappeared from most domestic cars around 1962. They're one of the easy things to get rid of to improve air quality. But the engine doesn't breath quite as well without them, and since the L-88 was a racer, it had a draft tube. Those little devils are so hard to find now. Dr. Miller found the part number and ordered it. It didn't come in. After two more tries and a couple of months, one arrived! It was filthy, with a yellowed tag that looked like it came through the war (Civil), but it was the genuine item. The doctor immediately ordered two more. "Sorry." came the reply, "That was the last one."

Sorry, last one!

WHAT MAKES A '67 L-88 A REAL L-88

Stamped suffix on engine pad:	IT
Block casting number:	3904351 (Same as the 1967 427/435 L-71)
Distributor:	#1111240 No vacuum advance on pot
Distributor cap:	Dark reddish-brown with copper contacts
Ignition wires:	Dark reddish-brown with no braiding or ground straps. Steel core.
Air cleaner:	Filter element mounted within specially molded duct in hood. Base mounted to carb has no flame arrester. Small diameter screen held to base by small metal top.
Fuel line to carburetor:	Same as 1966 427/425 L-72
Intake manifold:	Open aluminum plenum with thin wall (thicker wall in later L-88s)
Thermostat housing:	Uses spacer between housing and intake.
Valve covers:	Painted orange. Yellow and black "IT" tag on rear surface of right cover.
Fan:	High pitch, square tipped, 7 blade with large truck-type clutch.
Fan shroud:	None
Radiator core support:	Same as 1965 396/425 L-78.
Radiator:	Aluminum. Same as the 1965 396/425 L-78 replacement unit, which has longer neck than original equipment.
Heads:	Aluminum. Painted orange except under exhaust openings. Casting number 3904387.
Carburetor:	Holley 850 cfm #3418, specially calibrated.
Decals:	Square coolant decal in lower right section of inner hood, octane warning on console.
Wiring harness:	Heater lead wires present, but taped back. Transistor ignition.
Heavy duty brakes:	Power brake booster mounted between master cylinder and firewall. Front calipers use dual, long cotter pins. Special front pads. No boss for pin. Top of caliper is flat. Rear calipers stock. Special proportioning valve mounted below master cylinder.
Rear spring:	Seven leaf
Shock absorbers:	Larger in diameter with large, round flats at shaft ends.
Transmission:	M-22. Has drain plug on lower front corner on passenger side of case.
Interior:	Special round plugs fill holes made for heater control rods. No radio or speaker, but speaker grill is present. Heater block-off plate made of fiberboard on inside of firewall. Fuel warning sticker on very rear of shift console.
Engine details:	Road draft tube mounted into left valve cover extending down and backwards along side of engine block. Heater block-off plate covering firewall openings where heater is usually mounted. Special rubber cap on heater hose at base of overflow tank. Small tee block overflow tank

CHART INFORMATION COMPILED BY DAVE BURROUGHS AND BILL MILLER.

Many times parts can be located just by using some common sense. An absolutely correct carburetor for the L-88 was purchased by writing the manufacturer, Holley. Many times it is not possible to determine if a component was manufactured by General Motors or by a supplying vendor. And GM tends to be tight-lipped about who makes what for some sort of legal reasons. But when the manufacturer is clearly identified, as is the case with carburetors, a direct note to them often does the trick.

Dr. Miller found that visiting owners of the few other L-88 '67 Corvettes proved to be extremely helpful both in determining what he needed and where to get it. The problem present with all remaining '67 L-88 Corvettes is that most have been modified to some degree. But the owners of these models have practically formed a brotherhood to get at the truth. Even so, in the initial stages, Miller had to rely on a mixture of undisputed fact, disputed fact, rumor, guesses from former owners, salesmen, and GM employees, word of mouth, and an occasional stab in the dark.

The restoration itself was loaded with the usual trauma of such projects, especially the glueing back together of the body from numerous assaults on the race track. Co-conspirator on the restoration project with Dr. Miller was Dick Ferrando of D&A Corvette in Gillespie, Illinois. Dick went so far as to construct an elaborate jig to hold stock GM replacement body panels in place while fiberglass seams cured. The glassed body was left outside for several months in the sun, wind, and rain so that it would do all the stretching, shrinking and whatever else it cared to do before painting commenced.

Ferrando also constructed a roll-over jig that would spin the raw L-88's body over for easy access to the bottom so that it could be cleaned and refinished. That may strike some as over-restoration, but Bill Miller feels this way about it: "I want my Corvettes to be of a quality level that would be achieved at the factory if the car was walked down the line for a top executive." Interpreted, this means that he wants every part to be what the factory would have used, but he wants every part to be as perfect as possible. He would never dream of chrome-plating a latch that was originally

Last of the best

cadmium-plated. It'll be cadmium-plated, but it will also be perfect. Most of the Corvettes that leave St. Louis don't have admirable paint finishes, but the factory is capable of producing Corvettes with near perfect appearance. If Chevrolet's General Manager is in the plant watching his personal car being built, you can bet it'll be a beauty. It will have properly finished seams, correct panel fit, and a noticeable lack of overspray slop and carelessness. That's the quality strived for in a Miller restoration.

To sum it up, Bill Miller puts it this way; "I can understand why owners of an early '53 model would leave fiberglass mat texture visible in key areas because this can often authenticate the car's proper place in the production schedule. But to me, it makes no sense to purposely restore a mid-year Corvette to a flawed state."

As a further illustration of the type of enthusiast Miller is, just listen to this. Once he had the rolling L-88 chassis finished, he took it to the 1978 Bloomington Corvette Corral for everybody there to verbally pick it apart. Most people would have gotten the body on as quickly as possible to hide any construction errors. But Bill Miller wanted as many Corvette enthusiasts as possible to see it before the body went on. He figured that with thousands of people seeing it (there were 50,000 at Bloomington that year) some would have legitimate corrections to suggest. He had to wade through the inevitable, "Hey, a friend of my third cousin had one of those and I'm sure the engine was bright green" type of flak, but overall the experience helped him get a few steps closer to the 100% correct restoration.

The exterior appearance of a '67 Corvette with the L-88 option is no different than any other '67. Thus restoration of the body was no different than any other Corvette, except perhaps that extreme care was taken to get everything right the first time. The last thing Dr. Miller wanted to see was a seam letting loose six months after painting was complete. The Goodwood Green exterior color of this Corvette acts much like black in displaying the most minute flaw, but it's far more difficult to spot-in than black.

Once all the corrections were made to the chassis as a result of the Bloomington show, and the body was complete, the two were mated and a beautiful Corvette was re-born. The public unveiling of the completed car came at the big Knoxville Expo Corvette show. The reaction of people to this Corvette is almost as interesting as the car itself.

Goodwood Green Corvettes have a very elegant, but understated quality about them. As beautiful as Corvettes painted this color are, they simply do not turn heads like a red or certain shades of blue. Despite dressing up his L-88 with bolt-on wheels and side exhausts, Dr. Miller found that the Knoxville crowd didn't take special note of his Corvette as it was parked among the other cars. After all, an L-88 doesn't even have a badge or emblem indicating what lurks beneath the hood.

When the L-88 engine was started, the crowd likewise came to life. As Dr. Miller puts it, "Nothing, but nothing, sounds like an L-88. Fire it up in your driveway, and you'll have every neighbor within a mile wondering what's going on. The vibration alone shakes the windows of nearby houses." At Knoxville, lifting the hood of the L-88 brought knowledgeable enthusiasts in close for inspection. For many, it was the first chance to actually see an L-88 in person.

What does the future hold for Dr. Bill Miller and his L-88? For the near future, he will show the car. He doesn't particularly care if he wins trophies or not, it's meeting and talking with other Corvette buffs that Bill enjoys. During the time he shows the car, it will not be driven. After he's made it to all the major Corvette shows on his schedule, the L-88 will be sold. Then another start-from-scratch project will start. But before it goes, the L-88 and Bill Miller will get together for at least one long drive. Even though some of the L-88 engine components are as precious as gold and more irreplaceable, Bill says he simply cannot spend a couple of years on a restoration and not drive the result of that work.

That seems especially true when the car in question is an L-88, perhaps the fastest production Corvette ever made. And when the L-88 is installed in a '67, the last year of one of the world's great automobile series.

Historical Glances

1953-1955
Corvette Production

John Amgwert

Here was General Motors, the biggest mass-producer of cars in the world, planning to build a little two-seater with only limited sales appeal. Lunacy. And they were going to make it out of plastic.

Ridiculous. That brought back memories of Henry Ford's soya bean plans.

And GM was actually going to hand-finish this new car. Who was GM trying to kid?

Nobody. In 1953, Chevrolet actually became the builder of one of the world's lowest volume specialty cars.

There must have been a certain amount of romance, reminiscent of the days in 1912 when Louis Chevrolet's creative engineering ability (not to mention his superb talent as a race driver) built the first car to carry his name in the fledging company plant in Flint, Michigan. Although Louis very early left the company he had helped to start, millions of Chevrolets were built before his death in 1941. His motto throughout life was, "Never give up." Somehow, that motto must have been in the minds of the people who built the first Corvette, and all those who have followed.

Louis Chevrolet would have been proud of the first Corvette. Like his first car, the assembly of the Corvette started at Flint in a small Chevrolet Company building which had been known as the Customer Delivery Garage at Van Slyke and Atherton Roads. This was next to the big passenger car and truck assembly plant and the engine manufacturing facility. The construction methods used to build these first Corvettes were a mixture of mass production techniques and extensive hand labor, incredible at the time. The whole auto industry was watching this new car with its reinforced plastic body, to see if a steel substitute was the coming trend, or just a novelty to build a few experimental vehicles.

Hindsight tells us that the use of plastics in automobile manufacturing did not have that great of an impact at the time the Corvette was introduced. But years later, a fuel and cost conscious nation is seeing plastic replace metal in virtually every part of our cars. While Chevrolet is still the only major company using a fiberglass reinforced plastic body (the Corvette!) in production, in the not too-distant future, we're likely to see far more extensive use. But that's getting away from the subject area.

The original concept of the Chevrolet Corvette, beginning with the initial 1953 through 1955 models, has lasted for more than 25 years. That is not to say that the car hasn't been improved and refined in many ways during its first quarter century of existence. But in terms of its intended use and purpose, the Corvette since day one has remained over the years true to the idea of which it was conceived . . . a car that is fun to drive.

If we couple this "fun to drive" concept to the car's assembly using some parts shared with other vehicles in the Chevrolet product line, it becomes clear that the car introduced in 1953 was just as much a Corvette as the current edition is today. It could further be said that the present Corvette is

Lunacy

Who was GM trying to kid?

just as much alike and different from the Chevrolet Caprice Classic, as the 1953 Corvette was from the Bel Air.

When the Chevrolet Motor Division of General Motors Corporation decided to build a limited number of Corvettes for introduction during the 1953 model year, they chose to promote the car as "The First All-American Sports Car." The term "sports car" seemed appropriate enough, however that category denoted different things to different people and many presumed no American manufacturer could build one. All sports cars had to be European. If it wasn't built in England, Germany or Italy, it couldn't be a **true** sports car.

From an engineering, technical, and production standpoint, Chevrolet's original concept of the Corvette is best described in two papers presented at meetings of the Society of Automotive Engineers (SAE). The first paper, presented to the SAE Detroit Section Meeting at the Rackham Memorial Building on October 5, 1953, was written by Maurice Olley, entitled "The Evolution of a Sports Car. . . . The Chevrolet Corvette." Olley had come to GM in 1930 after being involved with Rolls Royce. He was an engineer for the Cadillac Division and Vauxhall Motors (GM-England) until he was appointed director of research and development at Chevrolet in 1952. It was Olley who did the design layout of the chassis for Project Opel, the Chevrolet Corvette.

It was Olley's contention that there was no universally accepted definition of the term "sports car." However, generally, "the engine must cruise at 70 mph without excessive piston travel, the power-weight ratio should be better than 25 lb./hp. (the Corvette was 21 lb./hp.), the car must have ample brakes, quick steering and light handling (the Corvette's steering ratio was an optimum 16 to 1), a low center of gravity, front to rear weight ratio approaching 50-50, smooth yet firm suspension (the driver must "feel" the road surface without causing occupant discomfort), and finally, it is a matter of safety that the response of the car should be immediate, but without oversteer."

His SAE paper went on to chronicle the history of road vehicles from the days of the two-place chariots of the 17th century, to 15 of the world's most

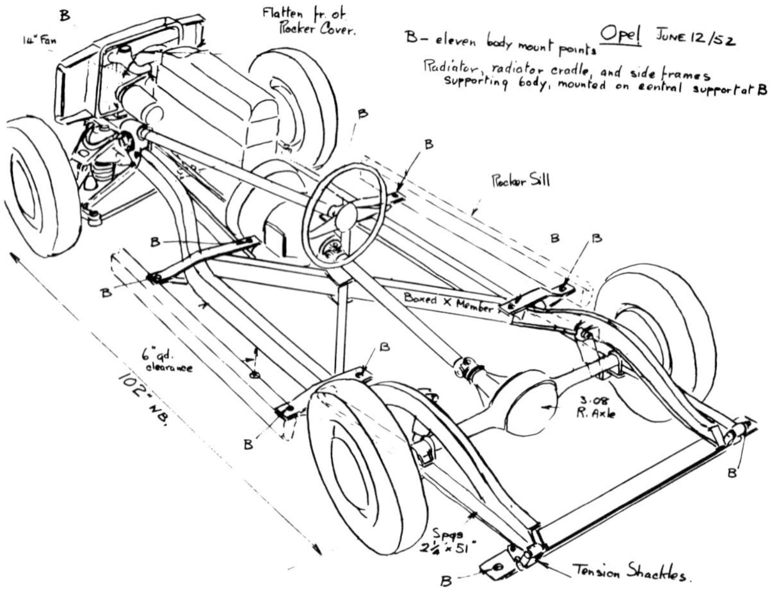

notable sports cars of the early 1950's. He stated his case well, comparing data to show that the new Corvette was a viable sports car, by European standards. He noted that the paper "should not leave the impression that the General Motors Corporation has lost all sense of decorum and is entering the racing car field."

Tilbury?

"The sports car is a serious form of transportation. It ranks with the tilbury (a light, two-wheeled carriage for two persons named after its inventor) the curricle (a two-wheeled carriage drawn by two horses) of the 1800's, and with the roadster of the 1920's as a necessary step in providing convenient, lively transportation for two people in a small package. Also, it is a bit of adventure: fun to drive, fun to build.

"One of the points of interest is that it is possible for a great mass production organization to step out of its normal role of producing over 500 vehicles an hour, to make 500 specialized vehicles in say two weeks. This is an interesting fact even outside the United States, where it is generally considered that American manufacturing methods are too inflexible

Left: *This is the original chassis sketch for the Corvette by Maurice Olley. Note the code name "Opel" and the drawing date of June 12, 1952.*

Olley struck back

to meet modern conditions. This was well disproved within our own knowledge by the wartime performances of the automobile industry. It is proved to the whole world by such a specialized vehicle as the Corvette." Olley was striking back, and setting the record straight!

To those who condemned the Corvette's Powerglide, Olley wrote, "The use of an automatic transmission has been criticized by those who believe that sports car enthusiasts want nothing but a four speed crash shift. The answer is that the typical sports car enthusiast, like the "average man," or the square root of minus one, is an imaginary quantity. Also, as the sports car appeals to a wider and wider section of the public, the center of gravity of this theoretical individual is shifting from the austerity of the pioneer towards the luxury of modern ideas. The performance curve shows that there is no need to apologize for the performance of this car with its automatic transmission." Olley's SAE paper was a bit on the defensive.

To further Chevrolet's move into the sports car market, a second SAE paper, "The Corvette Plastic Body," by Ellis J. "Jim" Premo, assistant chief engineer in charge of passenger car and truck body design at Chevrolet, was presented at the SAE Annual Meeting in Detroit on January 11, 1954. While this paper dealt largely with the building of an automobile body from reinforced plastics, it too referenced the Corvette's purpose:

"It is no secret in the automobile industry that interest in the 'sports' car has gained tremendous momentum in this country during the past ten years. Equally well recognized is the fact that, up to the present, this enthusiasm for a car that is 'fun to drive' has been catered to almost exclusively by European importations which for the most part are direct descendants of the 'race' car and primarily adapted to driving conditions and economic factors abroad.

"When Chevrolet decided to built the 'Corvette' and to produce a new type of sports car on a volume basis, there were many design factors to be considered. Essential sports car characteristics such as high performance and handling stability at all speed ranges had to be combined with the American public's conception of convenience, beauty and comfortable ride. Not the least of the problems to be worked out was that of an ideal body design.

"The Corvette, first exhibited at the Waldorf Show in New York in January of 1953, was designed as a straightforward approach to a practical two-passenger sports car.

"With a height of 34 inches at the door and 48 inches over the top of the windshield, an overall length of 167 inches, and an overall width of 72 inches, it is not too large for a vehicle of two-passenger capacity and still provides a passenger comfort that the American car owner is accustomed to, as well as adequate luggage capacity.

"The tremendous interest aroused by the Corvette wherever it has been shown leaves no doubt as to the public's desire to be able to buy an American-built sports car.

"By far the greatest part of this interest has centered on the reinforced plastic body. This is not only because of its novelty and its appeal as a natural styling medium, but because of the obvious advantages it has in overall sports car design.

"The whole history of the automobile industry is one of challenge to man's inventive genius. And, whatever the future role of reinforced plastics in the automotive field, the story of the Corvette body is, I believe, thoroughly in keeping with the tradition of continually finding new ways to do new things."

Now, it must be remembered that these SAE papers of Olley and Premo were presented after the fact; the 1953 Corvette was already in production. The reasons for the car's existence were merely being defined, and it is important to note that they still apply to the Corvette of today . . . a car that is fun to build and fun to drive.

Since the car's introduction, the name "Corvette" has been easily recognizable as Chevrolet's little plastic sports car. But the word "corvette" actually comes from several other words, all with related meanings. In Latin it was "corbia" (a merchant ship), or the word "corbis" (meaning basket) the symbol of the Egyptian grain ships.

From there the French/Portuguese used the word "corveta." The first "corvettes" were used by the

French Navy in 1687. These were small fighting ships carrying a complement of no more than 30 cannons, and using improved sails and keel construction so as to make them highly maneuverable and fast in combat.

In the 18th and 19th centuries the British Navy also used corvettes. In fact, by 1886 they comprised one-third of the Royal Navy's sea power. This ship was slightly smaller than a frigate.

Contrary to popular belief, the United States Navy never adopted the term corvette. Their version was first called the "sloop-of-war", and later "gunboat", and then during World War Two "escort patrol craft." The gunboat Panay, sunk by the Japanese on the Yangtze River in 1937, was an example of a corvette in terms of size and design, prior to the war.

Actual "corvettes", as used during World War Two, were ruggedly built escort ships weighing about 950 tons, mounting 4-inch guns and additional anti-aircraft armament and depth charges. Over 250 were constructed in England and Canada (starting in 1938) called the "Flower" class corvettes, adapted for combat use from a then commercial whale catcher design built by the Smiths' Dock Company. This allowed construction at non-naval yards as simplicity of building techniques was a main consideration. Once mass-building got underway, as many as eight corvettes a month were completed.

While their top speed was only 17 knots, they were highly maneuverable and deadly against German submarines. Though these ships were used chiefly by the British, French, and Canadian navies, a dozen other allied nations had them, including 18 corvettes used by the United States Navy as escort patrol craft. By 1950, many of these vessels were sold as war surplus and a few are still used today commercially and for coastal naval patrol.

How did Chevrolet come to use the name "Corvette?"

During mid-1952, as Chevrolet was in the design stage of the car, the engineering project was code-named "Opel", probably after GM's German division. About that time Chevrolet sought a name for the car which was to be their entry in the January, 1953, GM Motorama Show to be held at the Waldorf-Astoria Hotel in New York City, and later that same year on the production model.

The actual naming is an interesting story, as Myron Scott, a retired Chevrolet public relations executive, recently related: "Some 1,500 names were submitted to the top-brass at GM. Many of the names considered came from the corporation's advertising firm, Campbell-Ewald. All of these 1,500 names were rejected. A request was passed down through the ranks, soliciting additional suggestions for naming the car."

Scott said that Chevrolet wanted a name that began with the letter "C", and they were leaning away from "animal" names. With this, he simply went to a dictionary and began going through the words starting with "C". Scott remembers, "I saw the word 'corvette' with its definition of a small persuit ship which certainly fit the image of this new sports car. After saying 'corvette' to myself a dozen or so times, I found it rolled off my tongue. I sent a note to Ed Cole, then the Chevrolet chief engineer who later became president of General Motors, telling him that I was submitting the name 'Corvette' for the new car, suggesting that he say it a few times. Ed Cole called me about a week later to say that Chevrolet had decided to use the name I had submitted. The car was to be the Chevrolet Corvette!" According to Scott, the selection of the name "Corvette" came about four months prior to the Waldorf show.

The original Corvette emblem was created by GM Designer Robert Bartholomew, who relates how it happened:

"The original Waldorf Corvette show car was shipped from Detroit to New York but the emblems that adorned it when it left (Detroit) were never seen by the public. That first design (mine) had the checkered flag on the right side where it remains today. On the left side and crossing staffs with the checkered flag flew the American flag . . . all very pretty and rather optimistically signifying for the 'Old Blue Flame Six, an American winner.' A member of the General Motors Legal Staff blew the whistle on us and said, 'You cannot use the American flag on a commercial product.' The emblems had to be rede-

Right: *"Bag" method for producing early Corvette body panels helped get the car into production quickly, but process was slow and labor intensive.*

Corvette origins

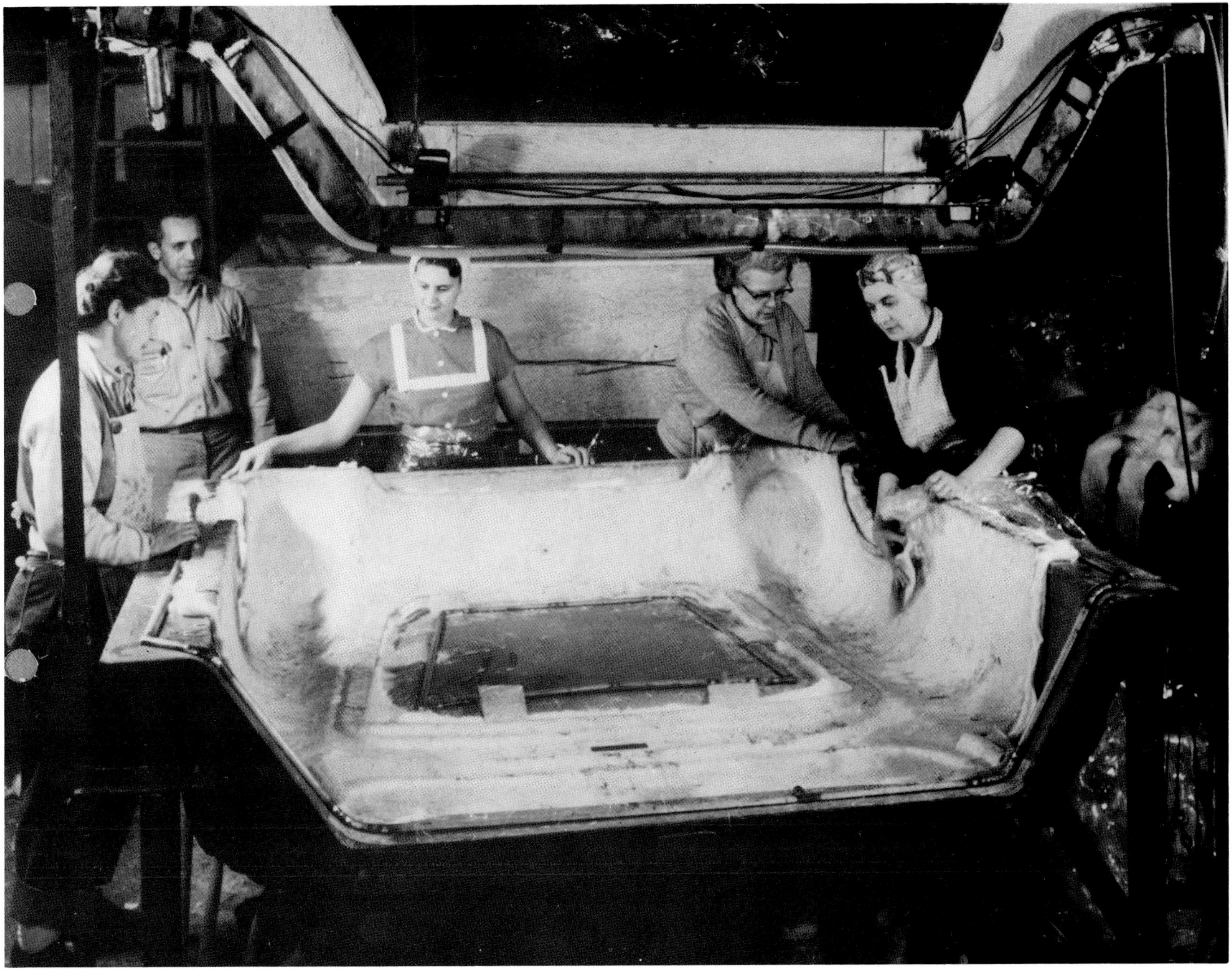

signed and fabricated in what seemed merely hours, then put on the car which was already in New York.

"Prior to the Corvette project, I had been working on emblems for the 1953 and 1954 Chevrolet passenger cars. I tried researching the Louis Chevrolet family in an effort to turn up a crest or some such item of heraldry, but I came up with nothing. Chevrolet is a French name, and the fleur-de-lis has always seemed very French to me, so I used these in conjunction with the famous Chevrolet 'bow-tie' for the passenger car emblems. I made the obvious move for the Corvette by incorporating the bow-tie and fleur-de-lis on a new flag to replace the American flag.

"Working directly with a plastics shop in Detroit, we soon had two completed emblems. The happy ending is that when the curtains were drawn and the public got its first exciting view of the Corvette, the proper emblems were in place."

Production of the Corvette showed that Chevrolet was examining two areas: 1) the growing interest in sports cars, and 2) mass-production of plastic bodied cars. Why did Chevrolet choose plastic? The answer involves several considerations: Tooling time, the soundness of plastics technology, expense, and the idea of experimentation.

GM had experience in plastic body parts prior to the Corvette. During World War Two the Cadillac division had scrapped expensive tooling dies used to make steel fenders and, following the war lack of replacement fenders, GM was forced to use cheaper service parts made of plastic. This was done while Ed Cole was Cadillac chief engineer, and he must have believed the process would work for making an entire body.

Tooling time is time lost forever, so the choice of plastics was logical for the Corvette, compared to the time and cost of a steel body for this completely new model. When Chevrolet said, "All plastic", they meant it, although some panels were held together with aluminum rivets (for positioning) and small steel backing plates were imbedded in panels where steel-to-plastic connections (such as hood and trunk hardware) were made. The only metal assembly in the body was the radiator mounting shell.

Left: *Myron Scott, the man who submitted the name "Corvette" to Ed Cole, after 1,500 other proposals had been rejected.*

Total weight of a trimless body was 340 pounds, compared to over 600 pounds for a comparable steel structure. The number of individual plastic parts used in the Corvette body was in excess of 100. Many of these, however, were partially assembled by the outside vendor suppliers and shipped to Chevrolet as complete, two or three part, assemblies (hood, trunk, top compartment cover, etc.). Chevrolet assembled some 60 parts, panels, and partially complete assemblies into the 24 major pieces of the Corvette body.

The eventual long-term plan for producing the plastic body panels was through the use of matched metal dies. These took time to build, so Chevrolet relied first on parts made through hand lay-up, vacuum bag molding. The bag method consisted of cast phenolic molds made from mahogany die models. These were first sprayed with a parting agent, then a resinous gelcoat to provide a smooth finish, then three layers of woven glass fibers were laid in the mold and a resin mixture applied by brush. A backup mold was then placed over the part creating a "sandwich". A sheet of polyvinyl plastic was added and air evacuated by vacuum (12 psi). The formed part was allowed to cure in the mold (for as long as 24 hours) by the addition of heat lamps.

24 hour cure

The parts made by this method were fabricated at several locations: GM Technical Center in Michigan, Molded Fiber Glass Body Company in Ohio, Lunn Laminates in New York, and Winner Manufacturing in New Jersey. Tooling was in a transitional state very early, from the bag method over to matched metal dies, and as the finished metal dies were completed, firms using the bag method would end production. Eventually all panels were produced by dies at Molded Fiber Glass in Ohio.

The matched metal die method was far more efficient as the parts were pressed, creating more uniform panels, and parts could be manufactured much faster. The smaller parts were the first to get matched compression dies, the larger parts took longer to ready. The largest single part of the Corvette was the underbody panel which measured 120 inches long, 70 inches wide, and 26 inches deep at its highest point. The dies for this part were completed and in operation during July of 1954, and represented the largest single plastic part ever compression molded (it weighed only 75 pounds). With matched metal dies this part took only 20 minutes to fabricate in a press compared to four hours using the hand-lay method, which required that part be made from eight smaller sections.

A significant feature of the matched metal dies was that curing time had been reduced, varying from two to seven minutes, due to pressurized steam flowing through the hollow interior which raised the temperature to 220 degrees.

The Flint Corvette assembly plant was actually a pilot-line designed to explore production techniques to be applied when mass-production began at St. Louis for the 1954 model. Only 300 hand-built units were assembled at Flint during the period starting in June, 1953 through December 24th. Production at St. Louis began on December 28, 1953. Valuable experience, though, was gained from the Flint operation.

Plastic body assembly required much more floor space and specialized hand labor than steel. Chevrolet wanted to find out, through Flint, if a moving, station-to-station assembly line was feasible for future production. The largest portion of the building was utilized for body assembly, flanked on one side by the painting booth, on one end by the trim area, and down the other side by a chassis line that could accommodate six cars.

Body assembly began with the large underbody panel. It was placed on a holding fixture at the start of the line and secured with clamps. Next, 180 holes to be used for attaching the body panels were made by lowering an electric hoist-mounted drilling jig, made from an actual underbody panel. Body sills and floor reinforcements were riveted in place for positioning and a bond mixture added to their joints. The assembled underbody was then placed on a movable "dolly" also used as a jig for placing the other panels to be added.

On feeder-lines, the front and rear sub-assemblies were built-up in their own jig fixtures, with panels such as bulkheads, fenders, and dash being positioned and bonded together with the aid of spring-loaded clamps, in an inverted state.

These completed sub-assemblies were then positioned on the underbody fixture. The front panel section was installed by locating the mount holes in the metal radiator support to the fixture. The door opening was measured for correct size, and the assembly bonded in place. The rear upper panel consisting of trunk opening and fuel filler box was similarly positioned and bonded, as were the side rocker panels across the length of the lower body. The final stage of body assembly was the fitting of doors, hood, trunk, and top compartment cover, which were then removed for the painting procedure.

In the adjacent spray booth the body shell received a prime-coat which, after drying, was dry sanded. Two finish-coats of Polo White exterior lacquer were applied as well as Sportsman Red trim paint and the "black-out" for the engine compartment and grill opening.

The procedure used for trim and black-out painting was aided by the use of large reinforced plastic "masks" which were fitted around the lips of the trunk, top, and engine compartments. These masks (easily set in place by the painter) shielded the exterior paint from overspray, and provided appropriate color parting lines.

The painting procedure was similar to that used for metal body finishing. The colorless plastic panels provided excellent paint adhesion to the fibrous surface. The paint was dried in a conventional baking oven using infrared heat lamps, followed by normal buffing and polishing.

The entire underbody on the Flint-built cars was left unpainted, except for the wheelwells which received black paint, and then a coating of thick black sound deadening compound running in a path about a foot wide from front to back.

From the painting area, the assembled body, still mounted on its dolly, was pushed to the trim line which could handle three bodies. Here, the previously fitted and painted trunk lid, doors, and top storage compartment cover were installed (along with rubber weather seals). The instruments, electrical wiring, and most body hardware including the windshield, folding top, gas tank, steering column, and lower body finish bright trim were added.

Left: *Views of Corvette construction at Flint plant, including body panel storage, panel assembly, and finish painting with "Polo White" on wheeled dolly.* **Right:** *Installation of '53 fuel tank.*

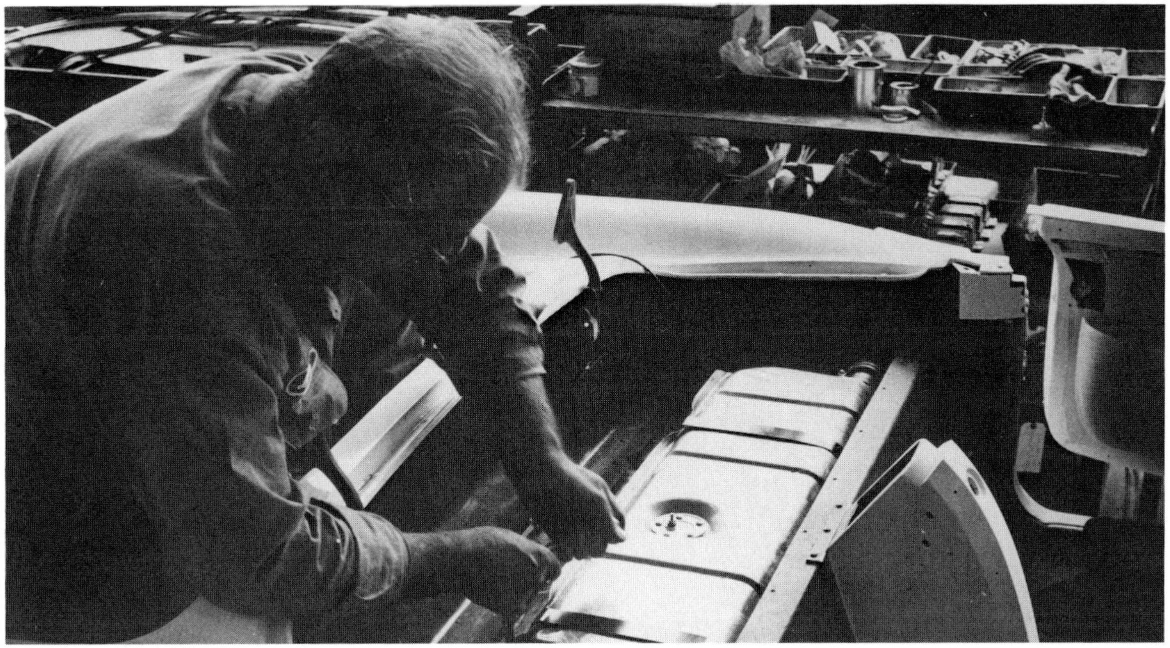

Six at a time

With the use of fiberglass templates, the drilling of holes used to mount the exterior chrome bumper trim and belt-line stainless steel mouldings was accomplished. These templates insured correct location and fit of the parts, as well as protecting the exterior painted surface from drilling damage. The 16 pieces of chrome trim which covered the four corners of the body along with the rear center bumper and side mouldings afforded little impact protection. They did, however, serve the convenient purpose of covering the flange seam used to secure the upper and lower body sections.

To aid installation of the body electrical system, a large display board was constructed and placed near the line. It served as an illustration diagraming the proper connections for the main wiring harness to all the components such as gauges, voltage regulator, radio, heater, ignition switch, and lights.

When the body left the trim area, it was by no means complete. The hood, all upholstery, windshield wiper parts, headlamp trim, trunk items, in fact many parts, were still to be installed. These, however, would not be added until after the body was secured to the chassis. It would be much easier to install these remaining parts later, as fitting, alignment, and adjustment could not be completed until the body and chassis became one rigid unit.

The chassis line was located adjacent to the trim line at Flint, and could accommodate six units in varying stages of completion from the bare frame to final vehicle assembly and drive-away.

The Corvette's chassis frame was designed by Chevrolet and supplied by the A.O. Smith Corporation. (That company, in fact, still builds frames for the current model.) The 1953 Corvette frame was a completely new design, sharing little with the passenger car. While the passenger car incorporated "hat-section" side frame rails, the Corvette utilized the "box-section" design. (By 1955, the passenger car adopted box-section frame rails.). Each box-section girder was composed of two full length channel sections welded together.

The frame's forward crossmember was conventional Chevrolet and served as a mounting for the front suspension. It had a formed, semi-tubular, flanged top section with a flat steel bottom plate welded across the flanges. An intermediate crossmember of the inverted channel section design was welded between the side rails at the "kick-up" over the rear axle and served as the upper mounting for the rear shock absorbers. The rear crossmember, riveted to the side rails, was a flanged channel section with a welded-on bottom plate and served as a mount for the rear spring shackles.

The rigidity of this frame was augmented at the center by the use of an X-member composed of I-beam sections welded to the side rails at the end of each leg of the "X", with long angular braces also attached to the forward section of the side rails. The use of an X-member brace on the Corvette was a carryover from the full-sized Chevrolet convertible model which, unlike the sedans, needed the extra frame strength. The entire Corvette frame weighed 213 pounds.

While the front crossmember was standard Chevrolet, the front suspension was fitted with a rather stiff stabilizer bar and redesigned center steering lever mounted to a double-row ball bearing. The entire front crossmember was bolted to the Corvette frame, rather than riveted as in the passenger car, to facilitate ease of removal in the future when the unit needed overhaul.

Assembly of the running gear began at Flint by placing the frame upside down on a rolling dolly fixture. This allowed for easy installation of the rear leaf springs, fuel and brake lines and hoses, and the heavy rear axle housing (complete with all brake components) which was dropped in place by an electric hoist suspended from an overhead rail.

Here again, the Corvette differed from the passenger car. While the Chevrolet's rear springs attached directly underneath the side frame rails, the Covette used inclined "outrigger" springs to aid ride and handling characteristics. The passenger cars had always used a "torque tube" which was a rigid structure containing the driveshaft and connecting the rear axle to the transmission. This tube absorbed all engine torque from the rear wheels, rather than using the rear springs as in the Corvette's essential Hotchkiss drive setup. The wheelbase of the Corvette was too short to allow for a

torque tube, so an existing Chevrolet rear axle (supplied by Chevrolet Gear & Axle) was adapted to the Hotchkiss drive's open propeller shaft. The 36 inch propeller shaft passed over the frame's rigid X-member brace (rather than through it as on passenger cars of the day), and this required the use of a woven cloth rebound strap attached to each side of the frame, limiting the downward motion of the rear axle housing. If the rebound straps were not used, excessive U-joint angles could occur, and the propeller shaft would strike the center of the X-brace.

Following assembly of all the components to the underside of the frame, the wheels and tires were installed. The wheels used for 1953 were 5 x 15″ covered on all surfaces with Sportsman Red Duco enamel paint, and fitted with 6.70 x 15″ wide whitewall tires. After their installation, the overhead hoist was attached to one side of the inverted frame, lifting the entire chassis off the dolly and moving it forward to the next station where it was lowered carefully and turned right-side up onto a raised platform. This raised platform consisted of two tracks on which the chassis could roll ahead through the remaining stages of assembly.

At this point the engine and transmission assembly (assembled and dynamometer test-run on a feeder line) was lowered into place by another overhead hoist. The 1953 Corvette engine was supplied to the Flint line by railroad car from Chevrolet's Tonawanda, New York engine plant; the Powerglide automatic transmission came crated from their Cleveland, Ohio facility. Again, standard Chevrolet components were adapted to Corvette usage.

The engine was basically the same 235.5 cubic inch Blue Flame-125 (horsepower) six cylinder powerplant used in the passenger car, except that it was modified for increased performance and installation requirements. This unique Corvette engine was named the "Blue Flame Special" and developed 150 gross horsepower at 4200 RPM using premium fuel.

The most noticeable difference was the addition of three Carter "YH" model sidedraft carburetors mated to a single aluminum intake manifold. Each was synchronized by the throttle linkage to two engine cylinders, with uniform balance of the car-

Page 74-75: *Chassis assembly at Flint. Note that frame at far left is inverted for easy component assembly. Frame was turned over between this station and next.* **Left:** *Oops!*

Duals, solids and three carbs

buretors aided by a small integral manifold surge passage. Each carburetor was fitted with a separate manual choke cable ganged to a single dash mounted control knob. Automatic choking could not be used due to fast engine idle. Triple carburetion provided more rapid acceleration and higher top speed, and side-drafting provided the necessary hood clearance.

A special dual exhaust manifold provided two completely separate exhaust systems which increased mid-range engine torque by eight to ten foot/pounds, as well as supplying a distinct sound. The three front engine cylinders exhausted through the front exhaust pipe, across to the right side muffler and tail pipe while the three rear cylinders were carried away by the rear outlet and down the left side.

Normal operation did not require exhaust manifold preheat of the incoming fuel mixture through the intake manifold during engine warm-up; it was not desirable or even recommended. While a provision was made for a heat valve using the front section of the exhaust manifold, a heat shield was installed between the two manifolds directing exhaust gases away from the intake manifold, and the heat valve spring was even installed in reverse, keeping the valve always closed. If heat valve operation became necessary in extreme cold weather, the heat shield had to be removed and the valve spring reversed.

Additional engine speed was also achieved by an increased cylinder head compression ratio of 8 to 1 (compared to 7.5 to 1 in the passenger car). A reduction of the overall combustion chamber volume in the Corvette's cylinder head allotted for the Increase. New light weight aluminum alloy pistons were used along with intake and exhaust valves incorporating advanced metallurgy to take higher engine temperatures. A high lift camshaft was used, allowing the valves to open further into the combustion chamber, and also featured an aluminum timing gear as opposed to a standard composition gear.

Hydraulic valve lifters normally would have been satisfactory for this engine. However, because engine speeds were known to exceed 5000 RPM, mechanical tappets and dual valve springs were required to prevent "floating" of the valve train. It is believed that the prototype Corvette used hydraulic lifters, but testing showed them to be inadequate.

The Corvette's ignition system was completely encased by metal shielding to prevent radio interference through the fiberglass body. A special ignition distributor was fitted to the engine incorporating a mechanical drive gear which was attached by a cable to the dashboard-mounted tachometer monitoring true engine speed. This distributor also used a beefed-up condenser and adjacent coil providing extra voltage at higher engine speeds. Longer point dwell was achieved by a modified distributor shaft ignition cam.

A vacuum advance diaphragm was used, and ignition timing adjustment changes (due to differences in gasoline sold commercially) could be made easily through an "octane selector" scale incorporated into the distributor mount clamp allowing for ten degrees of spark advance or retard from top-dead-center.

To provide proper engine cooling, a special high efficiency water pump capable of circulating 27 gallons per minute (at a normal 2000 RPM) was designed specifically for the Blue Flame Special Corvette engine. This pump, driven at 9/10ths engine speed, was far removed from a standard Chevrolet pump for two reasons; 1) frontal body design necessitated that the radiator be mounted at a steep incline requiring a large 18 inch four-bladed fan to assure more than adequate airflow through the radiator and around the engine block, and 2) the larger fan meant that the water pump had to be positioned lower or interference with the upper radiator hoses and underside of the car's hood would occur.

The lower pump mounting was achieved by the use of an adaptor, or backing, plate to which a centrifugal, permanently lubricated type pump was bolted. This was an expensive design as indicated by the replacement cost of servicing the two parts in the $40 price range, compared to $12 for a standard pump.

The Harrison Division-supplied copper cellular radiator, with its 393 cubic inches of frontal area, was inclined at such a severe angle that it placed the top below the plane of the cylinder head. This dictated a separate, chromed auxiliary coolant expansion tank, which was mounted along the upper right side of the engine. The completely "submerged" radiator drew coolant from the tank through a 1½″ diameter hose, and a small vapor hose was used to vent the system. Tests showed that radiator fan shrouding was not necessary.

A special thermostat housing was used for the coolant outlet at the front of the cylinder head, again a result of low hood clearance.

Further engine modifications from standard Chevrolet parts concerned the cylinder head valve rocker cover, crankcase oil pan, and vent tube used on the 1953 Corvette. The low profile hood, which was hinged at the front, required that a valve cover be designed with sufficient forward clearance and the oil filler opening relocated further to the rear for easy access. Hood clearance was so critical that the two top mounting holes in the cover had to be recessed. Additionally, two metal flanges were added to the right side of the cover for securing the top half of the ignition shield. The oil pan was shaped differently from the passenger car item due to the Corvette's larger central steering arm and the right side crossover of the exhaust, passing underneath.

It should now be clear that the engine modifications of the 1953 Corvette were much further removed from its passenger car counterpart, than those of the current model Corvette and a new Caprice.

The transmission was an improved version of the standard Powerglide, providing for the Corvette's increased torque. It gave full-throttle upshift at 4500 RPM (55 MPH) and downshift into low gear for passing up to 47 MPH. The major change for the Corvette Powerglide was the sliding 16 splines at the transmission output extension housing, essential to the Hotchkiss drive. The lightness of the Corvette made transmission oil cooling unnecessary.

The engines arrived at Flint less accessories (starters, generators, carburetors, fuel pumps, fans, crankcase vent tubes, distributors, and ignition shields, etc.). The cylinder head, valve cover, and

Left: *This photo shows Corvette number one being completed, with the number two chassis in the foreground.* **Right:** *"Built by hand" really meant something at Flint.*

both exhaust and intake manifolds **were** installed at point of manufacture in Tonawanda, and completely painted in standard Chevrolet blue/green engine enamel. The transmissions arrived painted in flat black. On a feeder line next to the chassis area, these two drivetrain components were mated and their remaining parts were added. Each completed engine was tuned and test-run on a dynamometer which was fitted with its own exhaust pipes and cooling system.

Once the assembly was given an okay, it was hoisted up by an overhead lift running on a conveyor rail, over to the chassis line. Two assemblers lowered the engine/transmission assembly onto the awaiting chassis. At this point the rubber engine mounts were secured and bolted in place, along with the rear transmission mount. The propeller shaft was connected, and the dual exhaust system installed and aligned to the engine and frame. The Delco-supplied battery was also installed and electrical cables attached. The chassis was complete! Down the remaining length of the chassis line, final vehicle assembly would be completed.

A hoist-operated scaffold running on an overhead rail would lift a completed body from the trim area and transport it through the air to the chassis. This scaffold was lined with fleece to protect the body paint. Four workmen were stationed at each corner of the chassis, with one operating the hoist controls, as the body was lowered and positioned on the frame being careful not to allow unnecessary contact of the two components. The body would be secured to the chassis at eleven locations and, as it was lowered, correct positioning was made using a large tapered drift tool at various mount locations. The body was aligned via metal shims (as needed for proper door and trunk function) placed between rubber bushings through which the body bolts would be attached and tightened to the proper torque specification.

Once in place, the remaining body trim and chassis parts were fitted, installed, or connected: the hood panel, all upholstery, carpets and seats, steering wheel, side window ventilators, wheel covers, exhaust outlets, luggage area trim and spare tire, radiator hoses and the windshield wipers and washers were added. The white "Blue Flame Special" lacquer decal with its distinctive lightning bolt was applied to the engine's valve cover. Assemblage of the Corvette was complete. Final inspection and a water test were carried out, followed by a test drive and any needed adjustments. The car was ready for shipment.

The very first production model 1953 Corvette was completed on Tuesday, June 30th (slightly more than one year from the drawing board) and Mr. Carl Jarema, an engineer at Chevrolet, was one of the plant personnel who worked on that car. He recently related that Harlow Curtice (then president of General Motors) had ordered, "The Corvette would be in production during the month of June!" The Flint pilot-crew made a mad dash to meet the deadline, completing both Jobs One and Two on the last day of the month. Full production, however, was still several months away.

Above: *Serial number #53F001289 (note "289 written on right-rear frame rail) body drop. Body hooks are wrapped to prevent scratching finish.* **Above right:** *The very first Corvette rolls off the Flint assembly line on June 30, 1953.*

The Flint test bed

Magazine articles published during the Summer of 1953 indicated that by the end of July only 15 units had been completed, and that total was raised to 40 by the end of August. During September approximately another 40 cars were built bringing the total to around 80. By Christmas all 300 of the Flint Corvettes were completed, with maximum production approaching the rate of six cars per day near the end.

As mentioned earlier, the Flint pilot-line served as a test-bed for exploring Corvette assembly techniques. Project engineers estimated that the actual cost of producing a single car at Flint was in the neighborhood of $4,800 to $4,900 (the retail price of the car was $3,250, of which the dealer paid Chevrolet $2,470). Assembly personnel were chosen for their craftsmanship skills. More economical methods of producing the Corvette had to be found before higher production rates could be achieved.

On Saturday, March 28, 1953, even before the first Corvette rolled away at Flint, Chevrolet's St. Louis, Missouri, assembly plant was notified that 1954 model production would begin there as soon as the pilot operation was closed down. The St. Louis facility at that time held the division's production record as builder of more Chevrolet cars and trucks than any other plant.

The Flint Corvettes were reminiscent of Louis Chevrolet's early auto exploits, but the St. Louis Corvette plant would be equally steeped in tradition and history. It dated back to 1915 when the Banner Buggy Company bought a franchise from Chevrolet to manufacture cars in St. Louis. General Motors Corporation (of which Chevrolet was a part) formed in 1917, and Banner's franchise was sold back to GM who built a new plant on 103 acres where Chevrolets (and for a short time, Buicks) would be produced. Since cars of that era used bodies fabricated with wooden framework, a "mill building" was the first to be constructed. That original mill building, some 35 years later, became the home of the Corvette.

The Corvette plant was small compared to the rest of the assembly plant, being packed into a 200 by 500 foot (100,000 square feet) area. It had to be geared to produce a projected 1,000 units per month.

Early in October of 1953, St. Louis Plant Manager William L. Moser Jr. and a group of essential St. Louis personnel went to Flint to see the Corvette pilot-line and what had been learned regarding plastic body construction methods. Since Flint was never tooled for volume assembly, new body fixtures and drilling jigs would have to be designed and in operation soon if St. Louis could ever hope to meet the scheduled 1,000 Corvettes per month planned for 1954. Luckily, much confident progress had been made with regard to mass production of the plastic body panels by Molded Fiber Glass Body Company in Ashtabula, as the majority of parts would be manufactured there via the matched metal die presses in early 1954.

On Monday, December 28, 1953, following Christmas weekend, the St. Louis plant began assembling 1954 model Corvettes. The shift in production was swift as the pilot-line at Flint had shut down

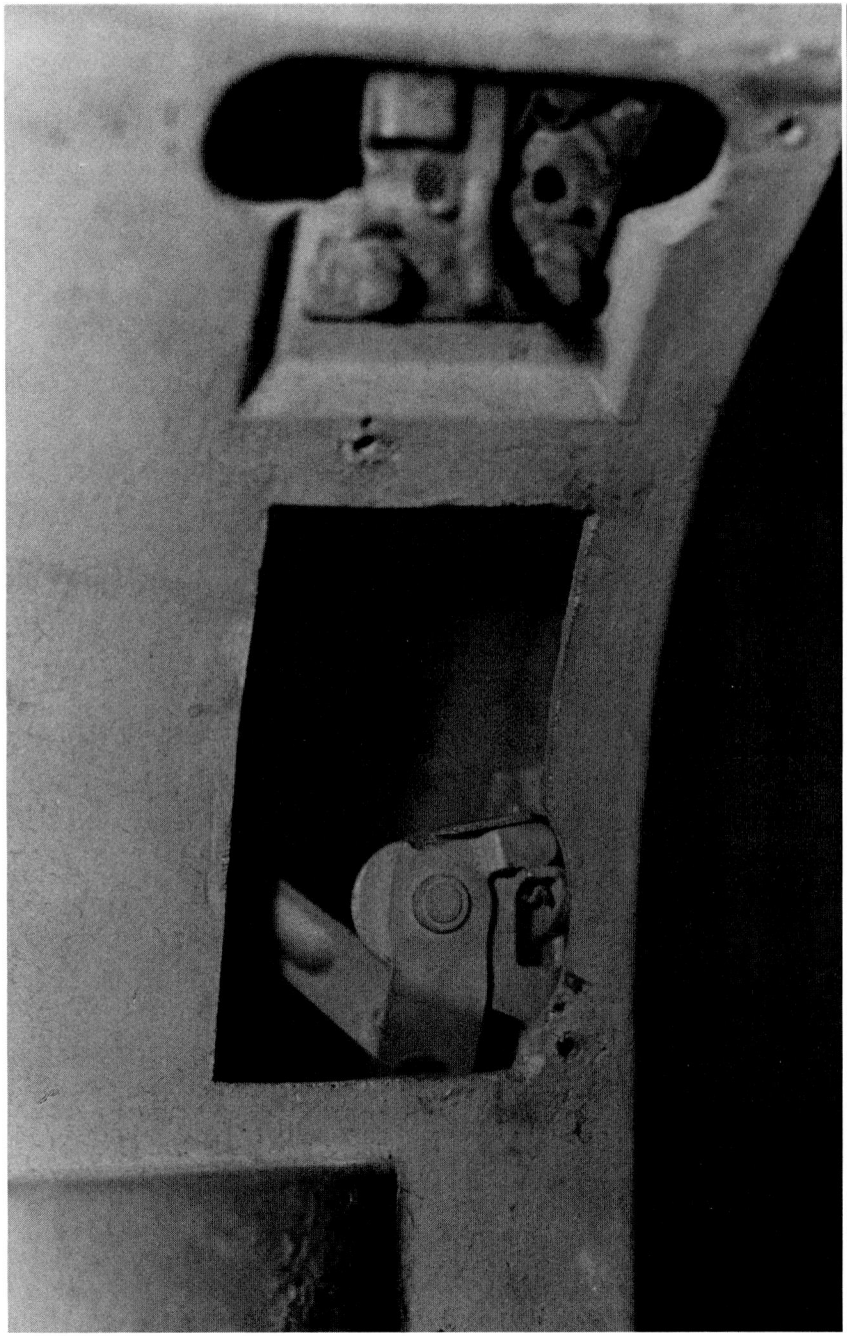

Left: *Running changes throughout 1953 and 1954 production were common. These photos show a change made to the inner door panel after production moved to St. Louis. The access hole for the opening mechanism was changed from square to round.*

Hand tailoring

just before the holidays. During the last few days of calendar-year 1953, 15 brand-new 1954 St. Louis Corvettes were built.

Improved techniques of Corvette plastic body assembly by St. Louis accelerated production. The large underbody panel (previously drilled) entered the first of three water-curtain scuffing rooms, called Mahon booths, where surfaces and bonding edges were prepared. These booths were very efficient in eliminating airborne and floor dust particles created as the plastic was scuffed and ground. An air downdraft forced dust into a cascade of water passing underneath a metal grate in the floor. The Mahon booth had been used previously in auto painting to control fumes and overspray, so it was a natural for plastic body construction.

After scuffing and installation of underbody reinforcements, the large panel was secured by clamps to an assembly truck attached to a power-driven conveyor track imbedded in the plant floor. It remained on this moving conveyor through all stations of body assembly, painting, sanding, oven drying, and trim installation, until it would be lifted off just prior to dropping on the chassis.

Simultaneously, the rear end body sub-assembly and front fender body panels were drilled and ground in Mahon booths at other stations. The rear section was accurately attached to the underbody with the aid of a gate. The headlight openings in the fenders were routed-in, and the housings hand-fitted. A headlight trim bezel was fastened into position and plastic resin puttied all around and ground flush (the bezel then removed for the next car).

The front body panel, complete with radiator support and inner fenders, would then be lifted off of its forward tilting fixture by two assemblers (it took four to do this in Flint, without the tilting fixture!), and carried to the assembly line. There it was positioned and bonded to the body shell, perfectly aligned by the use of a jig simulating precise door measurements. This jig also allowed marking of the door opening at the front fender, which was then ground to provide a close "tailored" fit.

Further minor assembly refinements were instituted at St. Louis. Previously, the access holes for the door opening mechanisms were manually routed, or saw-cut, in a square shape at the backside of the plastic panel. It proved much easier to make these with a smaller, circular hole-saw, eliminating the manual process and additionally providing a more solid door.

Special metal gate fixtures were employed extensively at St. Louis to aid in checking all openings such as the doors, hood, trunk lid, and the top storage compartment cover. In fact, about one third of the body line concerned itself with the fit of these items. Even the front grille opening was measured for precise fit with an inspection gauge before the body shell was bonded together.

A moving station-to-station assembly line had been achieved for body construction. Each station had a particular assembly function, supplied with completed sub-assemblies from feeder-lines.

Once the body shell was completed, it entered a steam cleaning room for the removal of all foreign dust and matter from the surface to be painted. It moved on to a moisture drying oven for one hour at 140 degrees which aided the curing process for the bonded joints. A prime coat was then sprayed in another Mahon booth and allowed to dry in a main oven which could hold four bodies abreast.

An extensive wet-sanding area was adjacent to both the prime coat and color painting booths, and handled bodies in both stages of finish at the same time.

Final exterior body and interior trim color lacquer paint applications were performed, followed by more baking, wet-sanding, and buffing and polishing before the body moved on to the trim area.

The most predominant color combination used on the 1954 Corvette was the Polo White exterior with Sportsman Red trim, just as all 300 Flint cars had been. Very early at St. Louis, exterior painting was expanded slightly with the addition of a few cars finished in black or Sportsman Red, both retaining the red trim as on the white cars. Published production reports however, indicate that by early Summer 1954, only the white cars, and a new Pennant Blue exterior with Shoreline Beige trim combination, were being offered.

The St. Louis trim line was comprised of 18 stations. Here the painted steering mast, seats, interior upholstery, dash instruments and speedometer, radiator, bumpers and bright trim, heater, radio, lights, horns and body wiring harnesses were installed. Unlike Flint, St. Louis installed the folding top and side curtains in their raised position, prior to body drop.

Normally, in more conventional auto assembly, many of these items were not installed until after the body drop operation was completed. But it was deemed too costly and time consuming to replace or adjust faulty items or installations further down the Corvette line. Even the body electrical connections and accessories were tested on the trim line prior to body drop, being temporarily hooked up to a battery. Repairs after final assembly had to be avoided.

The chassis line ran parallel to the body trim line, and frame build-up assembly was conventional, as it had been at the Flint pilot line. While the 1953 Corvette engines had been manufactured at the division's Tonawanda, New York plant, the 1954 powerplant was now being built in Flint and shipped to St. Louis.

Upon arrival, the bare engines were dressed up with all accessory components and attached to their Powerglide transmissions. Three dynamometer testing stands were used, and each engine was test-run for 30 minutes. During the test, the carburetors were synchronized, valve lash and timing adjusted, and the transmission checked for shifting, noise, and acceleration pressure under load conditions. The entire powerplant was ready for driveaway even before it was installed.

The Corvette chassis line had one of the first installations of a special on-the-car wheel balancing machine developed by the Hunter Engineering Company. This machine permitted balancing of two wheels at once, while the line was moving. Wheels and tires were spun at high speed by the operator with a motor drive attached across the chassis fixture, while a wheel-mounted dial indicator provided readings for weight size and location. As in 1953, all wheels were painted red, even those on the blue cars.

Following the body being mated to the chassis, the completed Corvette was driven off the line under its own power for a water leak test and quick trip around the plant grounds.

Above: *Wheel balancing of a '54 at St. Louis.* **Right:** *Body drop at St. Louis differed from Flint in that body was nearly complete, including folding top and side curtains in place.*

While volume assembly methods were achieved at St. Louis, Chevrolet's hoped-for schedule of 1,000 Corvettes per month did not materialize during 1954 (and it wouldn't, until December, 1957, when 1068 new 1958 model Corvettes were built that month). Just as production increased in early 1954, it was readjusted by July to 300 cars per month (Chevrolet said this cut-back was only "temporary"). In fact, at year's end, 977 new Corvettes were still unsold, out of a total 1954 model run of 3,640 units. The Corvette's future was in serious jeopardy due to lagging sales.

During the time that the division was designing the Corvette, work was also being done at Chevrolet Engineering to develop a new V-8 engine for the passenger car. Ultimately, an all new-passenger car chassis would be designed for a 265 cubic inch engine incorporating Hotchkiss drive, and was

NO SMOKING

These rare photos depict what apparently is the first factory installation of a Corvette V-8. Notes to production for necessary clearance modifications are scribed on the firewall and inner fenders.

eventually marketed on the Chevrolet product line-up for the 1955 model.

However, in 1953 during development of a V-8, and even before the final engine design was approved for passenger car production, one of the Flint-built pilot line Corvettes assigned to Chevrolet Engineering for testing was relieved of its stock six cylinder powerplant. This 1953 Corvette was fitted with an experimental prototype V-8 engine (of unknown displacement), apparently to develop and evaluate the technical practicality, and to design changes necessary to get this type of engine into an actual production model. Since the six cylinder engine had been highly modified from standard form for installation in the Corvette, a new V-8 design for a new passenger car chassis would likewise have to be modified to fit.

Again, as with the 1953 model, engine to hood clearance was a major factor. But unlike the slim sides of a straight-line six, the V-8 was a wider engine creating new fit problems in the Corvette's engine compartment. As fit changes and modifications were realized, written chalk notations were made directly to the areas affected on the prototype.

The motor mounting for this prototype installation was strictly "model-shop" made, being attached to the front of the engine block at the water pump and resting on the frame further forward than the six. This allowed the engine to set low. To simulate a yet undesigned air cleaner, a round piece of plywood sat atop the carburetor.

While the V-8 was wider than the six, it was also shorter, which meant the fan would be set further back and airflow through the radiator and around the block would have to be increased. A radiator fan shroud would be the answer. Further, an auxiliary coolant tank was impractical, so a filler cap would have to be added to the radiator.

It was determined that the left-bank cylinder head exhaust manifold on the V-8 would be positioned too close to the steering column mast jacket, so it was decided that the column would have to be moved slightly to the left of center. The left-side exhaust pipe also interfered with the Pitman arm at the steering gear during a severe left turn situation,

SHARK
Melbourne Brindle

STEELGARD
GOODYEAR
GOODYEAR
STEELGARD

so a bracket limiting arm travel would have to be added.

The right side of the engine also sat too close to the battery, so it was noted that the holding tray would have to be moved further to the outside. Relocation of the battery meant that the right inner fender panel would have to be changed allowing more room. Further, the hoses to the heater core would be routed further to the outside, as well as the engine starter electrical relay attached to the firewall.

The fuel pump attached at the right front side of the V-8 was resting too close to the frame rail, and any engine movement could cause interference. To remedy this, it was noted that the rail would have to be "bumped", meaning a recess area added.

Whether or not this 1953 Corvette with its prototype V-8 engine installation was actually a running vehicle is unknown. It is known, though, that during 1954 a 265 V-8 was installed in the actual 1953 Motorama Corvette showcar, which by then was serving as a test vehicle refitted with production parts. Through durability tests run on that car (and surely other Corvettes), it was determined that a V-8 installation was not only practical, but highly advantageous to improved Corvette performance.

This paved the way for a V-8 Corvette as a production reality in 1955. Whether there would still be a Corvette at all was another factor, considering the lagging sales. A philosophy of "Never Give Up", in the face of competition from Ford's newly introduced Thunderbird, allowed the Corvette to continue and it was hoped the V-8 would create new life.

Exactly when 1955 Corvette production began is not known, other than that it did not begin immediately following the end of the 1954 model run. Line start-up began later than introduction of the 1955 Chevrolet passenger cars, sometime after January 1, 1955.

The 1955 Corvette was offered in two distinct models, designated as 2934-6 (six cylinder) and 2934-8 (V-8). The six was an almost duplicate carryover of the 1954 model, except that now its horsepower rating was advertised at 155 (the five horsepower increase had actually been achieved during

1954 by a camshaft change, but was not mentioned in later 1954 sales literature). Chevrolet's new V-8 engine was a masterpiece! With 265 cubic inches of displacement the Corvette version was rated at 195 gross horsepower (passenger car ratings were the standard 162 HP, and 180 HP with optional "Power Pack"). While Chevrolet had had a V-8 back in 1917-1919, this new motor was an engineering sensation.

The cylinders of the cast alloy iron block were surrounded by full-length water jackets, and the crankcase provided for a main oil gallery to the crankshaft and two for hydraulic valve lifter lubrication. The engine was considered "oversquare", in that the 3.75″ cylinder bore was larger than the 3″ piston stroke.

The two cast alloy iron cylinder heads were interchangeable, either left or right side, and provided return passages for oil back down to the crankcase. Full pressure lubrication allowed engine oil to pass through an opening in the solid lifters moving oil up through the hollow push rods to lubricate the valve mechanism. The steel push rods were connected to the valve stems by independent, stamped steel rocker arms attached to the head via a new ball stud and lock nut design.

Other features included a forged alloy crankshaft with a front rubber mounted inertia balancer including timing-mark, connected by five main bearings, and press-fit piston pins at the connecting rods.

Not only did the new V-8 increase performance, it reduced engine weight over the six; approximately 570 lbs. for the six, to 530 lbs. for the new V-8.

A total of only 700 1955 Corvettes were produced, the majority of those being the V-8 equipped models. While the exact figure is unknown, partial production figures have been uncovered which indicate that six cylinder cars accounted for about only one or two percent of production; or 10 to 20 cars. Since only 700 were built, a six cylinder 1955 Corvette is considered extremely rare.

Little, if any, formal Chevrolet data exists which can accurately pinpoint the technical differences between the two engined models. An attempt to do so, however, should be made.

It had often been assumed that the 1955 six cylinder models may have been merely retitled 1954

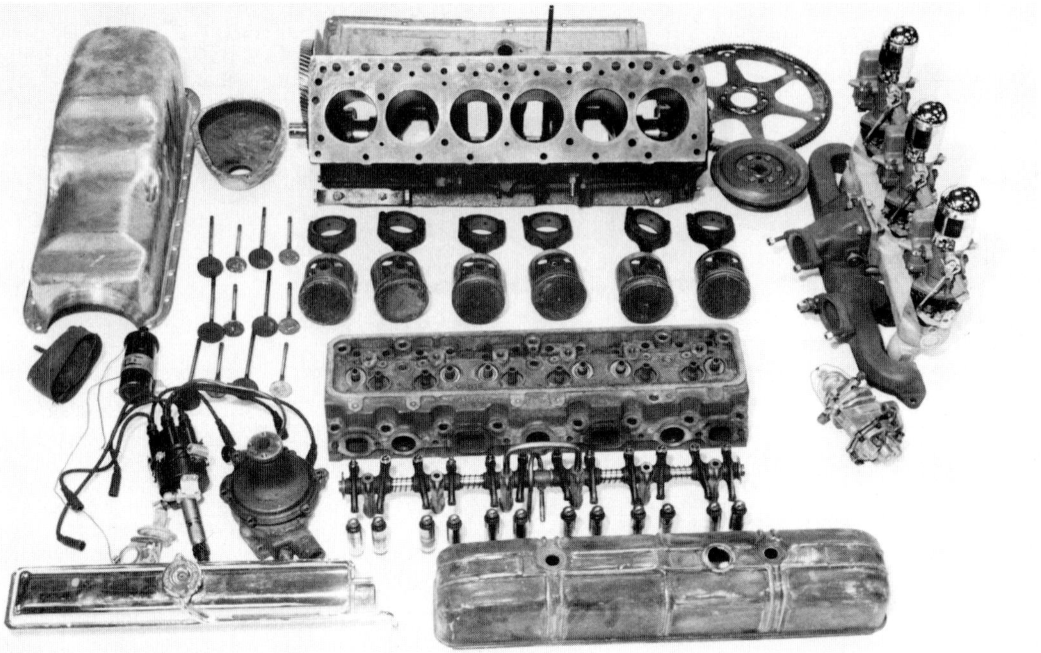

Left: *The components that made up the venerable "Blue Flame Six", and axle and transmission parts. All are typical for 1953 production models.* **Right:** *V-8 installation in a '55 model is denoted on the body exterior by a gold "V" overlapping the side "Chevrolet" script.*

"V" meant V-8

models left over at year's end, or at least exact duplicates. This apparently is not the case, as evidenced by at least one remaining six cylinder 1955 (others are known to exist).

External identification of a V-8 model was by a gold tinted "V" affixed over the small vee in the Chevrolet side script on each front fender. The six naturally did not carry these. However, the necessary mounting holes in the panels may have been drilled in the fenders on the assembly line, then filled in on a six-equipped car down the line.

The Vehicle Identification Number serial plate (attached to the left-side door post) was prefixed "VE55S" for a V-8 model, or "E55S" for a six. The plates carrying a "V" show a distinct difference in the stamping of that character when compared to the remaining letters and digits.

As noted previously, clearance of the V-8's fuel pump necessitated a relief in the right side frame girder, and different location for the motor mounting hardware as compared to the six, which didn't have the frame relief.

While the V-8's 12 volt battery and larger-sized holding tray were positioned farther to the right than the earlier 1953 and 1954 six cylinder cars, it appears that the 1955 sixes also carried the V-8 style tray and used an oversize six volt battery. Thus, the redesigned 1955 inner fender panel and routing of hoses to the heater core were apparently identical on both engined models. These changes have caused confusion today concerning authenticity of an actual six cylinder 1955 Corvette.

Hoods used on six cylinder Corvettes contained an "X" member center reinforcement panel on the underside. The 1955 with V-8 engine used a hood whose reinforcement was a single rib running perpendicular to the car's centerline for clearance of the air cleaner when the hood was closed. While the

Left: *She may be smiling, but Chevrolet executives were not, as Corvette inventory started piling up during 1954 production. Photo was taken at the holding yard of the St. Louis plant.*

Production went up but sales dropped

six cylinder 1955 model could also have shared the V-8's hood, the known example appears with the "X" type.

The new V-8 with its 12 volt system used an electric windshield wiper motor, the six retained a vacuum operated drive.

The Corvette's Powerglide, with its special extension housing, used a 36 inch propeller shaft. The V-8 Corvette for 1955, however, used the same output housing as the 1955 passenger car which also used Hotchkiss drive. Since this housing was a bit longer, the V-8 Corvette driveshaft was shorter, measuring 34½". This dictated a change in the shaft guard which had been a metal strap that bolted to the frame's "X" member and ran over the shaft on cars equipped with a six. The V-8 guard was a formed metal plate attached directly to the floor tunnel on the underbody.

Because the V-8 engine was positioned so close to the steering column, it was necessary to install a thick metal spacer between the frame and steering gear housing. Also, the column opening in the firewall had to be widened (by hand cutting on the assembly line rather than modifying the panel dies) and the resultant gap was covered by a metal plate. The addition of the spacer and cover plate moved the column sufficiently to the left.

To prevent the Pitman steering arm from colliding with the V-8 exhaust during a left turn, a raised boss which acted as a "stop" was cast into the arm, which lined up with a bracket attached to the column mounting to limit arm travel.

The six cylinder 1955's did not carry these steering modifications.

Other V-8 changes concerned the dash which eliminated the manual choke provision, and a new tachometer with dial increments of 1000 RPM rather than the six's 500.

Up to this point, only a Powerglide 1955 Corvette has been discussed. The public's desire for a manual shift brings us to the question of a 1955 Corvette with three speed transmission. Much evidence exists which substantiates the limited application of a three speed with the V-8 during 1955. Dealer price sheets, listings in the service parts catalog, blue prints and several verified examples authenticate its usage. The number so equipped has been purported to be 75, but no figure can be proven. Also, a six cylinder 1955 with a manual transmission cannot be completely ruled out according to some Chevrolet documents, but the actual existence of such a combination is highly doubtful.

The reason why Chevrolet chose to produce so few of the 1955 models can probably be attributed to the large inventory of the previous year's 1954 six cylinder cars left unsold. Because it **is** known that only a handful of 1955 sixes were built, Chevrolet calendar-year six cylinder Corvette sales figures indicate that pre-1955 models were sold as late as 1956; by then a brand new 1954 Corvette was still considered a two year old car.

ANNUAL SIX CYLINDER CORVETTE SALES
(Listed by calendar-year, not model-year)
Source: Chevrolet Motor Division

1953	183
1954	2,780
1955	869
1956	141
Total	3,973

Chevrolet surely wanted to allow the factory and the dealer network to deplete existing inventories, before building more new 1955 Corvettes, regardless of the new V-8 engine.

The early Corvettes did have their share of problems; any newly introduced vehicle does. From the very start of 1953 Corvette production, through the end of 1955, these models were constantly undergoing design and manufacturing changes: changes brought on by response from owners and dealers in the field, durability road and component tests, and new ways to produce more efficient or less costly parts. These are commonly referred to as "running changes" in that they are implemented on the assembly line during any given model run.

After several of the first 1953 Corvettes were test driven it was noticed that engine oil (thrown out the valve rocker cover venting slots) would exit the engine compartment at the rear of the hood and splatter the windshield. A production change was implemented adding a length of rubber seal to the rear hood lip, preventing oil escape and therefore remedying the problem. This occurred about ten cars into production, and it is reported that a service directive was released to correct this situation on the earlier cars produced without the seal (the first Corvette recall?).

The flat radio upper speaker grille had first been finished in chrome plate. Sometime early in production the grille's finish was changed to flat black paint, giving a better symmetrical appearance match with the speedometer housing at the opposite side of the dash.

A driver's door mounted rear-view mirror (affectionately called the "Guide Y-50") supplied by the Guide Lamp Division of GM has always been identified with the early Corvette. However, it didn't appear on the very early 1953's and was not mentioned in either the owner's handbook or the 1953 Corvette Parts Catalog. Improved rearward vision with the top up brought about the addition of this mirror as a standard item.

The standard windshield washer system on the first 1953's was actuated by a foot-pedal "squash" pump mounted on the floor under the dash. When the pedal was pushed, a squirt of washer fluid was sprayed at the glass and a Bowden cable would activate the wipers, which would return to rest position when the pedal was released. Somewhere between serial number 1175 and 1181 the washer system was changed to a vacuum coordinator pump operated by the dash wiper control.

An early gas filler door hinge was adapted from the passenger car item and did not provide adaquate room for easy removal of the Corvette's gasoline cap. A new hinge was designed allowing the filler door the swing clear for cap removal, and appeared between serial number 1083 and 1091.

A recently discovered 1953 change deals with the shape of the convertible top frame's left and right side link assembly support arms. For a yet unknown reason, early arms appear straight while later arms have a curve, the change probably occurring between cars 1076 and 1091.

An estimated 25 Corvettes were initially equipped with standard Chevrolet Bel Air full wheel cover discs, apparently used awaiting delivery of the special Corvette covers. Further, a first design Corvette

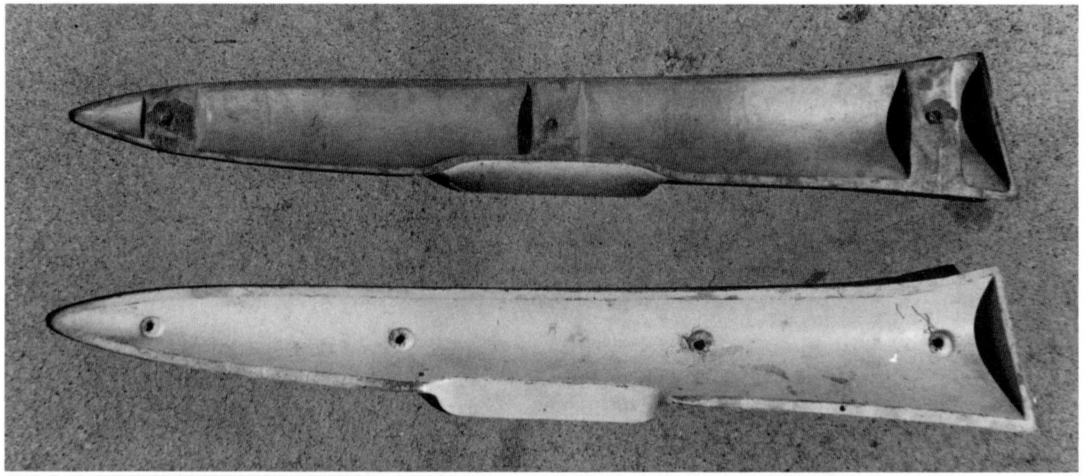

Page 94: *Inner door panel of '53 and early '54 models was unique with "hand lay" door pulls, distinguished by three attaching screws. This photo is of an early '53 with no door mounted mirror.* **Page 95:** *Also an early '53, photo shows interior details, including chrome speaker screen which was unique to the first '53 models.* **Left:** *This promotional photo is typical of Chevrolet's misdirected marketing efforts for the early Corvettes. This is another early '53, with perpendicular spinner-to-bow-tie hubcaps.* **Above:** *Perhaps the same early '53, this car also has the first type hubcap, and the 90° bend radiator overflow tube.*

cover was used which had spinner ornaments attached perpendicular to the center "bow-tie" emblem, while later covers appeared with horizonal spinners.

Under the hood of the 1953, early chrome auxiliary coolant tanks used an overflow tube containing a 90 degree bend at the end, directing flow downward to an attached rubber hose. During production this tube was shortened eliminating the bend.

A change in the Carter YH type carburetors used, occurred during 1953 when the switch was made from model 2066S to 2066SA; the latter using a different pump diaphragm, throttle shaft, shaft arm, and lever assembly. This seems like a minor change, but precise carb synchronization was essential to smooth engine running as the slightest difference in throttle valve openings above idle would be noticed. The connecting carburetor linkage also underwent a design change.

Almost immediately after startup of the 1954 model run, several assembly modifications were instituted. The A. O. Smith Corporation (frame suppliers) filed an engineering test report with Chevrolet on ride and handling qualities relating to the frame structure performed on a 1953 model. The Smith report contained several observations and criticisms of the test car. The rear spring shackle bolts had been installed in such a manner that removal was impossible. It seems that once the body was in place, there was not enough room between the shackle and the body to remove the bolts. Smith recommended that the bolts be installed from the centerline side of the shackle hence allowing easy removal. The change **was** made! Also, fouling of the trunk with exhaust fumes was noted, as well as staining of body paint at the tail pipes.

Zora Arkus-Duntov, then a newly hired engineer at Chevrolet, had already run exhaust tests on the

Corvette. Duntov found that exhaust fumes entering the trunk depended on the trunk lid seal. The solution to this came easily, with the weather stripping seal being installed in reverse fashion allowing for a tighter fit when the trunk was closed. He also determined that the solution to the staining of the tail pipe openings could best be accomplished by relocating the pipes to the fenders. This was not done until 1956, but a temporary fix saw the addition of longer exhaust extension tips which also directed exhaust down. The 1954 changeover to the longer exhaust extensions occurred in the 2500 serial number range.

The fuel and brake lines to the rear had been mounted along the outside of the right frame rail throughout 1953 with a special gasoline drain fitting located near the fuel tank. This continued early in 1954, but before the first hundred or so cars had been built, the lines were rerouted to run along the inside of the rail and the fuel drain eliminated. The lines would be afforded better protection in case of a collision and would not be subjected to stone bruising quite as easily since they'd be out of the tire's path. A similar shift was made in the mounting of the headlight dimmer switch passing through the floor at the driver's foot. Previously it had been located directly behind the left front tire splash shield in the wheel house. To prevent eventual road dirt accumulation on the switch body and wire connections, it was moved several inches inboard, just enough to place it in the engine compartment out of danger.

The six cylinder Corvette AC fuel pump was of "double-action" design (the same pump was optional on the passenger car). In addition to supplying gasoline to the carburetors, it provided reserve vacuum to operate the windshield wiper motor when engine vacuum dropped off during full acceleration or idle. The pump carried inlet gas lines which ran at a 30 degree angle to the engine block, and mounted a fuel sediment and moisture collector bowl on top, with added protection coming from a fuel filter placed just ahead of the front carburetor. Relocation of this filter occurred extremely early in 1954 production, being fitted directly to a new AC fuel pump containing parallel fuel lines accom-

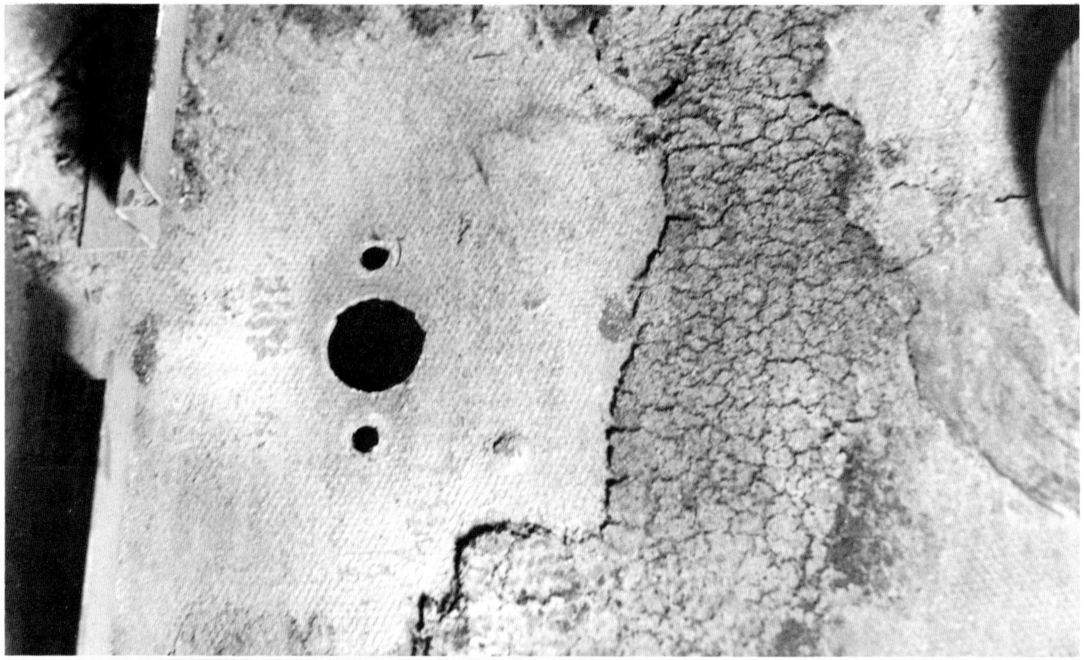

Left: *Illustration of the move made in dimmer switch location early in 1954 production. Top photo is original location and bottom is new location, inboard for better protection from road dirt and corrosion.* **Right:** *Another running change, the addition of Conelrad markings to the radio dial (round dots at "6.4" and "12.4").*

Civil defense

modating the filter. Why the filter was moved away from the left side is not known; it may have been done as a prevention against fire hazard near the exhaust manifold and pipes.

Two hood latch release cables with control knobs were mounted under the instrument panel on the right and left side. Since this caused awkward "reach-across" for the driver when unlocking the right hood latch, somewhere between 1954 serial numbers 1300 and 1336 the cables were ganged into a single control placed next to the parking brake lever at the right side of the steering column. Positioning of the ignition starter switch and the manual carburetor choking control knob next to each other on the right hand side of the wheel made starting the car similarly awkward. Between serial number 1981 and 2054 the choke and wiper control locations swapped places, placing the choke on the left side.

During 1953 and 1954, Chevrolet (in fact, GM) was replacing all braided fabric insulated wire with the then-new vinyl insulated type. As old stocks of fabric wiring were depleted, the vinyl wire would appear in the electrical system wiring harnesses. Another eventual changeover during 1954 concerned the addition of Conelrad Civil Defense markings to the station dial indicator at 640 and 1240 kilocycles on radios supplied by Delco.

Initially, the Corvette did not use carburetor air cleaners as we commonly think of them. Chevrolet didn't even refer to them as such in the owner's handbook, preferring to call them "carburetor air inlet extensions." These three chromed metal inlets (now referred to as "bullets") measured about four inches long, each with three openings covered by common wire screening. The housings of the inlets contained a "V" mark, which had to be installed in alignment with the boss on the carb's air horn. This alignment aimed the inlet's openings toward the ground allowing gasoline to run out should the carburetors flood (which they often did). Around 1954 serial number 2900, a far more efficient air cleaning system was introduced. This contained breather tubing ducts for each carburetor and two top mounted air cleaners with removeable oil-wetted aluminum mesh filter elements. Again, in case of

100

CHEVROLET MOTOR DIVISION
GENERAL MOTORS CORPORATION
CHEVROLET
SAINT LOUIS PLANT

flooding an air screen was provided at the bottom of the breather ducting.

The use of chrome-plated metal ignition shielding and rocker arm valve cover shows up on 1954 (and 1955) sixes, as opposed to parts painted in engine color. Their appearance on original cars surveyed today does not seem to fit any specific pattern, and there is no supporting Chevrolet documentation concerning the change to chrome from the specified painted finish. All that can be said is that this change did happen. These items, in chrome, begin to randomly appear on about 14% of the cars above serial number 1600. Further, cars may appear with a chrome valve cover while carrying painted shields, and vice versa.

The largest complaint lodged against the 1953-1955 Corvettes related to problems concerning water leaks and the function of the convertible canvas top. Wind noise was annoying at high speeds with the corner flaps being known to unsnap, and the front crossbar would lift off the windshield header and top fasteners wouldn't stay fastened. These problems were more than amplified by water leaks during a rain storm.

Never give up!

Little relief for the water leaks came during the three years of production, but some minor redesigning of the top bow structure was done during 1954.

Sometime during the 3000-3600 serial range the main bow was changed near its hinge area, where it came through the body. The earlier cars used a stainless body trim moulding containing a retractable "flipper" through which the bow entered as the top was raised. This trim moulding also provided the male snap for securing the top's corner flaps. Fingers and canvas were known to get caught, pinched or torn here, so the flipper (which also became bent or broken) was eliminated and the bow severely curved to clear the body and moulding; the outside seat back shoulder area also required a relief for the bow curve. Overall, this modification was more efficient and somewhat less costly in terms of the parts used.

The top was not easily raised by one person, so around serial number 4000 an operating instruction decal was affixed to the underside of the top's storage compartment lid. Also, the rear bow male latches which entered strikers in the lid were known to contact and scratch body paint during insertion. Late in 1954 a small metal tab protecting the paint was fitted under the striker as a cure.

When the 1955 Corvette was introduced, Chevrolet announced that convertible tops would be fabricated of a vinyl coated cloth material called "Co-tan." Beige tops (as used on all 1954 Corvettes) continued to be supplied on 1955's in canvas until stock was depleted, being replaced on the assembly line with a new white vinyl top. Other top colors were also available in 1955 depending on body color.

A top related running change that occurred during 1955 assembly was that of the dash-mounted rear view mirror used. Earlier mirrors had a fixed base, and when the top was raised the road behind could not be seen adequately through the rear plastic backlight due to mirror height. Soon after startup of the 1955 run, a new mirror with a built-in height adjustment and locking thumbscrew replaced the older mirror.

There were, of course, many other running changes and modification improvements made to the 1953-1955 Corvettes — and still others, that would not be incorporated until the introduction of later models.

Today we can look back at Chevrolet's original purpose for building that first, important 1953 model, "a car that was fun to drive and fun to build." The Corvette was and is today, as Jim Premo said, "thoroughly in keeping with the tradition of continually finding new ways to do new things."

When numbers are considered, it would have been understandable if Chevrolet had decided to throw in the towel on this expensive little white roadster. But the people who built the first Corvettes would not give up, and Chevrolet history through the next 25 years has been a whole lot brighter.

Louis Chevrolet would be happy today. In the face of seemingly impossible odds, with the prospect of utter disaster staring them in the eyes, the Chevrolet Division took Louis' words to heart.

Never give up!

1968 Co
THE TRUE SPORTS CAR FROM CHEV
'67 Corve
BY CHEVRO
CORVETTE
sports car

Dealer Promo Blitz

Les Curtner
of Corvettes Original

Remember the story about the farmer's mule which wouldn't pull the plow? The farmer tried everything, short of a stick of dynamite under the mule's tail, to get that mule to move.

No luck. The mule just stood there and refused to budge. Along came a traveling salesman (there's always one of those) who said he'd get the mule to move.

"Yeah, sure," chuckled the farmer. "Go ahead and try."

So the traveling salesman picked up a baseball bat (there's always one of those laying around in the fields) and clobbered the mule between the eyes.

The mule sank to all four knees, shook its head, and stayed there. Then, the salesman whispered something in the mule's ear. Immediately, the mule got up and started pulling the plow.

"Fantastic!" exclaimed the farmer. "What did you tell that mule?"

"Oh, I just said it would be nice if he started plowing."

The farmer was totally perplexed. "But why the baseball bat?"

"See," said the salesman, "First you have to get his attention."

End of cute story. But there's a point to it.

The Corvette didn't sell on sight during all its early years. First, GM had to get the public's attention.

And that's just what GM did. And not only during the first few years, but for many thereafter. Just about every kind of promotional item was used, and today many of those items are practically priceless to collectors of Corvette memorabilia.

The Find

Hidden away at many Chevrolet dealerships is a wealth of Corvette promotion materials. All of it is fascinating to the literature type and restorer as well, but from the standpoint of restoration a certain amount of caution must be exercised, since the automobiles portrayed in promotional materials were often not built exactly as shown. That's because prototypes are normally used for the promotional items, and changes occur between the time the promotional work is finished and cars are actually built.

Discovering the past in Chevrolet dealerships can be as exciting as opening Christmas presents, but take care. The owner may not be thrilled with someone poking around his attic. Personal injury suits, you know.

The best route is through the sales manager, or dealership general manager. He'll tend to be more understanding, especially if you find one who is a genuine auto buff to boot. Offer to pay for whatever you find. That will probably be refused, but make them take something for the coffee fund, at least. Promise yourself not to fall through the rafters, and start searching. Banners, albums, films, and favors remain undiscovered in dealerships across the land.

And when you find something, wow! It's like taking a time trip back twenty-five years. Share your find with other Corvette enthusiasts over a case of your favorite fluid, and suddenly the years fall away. Nostalgia becomes history, reflecting the development of America's only production sports car.

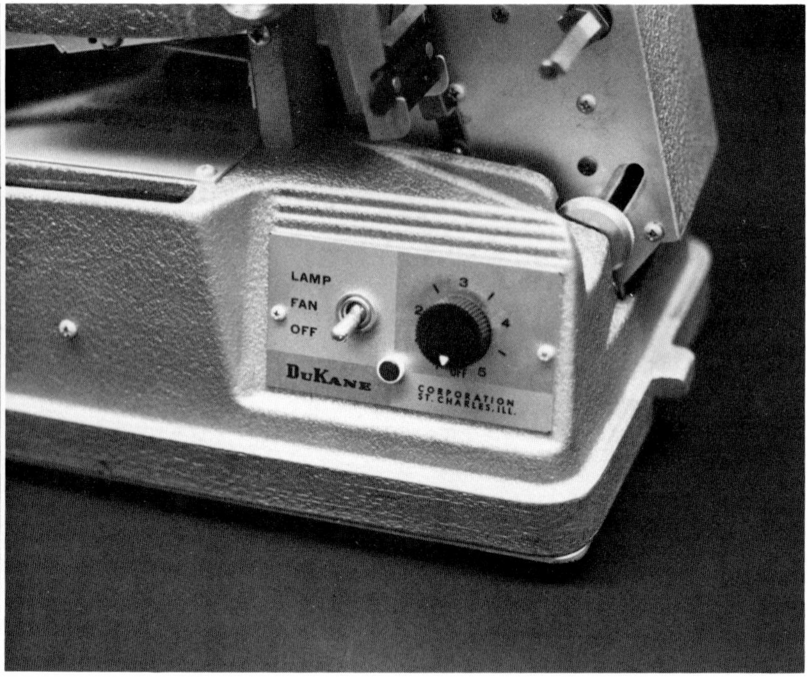

Above: *The DuKane film projector, complete with record-playing capacity.* **Above right:** *"Communications" dealer selling kit for 1966 models. Each small plastic canister holds a film strip.*

Films

Chevrolet couldn't very well give each of its dealers a movie film and a projector, so it did the next best thing. The Jam Handy Organization produced a number of "Product Training Kits" for the dealers. Ostensibly, these were used to train the salesmen of what a Corvette was, but they were surely used to whet the potential buyer's appetite.

They usually consisted of several strips of 35mm film with accompanying records, to explain what the pictures were showing. To view these photo strips, one needed a Dukane projector . . . sort of a simple slide projector.

A variety of these projectors was available, from a manual advancement job, to a projector with tone synchronization. This was the ultimate in marketing sophistication at the time, because the record made a little beep sound which signaled the projector to advance to the next photo. Find one of these Dukane projectors (they're similar to the ones used in schools today for visual education), and the accompanying film strips and records, and consider yourself fortunate. They're rare.

Most of Jam Handy's efforts were in the stillshot 35mm format, but an early movie was also made. The 1953 Corvette debuted in an eighteen minute motion picture narrated by Dave Garroway.

The film was entitled "Hall of Wonders" and apparently used a prototype of the 1953 Corvette. Shots covered the exterior, the interior, and even some engine views. Wonder of wonders, the prototype was shown hustling down an unnamed thoroughfare. But the biggest wonder of all was yet to come.

In 1954, a film strip was produced called "Fun on Wheels." Here were seventy-eight frames depicting that year's Corvette. But the wonder was that Corvette survived at all.

It's no secret that GM still was not sure what to do with the Corvette at that time. The typical buyer as portrayed by that film was a married man, preferably a business owner or executive, around forty-

Jowitt Jupiter?

five years old, and making about ten grand a year (which was a respectable salary in the early Fifties).

This was the infamous marketing blunder we have heard about. The entire film was summed up in its statement that "Here is spirit and speed and here is comfort—your invitation to driving for fun on wheels." The narrator made it clear that the Corvette was an American-made sports car built for American highways and for the all-American taste of driving for fun. It was pointed out that even in the days of the horse-drawn carriage "there were those young in spirit and heart that favored the light and quick handling of the two-seater."

The film went on to compare the Corvette's performance, style, ease of maintenance (just take it to your Chevy dealer), and general economy with the likes of Alpha Romeo, Lancia, Austin Healey, Porsche, MG, and (don't ask why) the Jowitt Jupiter.

Friends, the vision of a Chevy six-banger coupled with Powerglide did not exactly conjure up images of blistering speed. And those well-heeled business executives? After getting a few lap fulls of rain water whenever the weather got nasty, those executives decided they had had enough fun.

Bluntly, they got rid of those Corvettes like a boil in a bad place.

GM's sales expectations for the Corvette just did not meet the reality. Put another way, actual sales for '53 and '54 were godawful. Maybe, some brilliant mind must have thought, we aren't on the right track. Maybe "Fun" isn't the answer.

We know about men like Duntov and Earl who believed honestly that the Corvette should deliver what it promised. But that meant changing the marketing approach.

Certainly, it was time for a rethink. If that fortyish business executive wanted fun, he could buy a Schwinn. Meanwhile, a car was going to be built.

Performance was the new keyword. A 1957 silent film strip called "Date Line Daytona" told us that the Corvette could do something. The film showed Paul Goldsmith's No. 9 taking first place in the twelve hour NASCAR Class C finals, resulting in Corvettes taking the first three positions.

No mention was made of the Corvette's powerplant, but the film did boast that the production Chevrolet with ram jet fuel injection set a new world's record for the Flying Mile at 131.076 mph. More subdued, it admitted that the Corvette had managed only 91.301 in the measured mile. Still, this was enough for Chevrolet to brag that it was the leader in performance among the Big Three automakers in 1957.

Things were starting to look up. In 1957, another film entitled "Pleasure Package, the New 1957 Corvette" identified the Corvette as 2850 pounds of trim, smart design, with every ounce and feature designed for the driver's pleasure.

A return to the "fun" image? Not quite, because the film also promoted fuel injection with a statement from **Motor Trend Drive Report,** January 1957, which reported zero to sixty mph runs at 6.7 seconds.

But power was only part of the Corvette story. Its handling, according to the fact reports, excelled that of any production American auto.

Text continues on page 110

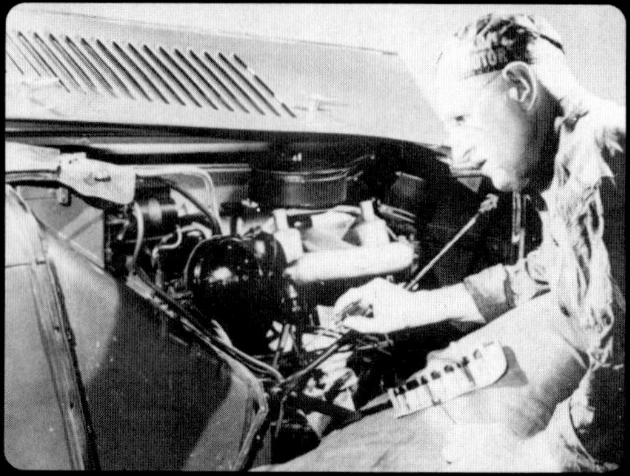

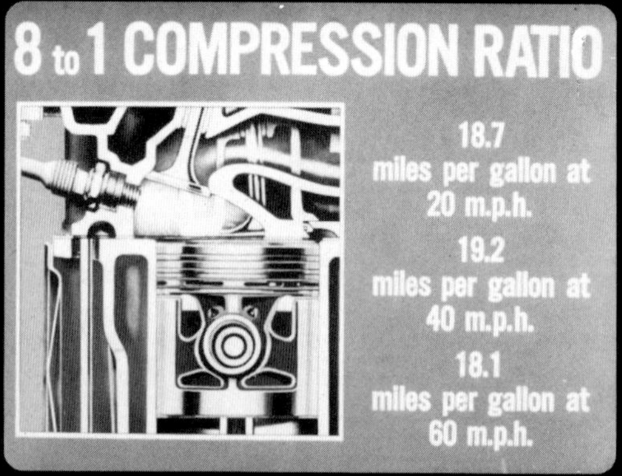

Selected photos from the 1954 "Fun on Wheels" dealer film clip clearly tell the story of the initial errors made in marketing the Corvette. Though they're humorous to look back on now, they nearly spelled doom for the Corvette at the time.

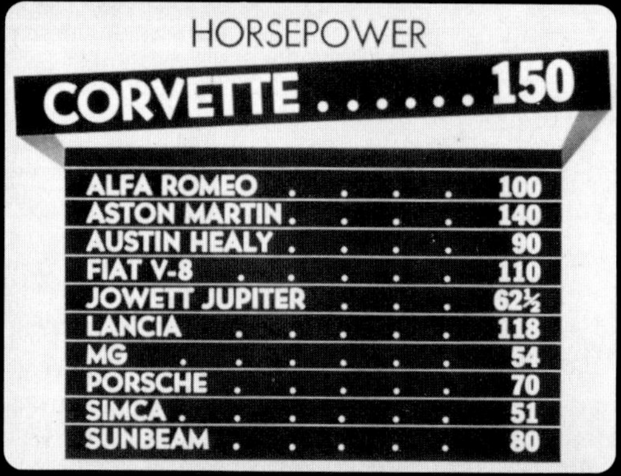

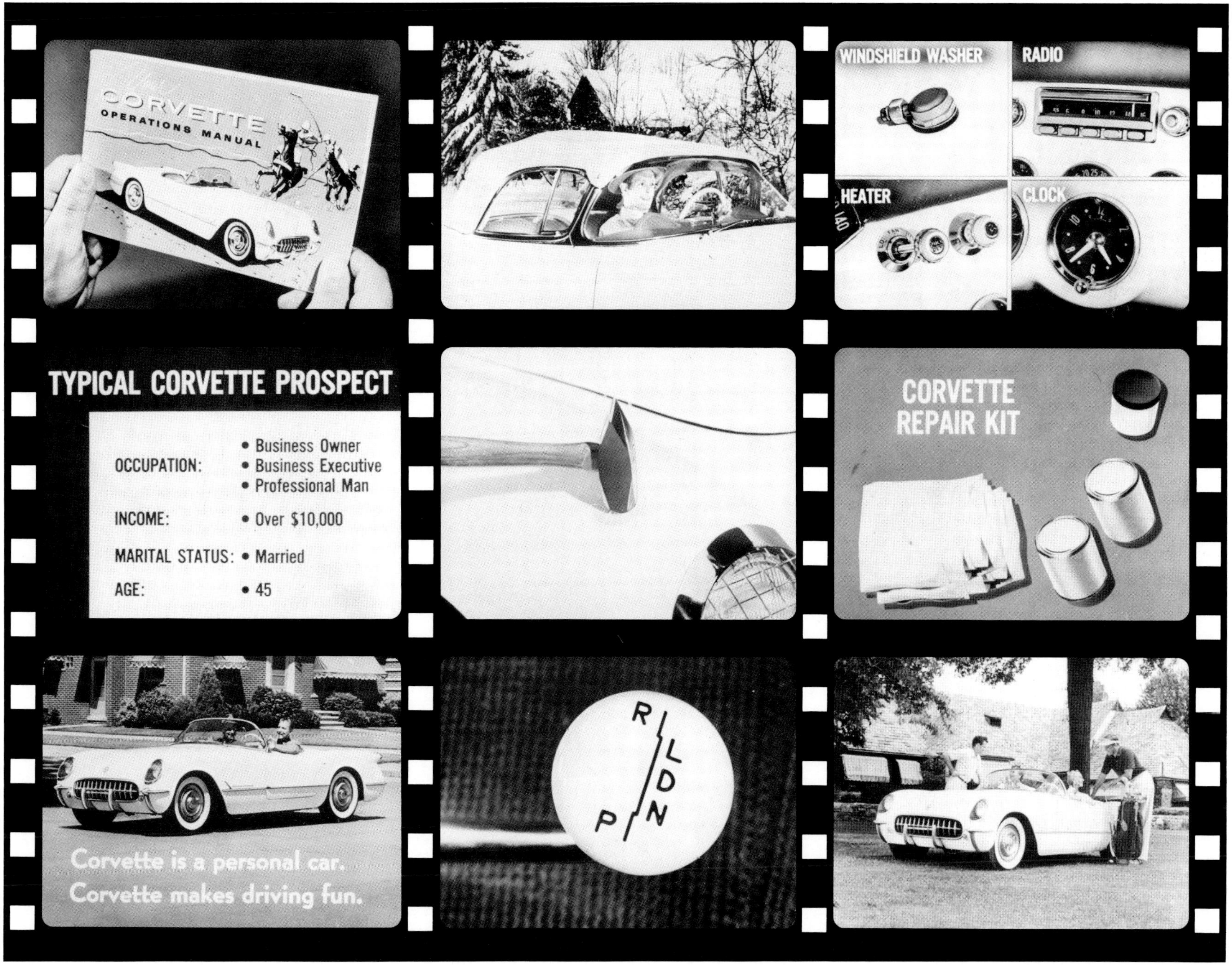
CORVETTE
OPERATIONS MANUAL
WINDSHIELD WASHER
RADIO
HEATER
CLOCK
TYPICAL CORVETTE PROSPECT
OCCUPATION: • Business Owner • Business Executive • Professional Man
INCOME: • Over $10,000
MARITAL STATUS: • Married
AGE: • 45
CORVETTE REPAIR KIT
R L D N P
Corvette is a personal car.
Corvette makes driving fun.

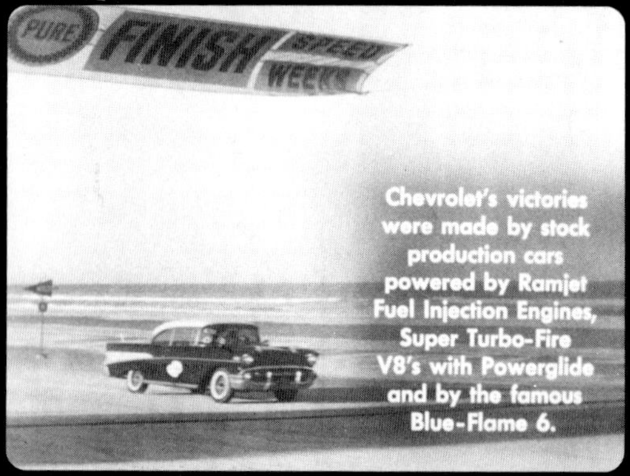

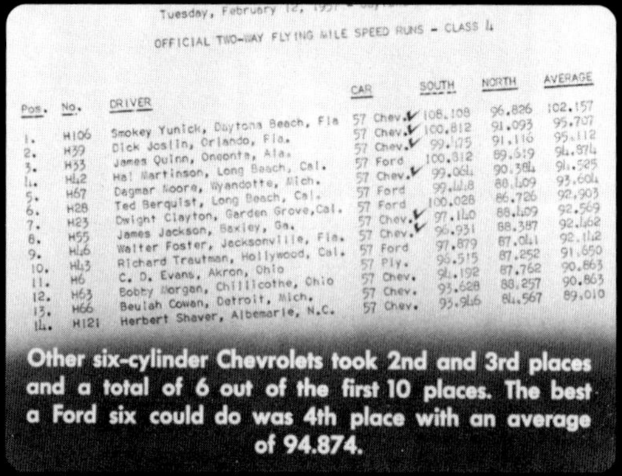
Tuesday, February 12, 1957

OFFICIAL TWO-WAY FLYING MILE SPEED RUNS – CLASS 4

Pos.	No.	DRIVER	CAR	SOUTH	NORTH	AVERAGE
1.	H106	Smokey Yunick, Daytona Beach, Fla	57 Chev. ✓	108.108	96.826	102.157
2.	H39	Dick Joslin, Orlando, Fla.	57 Chev. ✓	100.812	91.093	95.707
3.	H33	James Quinn, Oneonta, Ala.	57 Chev. ✓	99.175	91.116	95.112
4.	H42	Hal Martinson, Long Beach, Cal.	57 Ford	100.812	89.619	94.874
5.	H67	Dagmar Moore, Wyandotte, Mich.	57 Chev. ✓	99.064	90.384	94.525
6.	H28	Ted Berquist, Long Beach, Cal.	57 Ford	99.448	88.409	93.604
7.	H23	Dwight Clayton, Garden Grove, Cal.	57 Ford	100.028	86.726	92.903
8.	H55	James Jackson, Baxley, Ga.	57 Chev. ✓	97.140	88.409	92.569
9.	H46	Walter Foster, Jacksonville, Fla.	57 Chev. ✓	96.931	88.387	92.462
10.	H43	Richard Trautman, Hollywood, Cal.	57 Ford	97.879	87.041	92.142
11.	H6	C. D. Evans, Akron, Ohio	57 Ply.	96.515	87.252	91.650
12.	H63	Bobby Morgan, Chillicothe, Ohio	57 Chev.	94.192	87.762	90.863
13.	H66	Beulah Cowan, Detroit, Mich.	57 Chev.	93.628	88.257	90.863
14.	H121	Herbert Shaver, Albemarle, N.C.	57 Chev.	93.946	84.567	89.010

Pos.	No.	DRIVER	CAR	SOUTH	NORTH	AVERAGE
1.	K16	Al Simonsen, Cambridge, Wisc.	57 Chev.	121.008	116.017	118.460

108

In the National Sports Car Day Feature Event at New Smyrna Beach, a Corvette driven by Paul Goldsmith was class C production winner, beating out two Jaguar XK 140's which came in 2nd and 3rd.

In the 12-lap sports car race, Corvettes won 1st, 2nd and 3rd places in the class C production group, beating many expensive European sports cars.

In the two-way Flying Mile for class C stock production sports cars, Corvettes won the first three places.

Chevrolet learned its marketing lessons well and by 1957 the word was performance, as illustrated by these shots from the "Dateline Daytona" film clip. The Corvette shared the spotlight with the Chevy passenger line, but more than got its share. What a contrast to "Fun on Wheels", eh?

In the measured mile acceleration run for class C sports cars, Corvettes again took 1st, 2nd and 3rd places. The 1st place Corvette averaged 91.301 miles an hour. This beat the Ford Thunderbird which ran in class B.

The Thunderbird in class B averaged 89.708 miles an hour. Class B is for sports cars with engines over 305.10 cubic inches of displacement. The Corvette has a displacement of only 283 cubic inches.

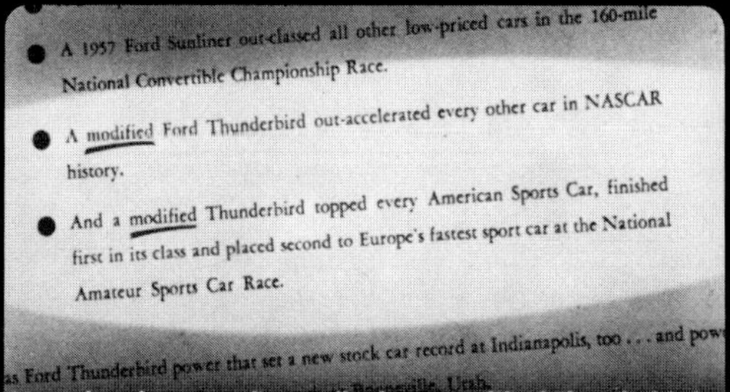

- A 1957 Ford Sunliner out-classed all other low-priced cars in the 160-mile National Convertible Championship Race.
- A modified Ford Thunderbird out-accelerated every other car in NASCAR history.
- And a modified Thunderbird topped every American Sports Car, finished first in its class and placed second to Europe's fastest sport car at the National Amateur Sports Car Race.

...s Ford Thunderbird power that set a new stock car record at Indianapolis, too . . . and pow...

Note that these two lines talk about modified Thunderbirds. This means that these cars have been custom-fitted for racing at a cost which often runs into $1,000 or more. These cars cannot be bought at a Ford dealership.

Chevrolet Corvette — first in Flying Mile and acceleration for class C production sports cars and still holder of Flying Mile record.

Chevrolet — first in points for the Pure Oil Co. Manufacturers' Trophy as the car with the best all-around passenger car performance in NASCAR competition.

The score —

CHEVROLET . .	574
FORD.	309
MERCURY . . .	165
CHRYSLER. . .	76
PLYMOUTH . .	73

Resale value was reported. A Red Book value guide noted that a three-year old Corvette was worth $110 more than a luxury convertible which had cost $800 more at the original sale. Even then, Chevrolet was telling what we all know today . . . Corvettes were smart investments.

GM was learning that the Corvette was an attention-grabber. Even if a buyer could not afford a Corvette, he walked into a Chevy dealership to look at one. The Corvette was a sure door-opener to sales of more affordable Chevrolet lines.

General Motors executives must have smiled. Marketing-wise, the Corvette was doing what it had been hoped it would do. Feeling more bouyant, the "Pleasure Package" film even went after its only real competition, the Thunderbird. The Ford offering was dismissed as a cut-down passenger car.

Film strips continued to educate the public and to train the salesmen. The early 60's saw the use of colored presentations, but Corvette had to share a film strip with the Corvair. In 1963, attention was given to Corvette's styling — redone for '63 — but the Corvette had to share about 50-50 of the limelight with the Corvair.

Perhaps it was felt some of the Corvette mystique would rub off onto the Corvair, because this film, entitled "Two Thrilling Sports — Corvette and Corvair" did not leave much unsaid about Corvette's performance. The viewer's attention was called to the sporty dual grills which flanked the hood wind split. (Oddly enough, they would be called distracting in 1966 literature and films.)

Behind the exciting styling, Chevrolet emphasized that the Corvette body was a structural network of steel combined with fiberglass panels. Issue was made of the new five crossmember frame. Strength, agility, and durability were the hallmarks of the new 1963 Corvette. An explanation of a warning buzzer that cautioned of excessive RPM's with the optional fuel injected engine really got the enthusiast's blood pumping.

All that came to a crashing halt when the viewer was reminded that many of these good Corvette things could be found on the Corvair. The rest of the film dealt exclusively with the Corvair, giving Corvette enthusiasts time to beat a path to the door.

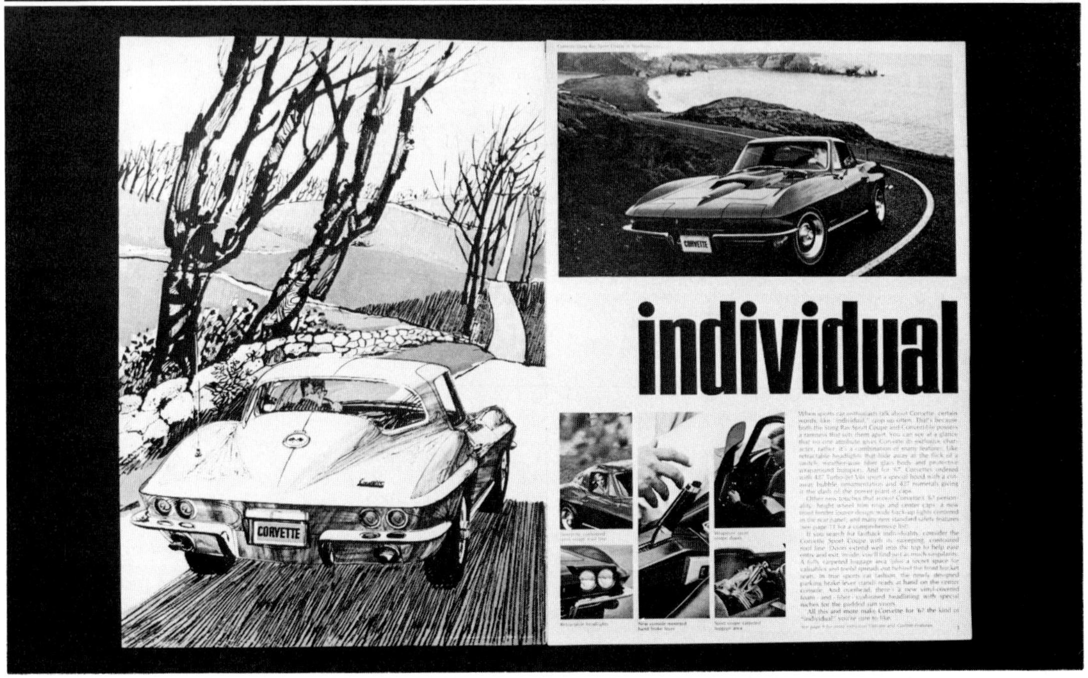

Sales Literature

Early Corvette sales literature played up the 'fun' theme, just as most of the other literature did. Ignoring the Auburn Speedster and the Stutz Bearcat, Chevrolet flatly stated that the Corvette was "America's First Sports Car." In 1953, correctly assuming that the Corvette buyer did not care beans about those earlier sports cars, virtues of the new Corvette were extolled in a turquoise binder.

Chevrolet was still unsure about fiberglass, so no mention was made of this revolutionary approach to car building. GM wanted more time to judge public reaction.

By 1954, the literature looked like Chevrolet meant business with the Corvette. Using the 'fun' theme, the literature was even called "Just for Fun." Approximately six variations of hand-out literature were produced, excluding the "Once Again Chevrolet" piece on the Corvair, Nomad, and Motorama car. "Just for Fun" folded out to thirty-three and a half inches, and used dynamic tones with high quality portrayals.

Blatantly, it promised sensational styling (depends on your definition of sensational), extra low center of gravity (true for the most part), and outstanding performance with amazing acceleration.

Stuck with the 'Driving for Fun' approach, Corvette relied heavily on illustrations that conveyed this fun potential. In so doing, Corvette made more performance promises than it could deliver.

Happily, this was not the case in 1956. A 1956 brochure entitled "A New Corvette by Chevrolet" was subtitled "Now even greater than the original in looks and performance." Corvette underwent a tremendous transformation and created a new era. The new era was ushered in with vibrant color and great artwork.

A three-fold splashy color folder warned of whiplash acceleration and boasted of cat-sure cornering. We were told that the Corvette was a true-blooded, tiger-tempered sports car in the noblest tradition. This was the real thing, gang, and don't forget it.

Action was the marketing approach. (The 'fun' theme was wearing thin by now.) The car was com-

fortable, too — a reaction to those lapfuls of water complaints. Plus, the public was told it was smart to be seen in a Corvette.

In 1957, the literature really had something to brag about. This was a special car for special people. Smack across the cover was the word "Fun." (Well, Chevrolet still hadn't shaken itself completely of that approach. Afterall, the car was fun.)

Fuel injection was introduced along with the all-new 283 cid engine. Chevrolet announced that, for the first time in automobile history, one horsepower was available for every cubic inch of displacement. 283 horsepower out of 283 cubic inches. (In truth, the Chrysler Corporation one year earlier had already tweaked 355 horsepower out of 354 cubes with its 300-B Chrysler, but the one-for-one ratio sounded good to GM.)

Missing from the 1957 introduction was any mention of the four-speed transmission. Apparently, shifting did not fit the comfort and fun definition, but four-speed and Positraction became available in May of 1957. Showing off its pedigree in every line of the folder, Corvette for 1957 was being heavily promoted as a champion. A strong pitch was made that service was as near as your handy Chevy dealer, and there was mention of more than seventy-five hundred dealers.

No doubt about it. There was plenty to talk about in 1957.

1958 hit like the landing at Normandy. There were enough styling changes that the styling was featured throughout its literature. Once again, emphasis was made that the Corvette was America's only sports car. The AMA had banned emphasizing performance in 1957, but it would have been difficult to prove that by reading Corvette's literature in 1958. In fact, the literature stated that performance was a sports car pedigree.

1958 sales pamphlets used the theme "A Way of Life Begins at the Wheel." And what a life! Once

Page 110: *Shown above is the '72 dealer brochure, an all-time favorite thanks to its exploded "body off" detailing. Below is a portion of the '67 brochure.* **Page 111:** *1968 dealer brochure shows a prototype Corvette with the unusual combination of both power windows (buttons on the console) and a manual window crank.* **Above:** *Beautiful lady and beautiful Corvette, from the "Silver Anniversary" brochure of 1978.*

1962
Sports car buyer's guide
1972 Corvette
1969 CORVETTE
Putting you first, keeps us first
'67 Corvette
BY CHEVROLET
CORVETTE
1960

4

Corvette Sting Ray Convertible in Marina Blue

personal

Sting Ray Convertible in Marina Blue with black vinyl-covered removable hardtop

Sting Ray Convertible in Marina Blue with black soft top

Sting Ray bucket seats and center console

Naturally, you'd like the sports car you drive to reflect your good taste. Corvette for '67 is just that kind of car . . . one that complements your way of thinking. If your favorite is the Sting Ray Convertible, then you have a choice of either the folding soft top – in black, white or new teal blue – or removable hardtop that matches your exterior color. Specify both and the additional cost is small compared to the all-seasons versatility. For a bit more elegance, order black vinyl roof covering available for the first time on the removable hardtop.

An impressive array of other personal effects is found on both Corvette models. Two that are new: a four-way hazard warning flasher blinks all directional signals simultaneously for roadside emergency parking; and a lane-change signal operates right or left turn signals by a slight pressure on the directional signal lever and cancels out when the lever is released.

Corvette has the power to please you, too, starting with the 300-hp 327-cu.-in. V8 and 3-Speed fully synchronized transmission, both standard. (This is only the beginning; you can order up to 435 horses.) More features worth mentioning: newly designed gas filler door and distinctive Corvette emblems; bright metal body and door sill moldings with black highlights; and your choice of ten Magic-Mirror exterior colors including four new hues – Elkhart Blue, Lynndale Blue, Goodwood Green and Marlboro Maroon.

From a personal point of view, Corvette for '67 is a car you can really call your own.

A detailed list of extra-cost Options and Custom Features can be found on page 9 of this brochure.

5

Left: *Apparently feeling the need to do a spectacular brochure in place of a not-so-new model, Chevy produced this handsome piece for the now-favorite '67 Corvette.*

Women's lib hits

again, the one-to-one ratio (actually higher in '58) figured prominently. Corvettes were as American as the "Fourth of July." It was so American, even the literature cover was red, white, and blue.

1959 told us to discover the fine art of sports car driving. Naturally, that meant born and bred for sports car performance with luxury and convenience. In other words, a Corvette.

There was not too much new in 1960, so little was said in the promotions which was drastically different from 1959.

In 1961, Chevrolet could have found other ways to describe the new rear end treatment. With the new styling look, the literature also took on a new look. Large scenic photos of the car in action highlighted the brochure. A center-fold depicted all the engineering advances of the 1961 Corvette with a full view schematic.

The same size brochure, now increased from three pages to four, returned in 1962. Chevrolet gave attention to Corvette's hustling power teams, but goofed on the centerfold. The photo showed the 1961 interior, calling it the 1962 interior. Power for the open road and obedience on the street were claimed for the new 327 engine.

1963 saw a completely new design change for the Corvette. This gave marketing men new ammunition, and they celebrated the birth of the Sting Ray. To cover all bases, two pieces of dealer literature were distributed to the dealers. One showed a black Corvette in a country setting, the other showed a red Corvette in the same setting.

In fact, the black Corvette photo is so heavily retouched that it lacks depth and modeling. Black is not thought to be a super marketing color, so the red version appeared soon afterward.

Between the design studios and the printer, a few other things happened. For the interior of the '63 Corvette, 1964 seat backs and seat belts were shown. A three-bar knockoff is shown on the last page of the black brochure, which is supposed to be correct for that year. But the revised red brochure shows a two-bar knockoff.

This appears to contradict the common assumption that a two-bar spinner option was available first, then was replaced with the three-bar. But documentation (Kelsey-Hayes drafting prints) does exist which indicates that the three-bar came first, was replaced by the two-bar, then returned. This would jive with the literature inconsistencies, though a third brochure with the three-bar never appeared.

For 1964, the refined Sting Ray styling was labeled to "puff up the pride of most design-conscious enthusiasts." Turn-about seemed like fair play, so instead of seeing 1964 seats in 1963 literature, we were treated to 1963 seats in the 1964 literature!

Looking closely, we can also see 1963 gas door lids. But the real change was happening in Corvette's understanding of the market. "Fun" and "performance" were dropping by the wayside, so GM went after the women. More mention was made that the Corvette was a sweet thing for sweet young things to drive. Women were shown, not just as admirers, but actual participants behind the wheel. Women's Lib, for General Motors, was closing in quickly. And the Corvette, with all its comforts, was deemed appropriate for women.

1965 got back to the nitty-gritty, with sixteen pages summing up meaningful changes. Chevrolet told about the smooth hood styling that lacked all those distracting depressions. Nobody seemed to mind that this seemed to contradict previous statements.

Somebody apparently wanted to know how many fiberglass panels were used to make a Corvette, because a complete illustration showed it took thirty-one to make a convertible and thirty-five to make a coupe. This may not have been world-shaking news then, but a restorer today drools over information like this.

If you were interested in structural specifics, that was there, too. But you first had to wade through statements such as "able to handle any kind of terrain," and check twice to make sure you had not accidentally picked up some literature on four-wheel drive vehicles.

"Sport Master" disc brakes replaced drums as standard equipment, but "Safety Master" drums were still available as delete cost "options." Even though the big block 396 engines were introduced too late to make it into the promotion, literature for

1965 remains among the most informative produced.

1966 boasted of the quartet of engine selections, with the 427 leading the list. Styling discussion seemed to have been waiting for the 1967 models. But, as rumored, the 1967 styling change was postponed. In 1966, the sales promotion people made do without much new to talk about, but they persevered.

1967 roared in, but without the styling change many expected. Corvettes had a plethora of required safety items, from the safety tire rim to the energy absorbing steering wheel, but not much to expand upon. Safety items are fine, but they do not get the blood coursing in a prospective buyer.

More exciting were the two pages devoted to engine selection. These told of the new 3x2 barrel carburetors and the walloping 435 horsepower mill.

1968 and the long-awaited styling change finally arrived, with raves by some and disappointed groans from others. Two editions of the pamphlet were released. The only real difference between them is that the revised edition carried a statement that readers should check with their local Chevy dealer about availability of the coupe, indicating that production was going to be a little late.

Aside from that, there were revised specs and some truly unusual optional equipment choices. As an example, first edition brochures showed power window switches along with manual window cranks. An interesting idea, to say the least.

Chevrolet should have played more on the new styling for 1968. Instead, bombastic narratives and photos were delayed until 1969. Again faced with revising the literature, the changes were focused on rewording a confusing statement about available axle ratios, and retouching the shifter knob to black from chrome.

1970 arrived and readers were given a nostalgic tour of vintage Corvettes. The newest Corvette was amply illustrated, but every other page featured Corvettes of earlier years. Basically, the same literature was used in 1971, with the appropriate changes in actual production options.

Chevrolet must have been saving their pennies to afford the treatment given in 1972. The 1972 litera-

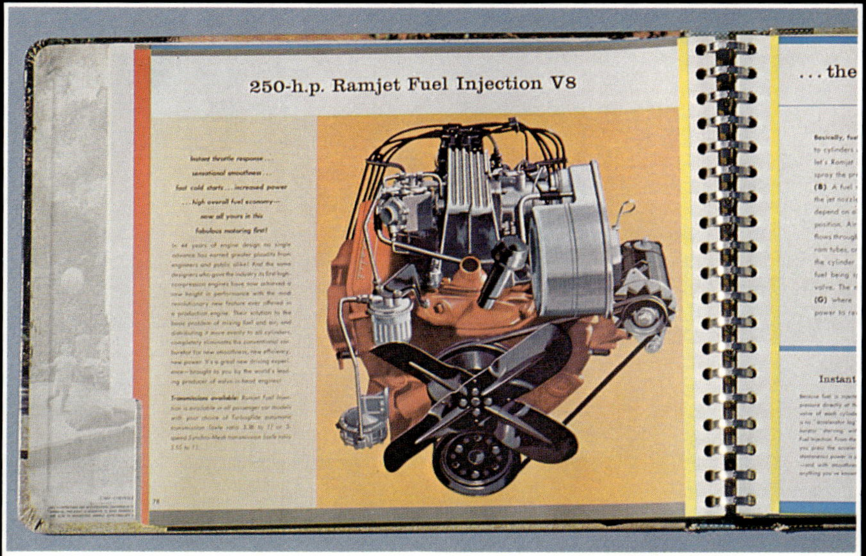

ture became one of the largest promotional pieces ever distributed, measuring a hefty 22 x 34 inches. This opened to an exploded view of body-off frame illustration and a fifteen point rundown of the new Corvette. Printing of this literature must have been limited, because the pieces are hard to find (despite their relatively recent origin), and their desirability is consequently high.

1973 compared the newest Corvette with a vintage 1953. Both were photographed in a pine forest. If nothing else, it was pretty. The copy proclaimed that "of all the cars built in America, only the owners of Corvettes wave to each other." Corvette was stating that its improvements were getting better all the time, and cited the all-new air induction hood and resilient body-colored bumpers as evidence.

Luxury dominated the 1973 and later year themes. Not a great deal was apparently found to talk about from 1973 to 1977.

But a silver opportunity presented itself in 1978. Corvette's Silver Anniversary and the Indy Pace Car replicas and derivations gave the marketing people plenty to yell about. And they did, with the most elaborate dramatizations since 1972. A complete rundown of the past twenty-five years of Corvetting was included. Since Corvette owners are particular about facts, contests were run to find the most errors in the six vintage Corvette photos shown, much to Chevy's embarrassment. All in all, the memories of twenty-five years of man and machine deserve the applause of every Corvette enthusiast.

This piece of sales literature is a must for every collector. Hopefully, you can still get hold of one without scurrying through too many dark attics.

Dealer Albums

Corvette entered this form of sales promotion late, but when it did, there was little left unsaid about the car's potential. With the 1957 dealer album, Chevrolet finally realized that the Corvette was becoming a permanent fixture for sport enthusiasts. Performance was not a dirty word then, and spectacular illustrations in the 1958 dealer album were headlined, "Ram Jet Fuel Injection — The Greatest Single Engine Advance in Forty-four Years". A little subtraction leads to the year 1914 when, we are to believe, Louis Chevrolet got things rolling and not much worth mentioning had happened since then.

1958 was Chevrolet's Fiftieth Anniversary, and the Chevy passenger cars were completely restyled. Corvettes, too, were redone in styling and performance.

Performance was listed as being one horsepower per every cubic inch, more than any other volume produced engine up to 290 horsepower. And Chevrolet's choice of words to describe **pebble-grained** was truly inspired. The ad boys called it "leather grained elascofab instrument panel crown for a more subdued glare." A 'more subdued glare' must have been reassuring. That's like saying 'less dead.' And 'elascofab' must have sounded more space-age than 'vinyl' or 'plastic.' Ah, shades of the adman's delight.

The 1959 album boasted of cleaner lines and minor refinements of the hood and deck. More importantly, Chevrolet salesmen were instructed as to the proper use of the album to insure a potential buyer would become a bonafide buyer. The instructions were quick to point out the Corvette section as a sure-fire attraction.

In 1960, part of the Corvette name was used to make "Corvair," in hopes that some of the magic could be transferred. Sixteen pages were devoted to the Corvair, while only four were allowed for the Corvette, which still was not allowed actual vinyl samples to illustrate its interiors.

No mention was made of the new carpeting "Tuxedo," but emphasis was instead made of "Equipment for Sports Car Meets." Chevrolet was taking performance seriously, with such offerings as RPO 687, a special brake package with air scoops and special fast steering adaptor.

With the 1961's styling changes primarily to the rear, illustrations in the dealer album limited themselves to those areas. A new superlative described the Corvette as a Classic Champion born to the Challenge of the Road.

Corvette finally received some rightful distinction. For the first time, photographs, and actual paint and fabric samples were used. Additional emphasis was made in describing the Corvette as a precisely tooled machine for the man who preferred a car different from the run-of-the-mill.

Illustrations in the 1962 dealer album showed the same narrow ribbed interior patterns, the same as in 1961. This might mean there was a last minute change of interior selection.

Each album cover was adorned with a shmaltzy photo of a Chevrolet passenger model. Finally, in 1963, the Corvette was given some exposure, even though it was a red roadster on the back cover.

A full sixteen pages documented the Corvette for the salesman. Chevrolet decided to give the Corvette the big treatment for performance and elegance. Curiously, there was no mention of the thirty-six and a half gallon fuel tank, nor of the Z-06 option, although the fingertip fact book devoted a full page in detail.

"Fun" had been replaced with performance, but performance became a no-no with the voluntary ban on racing. So marketing had to take another turn. 'Elegance' became the new catchword.

In 1964, the dealer albums stopped showing the engine views, and listing specifications. If a buyer was fussy, he could find those in the fingertip fact book only. In accordance with the new marketing approach, plush photos of the Corvette in action were featured. In 1966, even the full view photos on

Page 116: *Lovely '76 dealer brochure pictures Corvettes in desert scene.* **Page 117:** *1957 dealer album at top, 1963 at bottom:* **Above:** *1962 dealer album showing interior and top material swatches.* **Right above:** *Fingertip Facts for '67.* **Right below:** *Fingertip Facts books grew in 1964 to the bow-tie notebook binder.*

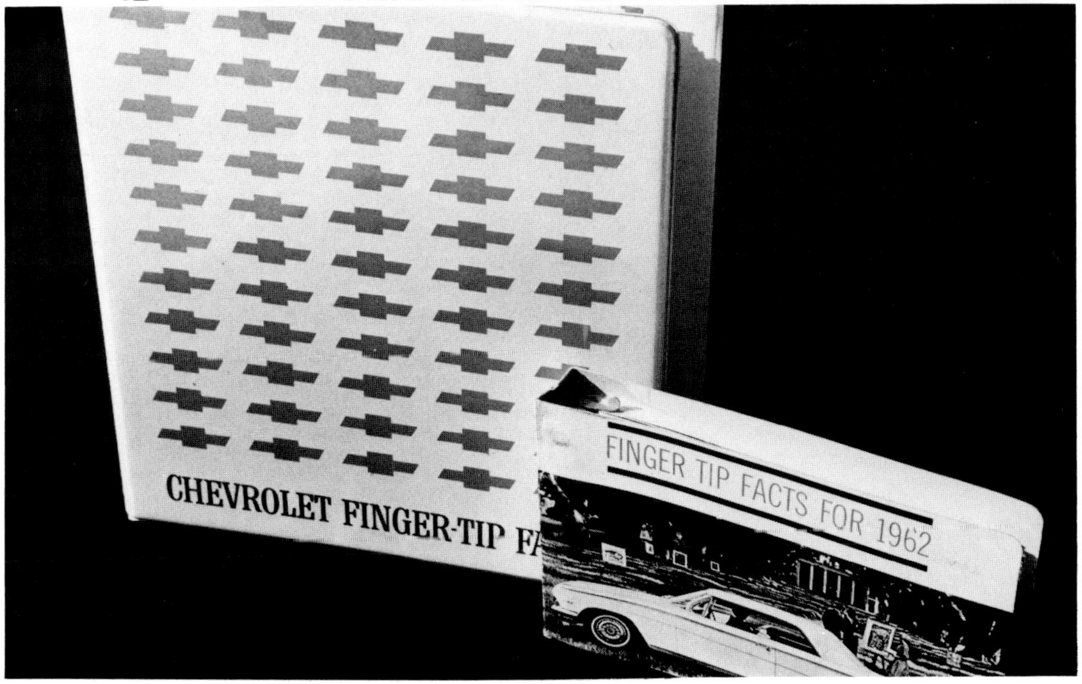

the album covers disappeared. They were replaced with plain binders with the Chevrolet emblem, and that style is still used today. Obviously, locating an early '60 album with a photo cover would be a monumental find.

1968 saw the last year for a totally independent album. That is to say, materials selected for this and previous year's albums were generally unique to the album. In 1969, much of the color photos and descriptive narration was duplicated from other dealer material, especially customer brochures. Find one of these albums, and lament. Compare it with an earlier album, and spend hours wistfully contemplating the changes in Corvette's promotion thrust.

Fingertip Fact Books

The fact books contained the details of optional equipment, as well as standard features. Often referred to as specification or feature books, they usually accompanied the big dealer albums.

Lucky for us they accompanied the albums because, with the shift away from performance, these are often the only places where hard information can be found without going through the GM archives.

Power teams were illustrated using engine photos. Basic engineering design, fuel and induction system specifications, body and chassis structure, mounting and suspension components; all were included.

Originally, these fact books were supplied in an 8½ x 5 inch binder which looked like mini dealer albums, since they used the same cover photos. Those lasted from 1957 through 1963.

But in 1964, the fact book grew in size to 10½ x 12. The cover was white with blue Chevrolet bow-ties. And nothing was done to it until 1968! A serious Corvette buyer found himself thumbing through last year's specifications until he found the current year's. Sure, revised guides were provided to keep the salesman aware of what was going on and, sure, that was fine if the salesman took the time to put the revised material in the book.

Usually, he did. Sometimes, he didn't. Hope he did, because those revisions are important.

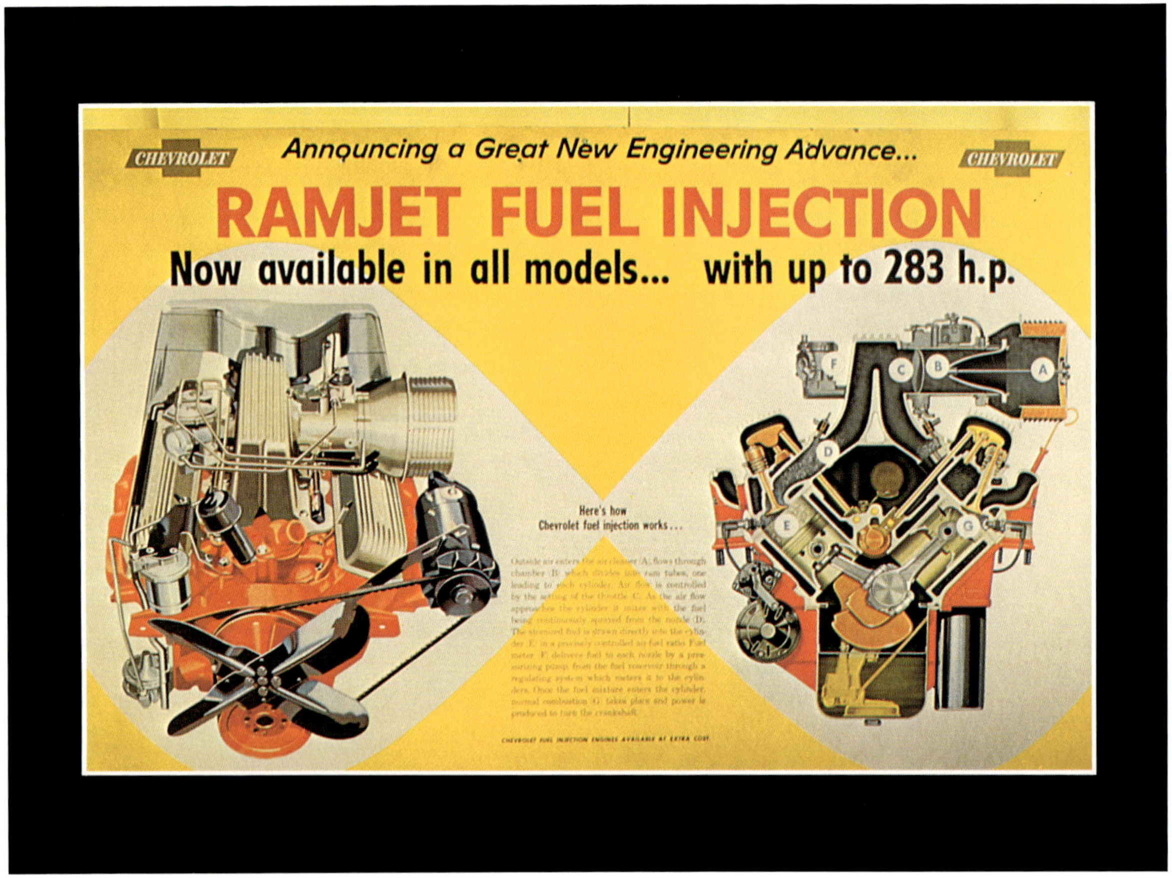

Left: *Beautiful, and as rare as they come, the '57 fuel injection wall poster.* **Right:** *"Chevyland Sweepstakes" game from the Milton Bradley Company, circa 1969.*

Heavy duty?

For instance, many production changes were apparently last minute. Without the revised guide, who's to know? The 1964 fact book illustrated the Z-06 special performance option available for that year. But the revised booklet cancelled that availability and offered F-40 special suspension and J-56 special brakes, complete with wheel air scoops and metallic brake linings.

The details of the F-40 option and the J-56 appear to be identical, but an important, though subtle, change occurred. The words "high performance" were no longer used. Instead "heavy duty" was used.

You did not have to be the brightest kid on the block to figure out what was meant, but there must have been some confusion at first. "Heavy duty" sounds like tractor suspension, but we learned.

Thereafter, "high performance" was used sparingly, but we all knew what was really going on.

Fact books are important today. Their use as sales tools are exhausted, but they serve as useful restoration guides; just be sure you are following a revised guide.

In the 70's these fact books were referred to as "Product Information and Illustration Guides." Their content became less specific, probably because features and appointments were under great overhaul and GM did not see the wisdom of constantly revising the revisions. If nothing else, these fact books are highly sought-after as reference sources.

No boardwalk here

Games, Miniatures, And Other Trivia

The Milton-Bradley Company produced a game called **Chevyland Sweepstakes** in 1969. It was sold at Chevrolet dealers, and was supposed to create the atmosphere of managing a Chevrolet dealership. It used the new 1969 Corvette in its artwork and playing board, and it was pretty much like Monopoly© except the player landed on a Corvette instead of on Boardwalk.

Caution was thrown to the wind to market the Corvette even before then. In 1967, you could buy your very own roadrace set for $5.95. It was made by Republic Tool for Chevrolet. This promotional item came with a 1967 Corvette and a 1967 SS Camaro that zipped around a miniature course called "Seeing the USA in your Chevrolet from New York to San Francisco." Before that, in 1966, you could buy your own 24½ inch long Corvette. Sold as Item No. 105, the red plastic car was manufactured by the good old Republic Tool Company of Los Angeles, and had an operable horn and steering. Dandy for the younger set, because the thing could be gotten onto by a three-year old.

It is impossible to gauge how many direct sales resulted from these toys, but maybe they influenced some kids when they grew up. But Chevrolet wanted sales right now, not fifteen years down the pike. However, considering the phenomenal sales of Corvettes during the past decade, maybe the strategy has paid off.

Many promotional items were free at the dealerships. Usually, a dealer ordered what was required of him and ended up giving it away to frequent customers.

For instance, in 1961, Chevrolet produced a vinyl record in a **Corvette News** issue. The record was also given away in dealerships during the 1961 new car showing. Primarily, it offered gutty sounds of a Corvette, with a narration by Gene Staley, then General Sales Manager for Chevrolet. It began with the exhaust rumble of a Corvette accelerating out of earshot.

Mr. Staley invited the listener for a ride. But first, he introduced Zora Duntov, Corvette's Chief Engineer. Zora explained the goodies on this performance-packed Corvette and away you went.

To achieve maximum sound effects, Zora went through so much double-clutching that the transmission sounded as though it had defective synchronizers. More seriously, the sounds of squealing tires, high engine revs, and enough shifting to wear out Godzilla's arm, made this record innovative and exciting. Credit the Jam Handy Organization for producing it.

Locate one of these, and you're in for a treat.

Miscellaneous

There was a give-away contest for a 1957 Corvette pedal car. These were offered through Chevrolet dealers to increase showroom traffic. Not many of them exist today, so if you're determined to have one, lots of luck.

Chevrolet Sales Promotion also made available a gas-powered version from 1958 through 1960. A 1961 was made for dealer distribution. All were made in Jackson, Michigan under the auspices of Yard-Man, Inc. The bodies were made in Ashtabula, Ohio, by the Molded Fiberglass Company in low volume, high costs.

Actually, Reed Draper of Draper Chevrolet in Saginaw, Michigan, came up with the idea. Reed remembers unloading 1,300 of these mini-Corvettes through his company of Pro-Mo, Inc. with the blessings of the Chevrolet Motor Division.

The bodies were engineered by Morgan Martin at MFG Co. Morgan remembers producing about six thousand bodies. The discrepancy in figures may be because those 1,300 Reed remembers were sold through Chevrolet. The rest were sold directly to consumers.

Either way, the vulnerability of these little Corvettes with their light-weight bodies and the rambunctiousness of their young drivers, mean few of them remain today.

Above: *Dream car for the young, a '57 Corvette pedal car.* **Above right:** *1966 and 1978 Corvette promotional models.*

Models of the real thing

Promotional Models

Scale automobile models date back long before the Corvette first appeared. The Aluminum Model Toys company produced a metal Ford sedan in 1948. A year later, AMT switched to plastic, but AMT's name stayed the same. Other model manufacturers in 1948 were Banthrico, National Products, and IMC.

AMT did not produce the first Corvette model, but they certainly boosted desirability of the miniatures as showroom promotions. PMC—the Product Miniature Corporation — became the sole supplier of miniatures to Chevrolet in 1951, '52, '53, '54, and '55. No models were produced in 1956 nor in 1957.

Beginning in 1958 and lasting for nine years, AMT supplied the models. In the early Sixties, a new plastic was developed. Collectors have found that earlier models had a tendency to warp and distort, due to the acetate-based plastic being used.

A shift was made to the new Cycolac plastic, and greater molding tolerances could be held. AMT used the new plastic first, but it was quickly adopted by other manufacturer/ suppliers. By 1968, AMT was responsible for models of the Corvette, while the Molded Production Corporation of Mt. Clemens, Michigan, became the supplier to Chevrolet in general since then. Exceptions were the years 1969 and 1970. The miniature car business was as competitive as its big brother. By 1972, AMT was out of the business of producing promotional models.

Not all the models were dealer oriented. Through the 1962 year, friction-powered models were purportedly sold through retail outlets by AMT, MPC, and other suppliers.

Postcards & Posters

Here is a controversial area. Nobody knows for sure how many promotional postcard subjects were used. Reliable sources seem to agree that twenty-three separations were utilized, but those do not include the various tints of the cards, nor the black and white Brussels World's Fair Experimental Corvette Motorama card which was not intended for dealer distribution.

One thing is usually agreed upon: there were no postcards in 1955, 1956, 1957, 1967, or 1970. Why not is unclear, but some interesting theories have developed.

The 1967 card may have been scrapped because it might have shown the Sting Ray styling which was scheduled for that year, but was held off for a year. In 1970, production of the Corvette was just delayed, so there may not have been time to produce a card. Who knows about the other years? Could be that Chevrolet did not plan any for those fifties years.

Besides Corvettes, post cards showed the entire Chevrolet stable most years. Scenic backgrounds were used from 1959 to 1965. After then, studio shots were used, or no background was used. For some reason, the scenic backgrounds bit the dust.

Nearly all the postcards have been reproduced to create showroom posters which measure 18 x 32 inches. Ordered in assortment, these full-color posters provided year-round promotions, including the Corvette.

With 1961 and later, the showroom posters bore exact enlargements of the postcards. Prior to the individual posters, full line wall posters, measuring around 40 x 60, were used. These selling aids featured the regular Chevrolet line as well as the Corvette. They were printed in full color, and were designed to fit into aluminum frames for wall hanging or on easel tripods for window display.

The Sales Department was not the only department to receive Corvette wall hangers. The Service and Parts Departments often received materials, but these were more informative than merely showy. Consequently, many enthusiasts find these more desirable.

One favorite poster illustrates the 1957 Fuel Injected Engine. It displays a full view of the 283 fuel injected engine, with a frontal cutaway explaining the workings of this new engineering milestone.

With all the furor over the 1978 Pace Car, one item went largely unnoticed. Many dealers report receiving a Pace Car sales promotion Calendar poster sometime prior to May, 1978. It often went unnoticed, because it was included with the Parts Department material. Usually, the Parts Department pulled out what it needed, and ignored the rest. That is a shame, because the calendar included photos of the four previous Chevrolet-made Pace Cars since 1948. It may not be too late to find one of these.

If you find one, hang onto it like the family jewels. It will surely become rare and collectible.

For sheer impressiveness, an early car color display board takes some awards. This was designed to impress showroom customers, and showed the full lineup of Chevrolet and Corvette colors each year. Often, a picture of a Corvette was shown, with the 1959 and 1960 versions showing the color variations possible with the side cove treatment.

Left: *Corvette postcard selection.* **Above:** *1961 Corvette was dubbed onto scenic background to create this striking wall poster.*

Nostalgic history

Talk about class! Each 'Magic Mirror' finish was sprayed on curved plates to duplicate highlight reflections. A hand-rubbed finish was simulated to add sparkle and luster. But costs were rapidly building to produce these.

By the early Seventies, cardboard and paper paint chips were used. Need we mention what one of the original selection posters would be like to find?

A personal invitation to come into the dealership and try a Corvette was also tried. A special Corvette brochure "mailer" was sent out, but the use was short-lived, because they were apparently only used from 1958 through 1960.

Pick Of The Litter

It is impossible to know what the future will bring, just as it is impossible to pick the best items for the collector. Notable items have been listed, but there is no easier way to appreciate the Corvette than by collecting its memorabilia.

You do not have to be a Corvette owner, nor a student of marketing, to appreciate these reflections of the past. There's a little nostalgic Corvette history in every one of the hundreds of devices used by Chevrolet dealers in selling the Corvette.

Corvette People

SHARK
Melbourne Brindle

William L. Mitchell

110 million cars

Just stop and think about this for a moment. William L. Mitchell was the vice president of General Motors in charge of the design of all General Motors automobiles for the twenty year period from 1958 through 1978. He was only the second man to hold such an influential design position within the hierarchy of GM. The first was the legendary Harley Earl, whom Mitchell succeeded.

Considering the proliferation of automobiles during Mitchell's tenure, it is probably safe to conclude that no other single man has had more impact on what automobiles look like today than William Mitchell. General Motors itself has produced well in excess of 110 million cars during the Mitchell years. And Mitchell designs have served as inspiration for millions of other cars from GM competitors.

If not for a few twists of fate, Bill Mitchell could very well be just now retiring as the successful proprietor of Mitchell Buick Inc., Titusville, Pennsylvania. His dad ran a Buick dealership there as young Bill grew up and, as most dads do, had visions of his son following in his successful footsteps.

It could have happened that way. Bill Mitchell grew up loving cars. Buicks were great, but his dad's personal cars, like Stutz Bearcats and Mercers, were even better. Race tracks were scarce then, but Bill's dad could stay with the best of them on the back roads. And if someone did beat him, he'd be so infuriated that he'd try to buy the other car on the spot.

In addition to loving the cars, young Bill also loved to draw them. Those two loves would seem to point clearly to auto design as a career, but Mitchell first turned his interests to advertising illustration.

At the age of fifteen, Bill Mitchell landed a summer job as office boy at the Barron Collier advertising agency art department in New York City. Part-time turned to full time upon high school graduation when Mitchell was offered an illustrator's position. His self-taught rendering techniques were honed by attending night school classes at the Art Students League on 57th Street.

Collier's did a big business in beautifully illustrated ad cards for display in buses and other public transportation. Autos were but a part of the subjects displayed, but Mitchell's particular talent for illustrating automobiles was soon evident to the Collier brothers, sons of Barron Collier Sr. As luck would have it, the sons, Barron Jr., Sam, and Miles, were bonafide auto enthusiasts. Before long the Colliers and Mitchell were racing together and sharing the joys of that era's fascination with automobiles. When the Colliers formed the Automobile Racing Club of America, it was Mitchell who designed the club's logo and format for the ARCA magazine.

The winds of fate

Then the winds of fate really blew his way. At one of the Collier-sponsored races, an insurance executive named Walter Carey saw some of Mitchell's sketches and wanted to know if he had ever considered a career as an auto designer. Mitchell hadn't, but wasn't exactly opposed to it either. Walter Carey asked Mitchell to work up a portfolio and submit it to Harley Earl, who was head of General Motors Art and Colour, the predecessor of today's corporate auto design departments. Harley Earl, you see, was a close personal friend of Mr. Carey. Small world.

Harley Earl saw Bill Mitchell's work and liked it. Six months later, at age 23, William L. Mitchell began his career with General Motors.

At age 24, Cadillac's chief designer

Being the son of a Buick dealer naturally meant that Bill Mitchell's dream was to design Buicks. But Harley Earl's love was Cadillac. And quite apparently, Earl saw something in young Mitchell that he liked, because within one year of joining General Motors, Bill Mitchell was Cadillac's Chief Designer. That was a fast move, though the size of auto design groups then was on a completely different scale than now. It was only earlier that same year, 1936, that Earl had segregated design of GM's different divisions. Previously, it had all been done in the same room.

Mitchell proved quickly that Earl's faith in him was not without substance. Mitchell turned his first big assignment under Earl's supervision, design of the 1938 Cadillac Sixty-Special, into an instant classic. In typical "I don't care what everybody else is doing" fashion, Mitchell styled the Sixty-Special without running boards, the first such car of its class ever.

Mitchell's design career with General Motors was interrupted by World War II. He enlisted and, surprisingly, the Navy actually made excellent use of his talents by assigning him the job of producing and illustrating flight training manuals. Among others, he did the standard training manual for instrument flying, **Flight Through Instruments.**

Bill Mitchell returned to Cadillac after the war and stayed until 1949. He then left to establish an industrial design firm in Detroit. The financial backing came from Harley Earl, who wanted to set up a company with his sons. For his efforts, Mitchell was rewarded with ten percent of the gross receipts, a generous deal by any standards.

Strange that GM would go along with such an arrangement, that of a vice-president operating a consulting design firm through a former GM employee, but Harley Earl wielded tremendous power at GM. He got what he wanted. And in 1953, he wanted Bill Mitchell back.

And it was in 1953, five years before Harley Earl was to retire, that Mitchell learned from Earl that he, Earl, had selected him, Mitchell, to be the next General Motors vice president in charge of design. Earl also informed GM's chief executive officer, Mr. Sloan, of his wishes. This was all providing William L. Mitchell didn't somehow blow it.

He didn't. Upon Earl's retirement in 1958, Mitchell was in. And it is here that the Corvette starts to figure prominently in his career. Because, while Mitchell was clearly Earl's protege and while he got things done the way Earl wanted them, the design preferences of the two men weren't on parallel roads.

Earl loved heavy, rounded, stately cars. Mitchell now believes this was because Earl himself was a large man from a prosperous family engaged in custom coach and auto body building. Earl came from the chrome era, the era when pounds of chrome were in direct proportion to desirability of car. Cheap little car, no chrome. Big expensive car, lots of chrome.

Mitchell's early influence from his days with the Collier brothers was heavily European. He liked sharp, sheer lines typified by the European classics. He also loved the specialty cars, sporting cars, and racers. His great inspiration came from the Italian designer, Pininfarina.

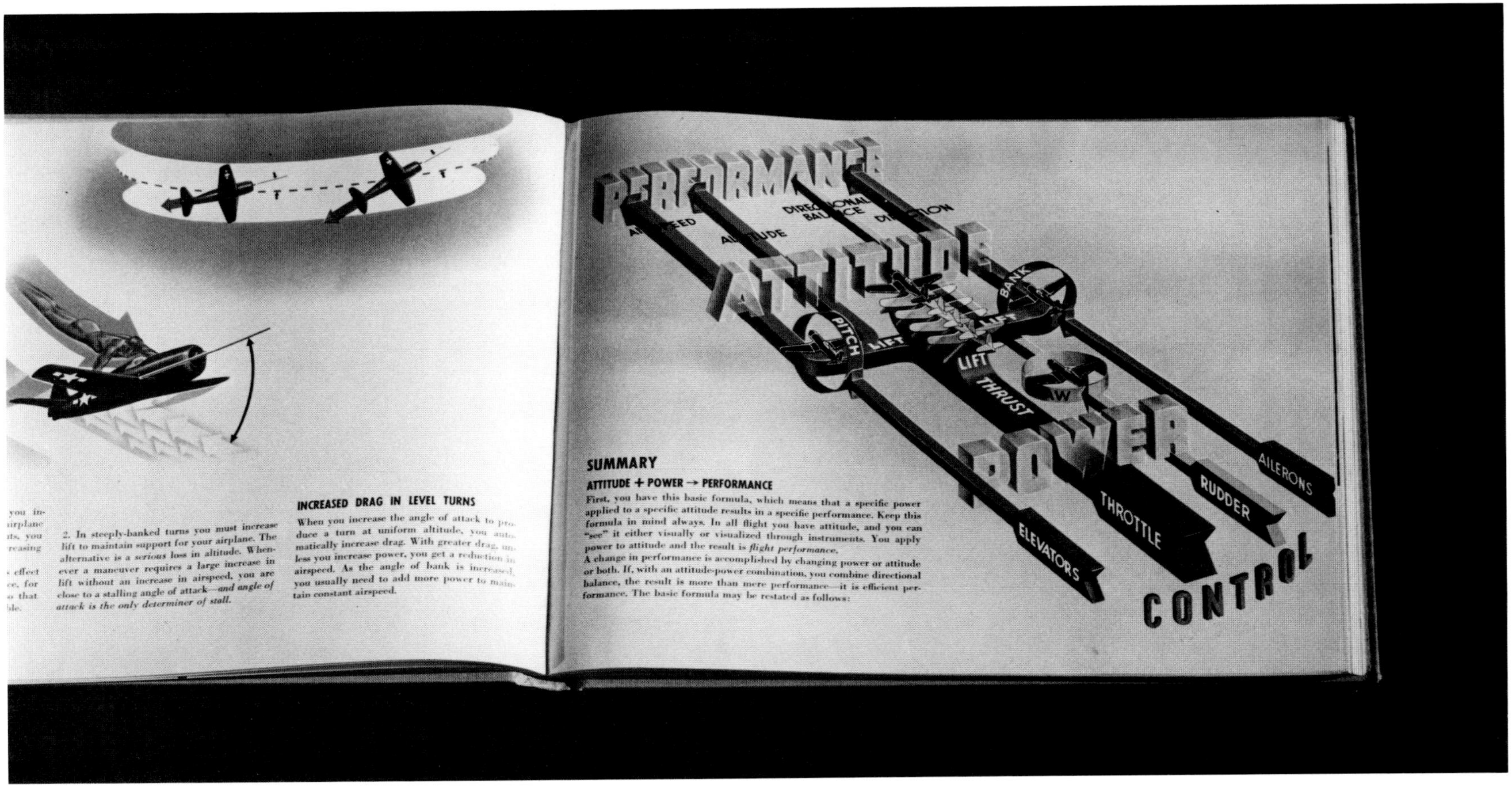

During World War II, Mitchell illustrated the "Flight Through Instruments" training manual for the Navy. His descriptive renderings, full color in defiance of the budget, revolutionized training techniques.

When he assumed full design responsibility for General Motors in 1958, Mitchell was fully aware that any new Corvette was at least three to four years away. A sleek new body had been proposed for the 1960 Corvette which was to include a radical new Duntov chassis with aluminum engine, rear-transaxle, and inboard brakes. But GM management axed the project as prohibitively expensive.

Mitchell-inspired regular production vehicles were several years away as well. Anxious to let the world know that his design philosophy was not that of Earl, Mitchell hatched a plan.

Mitchell was dying to get the "Mitchell Look", that of sleek shapes with windsplits, into a Corvette the public could see quickly. He asked Ed Cole, then Chevrolet's general manager, to let him have one of Duntov's Sebring racing chassis. Mitchell's plan was to put a new body of his design on the chassis and race it as a Corvette prototype. The exposure would be a great public test of the shape that Mitchell envisioned for the next production Corvettes. In addition to that great selling point, Mitchell had another motive. A Mitchell-inspired car would be public and the change of design emphasis from the Earl era would publicly begin. Not four years out, but in a matter of months.

Cole was a racer too, but the corporation was committed to a no-racing policy. This Mitchell plan would never fly. If that's the case, Mitchell countered, how about if he bought it himself and paid for

Left: *A young Bill Mitchell during his early days with Cadillac.* **Above:** *Mitchell designed the ARCA racing logo while still with the Collier Advertising Agency in New York City.*

the racing program out of his own pocket? Cole agreed.

Mitchell promptly set up a secret design studio in the basement below his office with his favorite designers, and the racing Sting Ray was born. It was campaigned for two years with moderate success. For Mitchell though, it was complete success. He'd achieved his goal of getting a "Mitchell" car out quickly before the public. The public loved it. The racing Sting Ray led the way to the Sting Ray production series starting in 1963, which the public loved as well.

Though the Corvette is a peanut in the overall picture at GM, Mitchell's association with it is so strong that the mention of "Mitchell" and "GM Design" immediately brings thoughts of Corvette. From Mitchell's secret "X" studio poured forth a steady stream of tantalizing Corvette dream cars. The XP-700, the Shark, the Mako Shark, the Manta Ray, the Astro series, the rotary Corvettes, and the Aero-Vette are but some of the famous ones.

Bill Mitchell's career with General Motors spanned forty years, the last twenty of which found him at its top design decision making position. In 1978, he retired. But retirement for Mitchell simply means a new office and new challenges. He is now president of his own design consulting firm, titled appropriately enough, "William L. Mitchell." He's not allowed to do any auto design under retirement provisions of General Motors, but the field is open for everything else.

Everything else includes Goodyear tires and petrochemical products, Yamaha's motorcycles, all 3-M products, and a better way to build a car-hauler for Bridge. He splits his time between his studio in Birmingham, Michigan, and his new home in Lost Tree, north of Palm Beach, and its studio-office next door with years of Mitchell treasures. He says his wife thinks they should travel more, spend some time in Europe. He says she's right, but there's still so much he wants to do.

Someday years hence, someone will be writing about the golden era of the Corvette's first quarter-century. The subject of engineering will come up, and Zora Arkus-Duntov's name will filter in. Management will be discussed, and Ed Cole will be remembered. Then design . . . and William L. Mitchell.

Cole was a racer too

CSA talks with Bill Mitchell

CSA Were you involved in the development of the first Corvette?

Mitchell No, Harley Earl created the Corvette, not me. He always said that there was never a true American sports car. You see, Harley Earl was from Hollywood and that was a different world. I can remember going to California in 1941. There were sports cars everywhere out there. True, they might have been foreign, or even home-made, but they were there. But in Detroit, none at all. The love of the automobile was not here at that time. Here it was just production.

Harley Earl unveiled the Corvette at a GM directors' meeting at the proving grounds. We often spring one like that, something nobody knows about. All the who's who are there. You let them see the regular models first, then bring them into a specially lighted room where you have your surprise waiting. "What do you think of this?" They sure loved the Corvette. It was fiberglass, the first thing we'd done that way. We really developed fiberglass for automotive use. Sure, we got help from Goodyear and Monsanto and others, but we were the ones who really guinea-pigged it along. We were the leaders.

There was such enthusiasm at the directors' meeting that we decided to put the Corvette into the New York motorama show. The rest is history. The public response was tremendous and we built the first production cars almost exactly like the show car.

Harley Earl was one of the great showmen of automotive history. He believed so strongly in the show car, the dream car. But he didn't build them to say, "Hey, look what we can do." He built them to get public response. The public loved the Corvette right from the start. Their response was, "Why don't you build this thing?" Which Mr. Earl of course knew would happen and would give him the necessary leverage to get the car into production.

CSA Why fiberglass?

Mitchell I'm not really sure. At the time, it just seemed like the thing to do. There were probably good technical reasons, but it just boiled down to an innovative new material for an innovative new car. Some of those early cars weren't the greatest. But the real beauty of fiberglass was that it allowed not only the designers, but the owners as well, to change the car easily. I just love what some of the kids do to their cars.

I've been going to Elkhart Lake now for over twenty years, even staying in the same hotel room. I remember years ago seeing lots of Porsches there parked together and I thought, "Hell, why don't we do this? We've got more cars than they do." So Joe Pike put together the Corvette Corral up there. Oh, that's a beautiful sight to see. To me, the Corvette has become like a Ferrari. It's ageless. You go up there and you see those Corvettes and they're all beautiful. One guy has a '55, another a '63, another a '75. And they all look like new. That's the beauty of fiberglass. Then the owners customize their cars and that's the beauty of fiberglass too. I love them all and I sure hope fiberglass stays.

But don't think for a minute that a fiberglass Corvette will always be a sure thing. We're limited in our current capacity to making 40,000 to 50,000 Corvettes a year. You just can't squeeze out many more. There are constraints in the production of the car, especially related to fiberglass, which prevent the production from going much higher. Now, there are plastics coming along that can actually be stamped out in sheet form in a press like metal is now, and the proposed new Corvette assembly plant in Kentucky could change things, but don't think that when someone points out how easy it would be to get production up to 150,000 per year by switching to metal . . . don't think some of the corporation's directors don't listen.

"Harley Earl was one of the great showmen of automotive history."

"Don't think for a minute that fiberglass will always be a sure thing."

CSA Was Harley Earl a visionary? Was he really behind the Corvette, and do you think he could actually see what was coming?

Mitchell Yes, definitely yes. Let me give you a little history on all this.

After the war, a large number of young men, some still in the service and some out, returned to the United States. They were restless and looking for things to do. One activity that flourished was auto racing. But tracks were scarce so many races were held on old airstrips, with the blessing of the Air Force. Sebring is the classic example.

Mr. Earl was close friends with General Curtis LeMay and LeMay loved cars. I remember he had a Jeep with a Cadillac engine in it and he'd love going out on the highway and cleaning everybody. Through Lemay's and others' influence, General Motors encouraged these racing activities by giving parts and assistance to the servicemen to build their cars and go racing on the airstrips.

Harley Earl wasn't the type of man you'd normally associate with dinky sports cars. First of all, he was a physically big man. He came from a wealthy, prestigious family. He loved big cars. He loved elegance. He loved Cadillac. But LeMay loved all kinds of cars and he got to Mr. Earl. He saw what was happening with the servicemen racing and through him Mr. Earl saw it too. LeMay wondered why GM couldn't build a real sports car. Pretty soon Mr. Earl was wondering too.

Yes, Harley Earl saw it all coming. He wanted an American sports car and he wanted General Motors to build it. And today the Corvette is still America's only sports car.

CSA It's ironical that most people don't relate racing to the early Corvette at all, but tend to relate the later racing efforts and success starting around 1956 as one of the Corvette's paths to stardom. But the story you've just related implies that the Corvette owes its very existence to the racing enthusiasm of servicemen returning from World War II.

Mitchell It is ironical. And it's true.

CSA Was Harley Earl himself a good stylist?

Mitchell Well, he couldn't draw. He came from the days when you laid it out full size. He loved preci-

sion. He'd never make an instrument panel that looked like a whore's top dresser drawer. He'd always personify the engine on the dashboard with instruments, machine turning and masculine touches. He liked emblems that looked like Cartier made them. Great taste, great finesse . . . very demanding.

His father was a carriage builder who eventually turned to cars. At the big custom show at the Commodore in New York, Mr. Sloan and the Fisher brothers noticed that all the good looking Cadillacs had Earl bodies. So Harley Earl was brought to Detroit as a consultant to Cadillac and the first thing he came up with was the beautiful LaSalle. Then Sloan said, "Hell, if he's that good, let's have him design all GM cars."

Earl was a big, tough man. He came from California, but his vocabulary sounded like the New York waterfront. He could eat people alive.

CSA Is it true that you were his hand-picked successor?

Mitchell Yes, he told me five years before he retired that he wanted me in there. He told Sloan and Curtis too.

CSA How did that happen? What did you do to catch his eye?

"Earl was a big, tough man. He could eat people alive."

"If it went good but was ugly, like the Cobra, you'd have no market."

Mitchell I've been asked that before, and I don't know. It was just chemistry, I guess. You know, you can travel with one guy and have a great time. With another guy, you don't even know what to say. You can get along great with one neighbor, but not another.

I knew what he was thinking about. I didn't "yes, sir" him, but I could understand him . . . sense him. Oh, he ate me out, but damn seldom compared to some others he worked over.

Up until the day he retired, he was never easy on me. I'd do something great, and he'd tell me to get off my rear and go get the trucks done, or why wasn't I doing this or that. I remember telling my wife that I didn't think I could last. But he whipped me into shape.

CSA What has made the Corvette so successful?

Mitchell If you're looking for a single item, I'd say Cole's V-8. It doesn't matter if it's a Ferrari, a motorcycle, or even a horse. It can be the most beautiful in the world, but if she can't go, it doesn't mean a thing. Prior to the introduction of our V-8, Jaguar was killing everybody. Then came Mercedes. When the V-8 Corvette finally came along and beat Jaguar, that was a big thing. But when we started knocking off Mercedes, that really got people thinking. All of a sudden the Corvette went the way it looked. And that inspired the designers. We weren't just designing a cute little car that didn't do much. The six was good, but the V-8 was just better.

CSA How important has styling been to the success of the Corvette?

Mitchell Oh, very. I've always said that if it doesn't look good, why bother to even get in? It's just like Jaguar. Its looks have been as important in its success as its performance. They go hand in hand.

First of all, if the Corvette looked good but didn't go, the real sports car enthusiast would call it a phony. If it went good but was ugly, like the Cobra, you'd have no market. It has to be beautiful too. And the Corvette is. Women love it, kids love it, everyone loves it. It's the same kind of appearance-performance success as the Camaro/Firebird.

CSA When you see one of the first Corvettes on the road or at a show, how does it look to you today?

Mitchell It looks good.

CSA How about a '56 or '57?

Mitchell They look really good.

CSA How about the '58 through '62?

Mitchell I think they look good too. I always thought the dual headlights looked like a shotgun barrel. Overall, they were pretty well done. I suppose if I should be criticized for anything, it would be the rear end of the '61 and '62. We tried to update the car by grafting on the Sting Ray rear. That was the wrong thing to do. A car like the Corvette shouldn't

be changed that way. Sure, we face-lift regular production cars with new grills, taillights and trim, but that's different. A car like the Corvette should only change when you're making a complete change. You should definitely change the body when there's a major engineering change. For instance, if we go to mid-engine, the Corvette's appearance should telegraph that.

CSA How do the Sting Rays of 1963 through 1967 look to you now?

Mitchell They're out of this world. I personally have a taste for sheer shapes. I don't like boxy cars. I like sheer shapes with accents. Like if you took wings off a fighter plane, the shape just wouldn't come off. You need the tubular shape plus the windsplit. The first Corvettes had a little too much turtle look to me. When we got the look of the Sting Ray racer into the production car, we were home. To me, it was the introduction of the Sting Ray that really sent the Corvette on its way. It took off then.

CSA Is the styling of the current series Corvette pleasing to you?

Mitchell Oh, yes. I have to say that we borrowed a lot from Ferrari for the later Corvettes. I remember once I was driving with my daughter — she was about fifteen at the time — in a new Corvette and I pointed to a car approaching and said, "Look at that new Ferrari!" She said, "Dad, that's a new Corvette, just like you're driving." That was sure embarrassing. I'd seen the Corvette a thousand times in the studio, but never on the road.

It's a funny thing with auto design. You never know what you have until you see it on the road with other cars. I used to say that a car in the studio is like a horse in the kitchen. Nothing's relative. Put a car with other cars and you know what you've got.

The range of Mitchell's influence is evident in these photos, at top left the wild Astro II show Corvette, at right the Monza SS mini-car.

"A car in the studio's like a horse in the kitchen."

Left: *A dramatic studio view of the "split window" Mitchell fought so hard for.* **Above:** *The large back window treatment starting with the '78 wasn't Mitchell's favorite, but he agreed for utility reasons.*

You have to see a Corvette on the road to appreciate it.

Anyway, the new Corvettes have that long Ferrari nose. Due to the federal bumper standards, the nose of the newer Corvettes has gotten too long to suit me. But we had to do it.

Sometimes I think I'd like to see the headlights exposed on the new Corvettes. Headlights are like the eyes of a person. They have a lot to do with the character of a car. I exposed the headlights on my pace car by flushing glass over them. There are no more rolling doors or flaps to monkey with. You know, for years the Europeans didn't want to see cars with hidden headlights, automatic windows, six-way seats, tilt steering wheels, or any of that sort of thing. They'd rather have you spend your money on the engine, suspension, and maybe leather seats. But the desire for luxury and special appointments just can't be held back. Cadillac gives you so many things that Rolls doesn't. Now Rolls is buying from us as fast as they can.

CSA If you were to exclude the visual impact of the Corvette, and also the V-8 engine you've already mentioned, what would be the next most important factor in the Corvette's success?

Mitchell Handling. Duntov and that group over there worked magic with the Corvette's handling. Not everyone is a race driver. They might think they are, but they're not. A fast car can be a dangerous car. If the suspension isn't just right, you can be in trouble before you realize it. Chevrolet worked long and hard to make the Corvette a car that could compete with European sports cars on the track, but still have predictable enough handling for an average driver to drive it safely.

And the Corvette is an American sports car. I'm quoted sometimes as saying the Mercedes is antiquated. People ask, "Well, what do you mean?" I tell them that the Mercedes was designed for flat-out driving on rough roads in Europe. You get it over here on the boulevard and it feels like a twenty-year old truck compared to a Seville.

We were going to put a hotter engine in the Seville because the Europeans said you had to be able to drive it 130 mph all day long. Well, they may still be able to drive like that, but not for long. And we certainly can't here. Times change, and cars better change with them.

CSA Here comes the standard Corvette interview question. Of all production Corvettes, which is your favorite? As a bit of background to ponder, Duntov has expressed his favorite as the '65, because of the availability of fuel injection and disc brakes simultaneously. That's the engineer's dream Corvette. Larry Shinoda has picked the '63 split window coupe. That's one stylist's choice.

Mitchell Well, I sure had to battle everyone to get that split down the window. And it didn't stay long. I admit that it annoyed you when driving, but I just liked that windsplit continuing right through the glass.

To answer your question, the newer Corvettes are my favorites. I don't mean the '78 and later with the filled-in backlight. That I don't like. I don't disagree

Left: *SR-2 in show form.* **Right:** *SR-2 in racing form, and the '77 Corvette, Mitchell's personal favorite.*

with the decision to put that big window in and we did it for a reason. It used to be that a young married couple with a child just couldn't tolerate a Corvette because the space behind the seats was useless. But opening the rear up with that backlight makes the space so much more usable. There's actually room for a kid to crawl back there and take a nap. It's a question of utility. But to me, it sort of mis-mashes the Corvette with the Camaro/Firebird. I like the Porsche 914 type scooped-out backlight treatment better. I wanted to put the Manta Ray rear backlight treatment where we brought the scooped-out area to a "V" in the production car, but that just didn't work out. So anyway, my pick would be the '77, the newest of the current body with the small rear window.

CSA An addition to the previous question was the fact that Larry Shinoda said he liked the '63 because it was the closest production car to the racing Sting Ray. Even though the story has been told before, could you relate how and why you came to build the original racing Sting Ray?

Mitchell That's a great story. Well, let's see, At that time, Gordon was the president of General Motors. The National Safety Council was always close by and they put the heat on GM to get out of racing. Prior to that of course, we'd raced openly at Sebring and other tracks. And before that, we raced the SR-2 on the sand at Daytona. That was the job that had the bubble over the driver like a fighter pilot, and pipes dumping straight out from the engine. We went 169 mph in it. Oh, that was a mean SOB.

In the late fifties, Cole was running Chevrolet and he flat-out wanted to go racing. But Sebring in '57 generated so much Corvette racing publicity that Gordon finally had to say, "That's it, we're out of racing." Well, I knew there were a couple of chassis from that Sebring effort left over. So I deviled Cole to get me one and he did. To make it legal and get around the corporate racing ban, I paid $500 for it,

"Duntov had designed a very elaborate braking system."

with the understanding that I'd sell it back to the corporation when I was finished.

That reminds me, I never got my $500 back . . .

CSA This was the "mule" chassis for the Corvette SS, was it not?

Mitchell Right. The ugly car that ran great. To that chassis, we mated the Sting Ray body. It was all done in super secrecy in the special "X" studio below my office. There were just a few hand-picked guys involved.

Once we got the car designed, I had some of the Chevrolet engineering guys work on the suspension and engine on their own time.

CSA Duntov wasn't involved?

Mitchell Not too much. The chassis was his design, of course. But he couldn't get too involved in the Sting Ray racer project. Everything was being watched so closely and we had to be very careful. He helped where he could.

CSA But you did actually style and build the body at GM?

Mitchell Sure.

CSA What was the first race outing like?

Mitchell It was at Marlboro and our driver was Dick Thompson. He'd been driving Corvettes already for a couple of years and he was fantastic. The Sting Ray was red. We did pretty well, but there were a lot of problems. Duntov had designed a very elaborate braking system for the car. Electric switches on the dash to proportion front to rear pressure . . . things like that. I mean that as no disrespect to him, but these were just things that needed a lot of sorting out.

I remember I did one thing at that race that Duntov never thought I'd do. I had an intricate set of louvers on the hood, but the engine was running too hot and we figured those little louvers weren't letting enough air through. So I had them cut the louvers

111

Left: *Dick Thompson and the original racing Sting Ray, probably the most significant sports vehicle of the Mitchell tenure at GM.* **Right:** *The Sting Ray in action.*

"Hacked 'em out with a saw right at the track."

out right on the spot. Hacked 'em out with a saw right there at the track. Later we put styled screens over the holes and these ultimately made it into the '63 production car, though they weren't functional in production form.

Our racing the Sting Ray almost got nipped in the bud. One day during an engineering policy group meeting at GM, Jack Gordon stood up. I'd known him for years. Before his rise to the presidency, he'd been chief engineer at Cadillac when I was still a designer there. He stood up and said, "I thought everyone understood that we were out of racing." Didn't say anything else about it. I waited until after the meeting and went up and said, "Jack, were you talking to me?" He said he sure as hell was and walked out. He was one tough customer.

I thought it was the end of the world. I didn't know what to do. After thinking about it a while, I got Bob McLean and some of the other fellows to help me write a letter to Gordon. I spelled out that I got my job through racing, that I came to GM with it in my blood, and that my whole inspiration to design a car was through racing. It was my life. And since I was spending my own money to campaign the Sting Ray — and it was the Mitchell Sting Ray then, not the Corvette Sting Ray — so what was the harm?

A few weeks later he came out to Styling and as he was leaving I said, "Did you get my letter?" He said, "Yea, you're a pretty good salesman." He said, "You go ahead, but keep that thing off the property. I don't ever want to see it around here. And you spend your own money."

So I rented a garage on Twelve Mile road, moved the Sting Ray there, and we kept racing. I paid for the tires, the transportation expenses to the races . . . everything. It seemed expensive then, but an individual couldn't begin to do it today. I did battle with the IRS and managed to deduct some of the expenses from my taxes for the two years that we raced. After two years, GM finally said enough is enough.

CSA How did the Sting Ray fare on the track?

text continues on page 150

GOODYEAR

Mitchell We didn't win so many races as we broke track records. It was really something to go out there and beat people like Briggs Cunningham. We always seemed to have some minor problem that would cost us a victory, but that Sting Ray always gave 'em hell, I'll tell you that. They knew who we were.

It really spoiled me too. When you go to a race, and it's your car out there . . . man, you're watching, timing . . . it's really something. And Thompson drove like a madman. He was unbelievable. I remember at Elkhart Lake, I'd always get up by the lead turn at the start of the race and Dick would always come roaring through first . . . vroooom! Lord, what a thrill!

CSA Is it true that you drove the Sting Ray back and forth to work after you retired it from racing?

Mitchell Sure did. And we hardly changed it at all. Just a few little things to make it street legal. For a while, I went to four Webers in place of the fuel injection. That wasn't so great. I went back to fuel injection and that's the way it is today. That injection made a monkey out of the Webers. Even when we were racing, the fuel injection never gave a minute of trouble. Never. It was always some other little dinky thing.

CSA How did the crowds respond to the Sting Ray?

Mitchell Oh, terrific. They loved it. It was so striking on the track. With the right light, that sharply undercut side would go into shadow and the brightly lit upper surface made it look like a hydroplane darting around out there. After realizing what the light did to it, I changed from red to silver to highlight it even more.

CSA Where did the Sting Ray name come from?

Mitchell I cooked it up. As a kid, I'd lived some in Florida, and grew up loving fish and water. The Manta Ray, the Shark . . . they were all my names. Mr. Gordon hated them and the foreign names too. But I thought they were descriptive. You see a shark in the water, for instance, he's exciting to watch. Sleek, nervous, nimble, darting around. You need to put a little of that look into a car. Make it look like it'll do something.

Mitchell's love of exposed side exhausts is evident in these photos of the Shark show Corvette at left, and a '64 Corvette prototype above.

I was very contemptuous of foreign racing cars at the time we did the Sting Ray. They were all hammered out of metal overnight. You know, I'd hear about the new Ferrari, rush down to see it, and it'd be ugly. No attempt to style it whatsoever. The back end was like a potato and the front just sort of drooped over. They were all go, but no looks.

I wanted to make a race car that looked good too. A sharp, styled racer. I had to kick some of my own designers' butts on occasion. They'd want to do this or that to the Sting Ray and I'd say, "Never you mind, this is **my** car. Get out of here!" Even those sleek show Corvair Monzas, some guys wanted to make them look like potatoes too. Jeez, I didn't want that. I like pants that are pressed, you know? Direction. Like when I was in the Navy, I couldn't wait for the Army planes to come in. Our flying barrels looked like hell, but when an Army P-38 came in with that sharp nose and those twin tails . . . action! See them and you knew they could do something.

CSA You played a major role in the shelving of the four-place Corvette planned for 1963, didn't you?

Mitchell Oh, yes. I'll never forget that. Ed Cole made me get the windshield pillar up high enough so we could turn it into a four-placer. It looked gawky. Still does.

CSA You mean the windshield angle had to stay even after the four-place was dropped?

Mitchell It stayed. Still bothers me when I look at it today. It makes the car look narrow and high.

CSA How was your relationship with Cole?

Mitchell I loved that man. He did more for me than anybody in General Motors. When the engineers would get in my way, he'd say, "You get the hell out of here. Mitchell's designing the car." Cole was a great engineer and he was personally into everything. But he never bothered me. Design was mine. He was just great.

Cole probably knew more about an automobile than anyone ever did in the industry including Henry Ford I, Kettering, and all. And that was probably a weakness in him as an executive. He wanted to design the engine, transmission, carburetor . . . everything.

He had endless energy and enthusiasm that was contagious. He inspired me and all my designers. But fortunately for me, he did not try to style the car.

CSA In one of our previous publications, we featured an article on the 1955 Corvette. In the article we speculated on the reasons the '55 model managed to survive some very difficult and unprofitable times. Some have speculated that it was Duntov's engine work that saved the day, while others credit the competitive spirit within GM aroused by the introduction of the two-seat Thunderbird by Ford. Our article concluded that it was plain and simply Ed Cole and his unswerving support of the Corvette that saved the day. Would you go along with that?

Mitchell Yes, I'd agree. I saw Ed Cole stand behind the Corvette in front of a lot of GM top brass. He wanted that thing to go and that was that. And it wasn't easy. You know, General Motors is a profit-making corporation owned by stockholders. You talk about neat cars that don't have profit potential, and you won't get much attention from the people who count. And I'll tell you right now that many of the people who run or who have run General Motors are not car lovers in the sense that you and I are. I mean no disrespect by that and maybe that's the way things have to be. You need a lot more than a love of automobiles to run a company like General Motors.

Knudsen loved cars. Lord, he loved cars. He was always doing something special. While Cole was an engineer, he didn't care so much about what he drove. Except when he was dating Dolly, then he'd like to borrow my Silver Arrow. Harlow Curtis loved cars. We had Pininfarina do some special bodied cars for him to drive.

But the average executive at General Motors wasn't that way. They just didn't care. I'd feel guilty. I'd have six or seven special cars around. I'd offer them something to drive for the weekend. They'd say, "Naw, I'm going fishing" or something like that.

CSA Corvette enthusiasts love to know how other cars, people, and events have influenced Corvette history. Whether there is a Corvette connection or not, could you respond with your gut reaction to some one-liners?

Mitchell Sure.

CSA The Pantera.

Mitchell To begin with, I've always felt that Ford had no feel for an automobile. Bordinat, their Design VP, has heard me say that they have no gasoline in their blood. The only cars they ever designed that had automotive feel were the cars they raced, and the Pantera sorta came out of that.

The Pantera was hard to get into and its overall packaging wasn't at all good. It wasn't really a saleable product. Its styling was interesting.

CSA The Pantera obviously didn't affect Corvette sales much, but did its introduction influence you or the Corvette in any way?

Mitchell No, not at all.

CSA How about the Bricklin?

Mitchell Ugh. They called that the safety car. It looked like folded cardboard to me. Insert tab "A" into slot "B". DeLorean's car has that same look and you see it all over Europe. It comes out of Italy and I'm really sick of these cars. I'm just now working on an article about what's happening today to automobile design . . . the loss of the real beauty of a car.

You know, years ago when you went to an auto styling department, you found sweeps . . . racks of them. Now they design them with a "T" square and a triangle. No beauty, no flow. It's like this crazy disco music you hear now Arrrrahhhhhh . . . yoooop . . . yoooop. Yuk.

CSA The new Ford Mustang?

Mitchell Awful. I think the whole Ford line is awful. To me, their cars look like they put six or eight proposals together in a room, the execs come in and say, "Gimme the hood off that one, the door off that one over there, and stick some gills up here." Committee design at its worst.

The Japanese are much better. They haven't gotten sucked into that Italian box business. They got the jump on VW, then VW went to Italy for its new cars and they're all boxes. I think the Japanese Mitsubishi that Chrysler sells is much better looking than the Rabbit. Ford has become enamoured with European designers and they're moving them in. They keep that up and they'll be in real trouble. All these guys speak is function . . . everything has to look function. I say a car doesn't have to be ugly to be functional.

CSA You mentioned the DeLorean car. What do you feel about that whole project?

Mitchell I'd rather not say too much about it. I've just blasted everything that comes out of Italy, but I have to admit that his car is rather striking. John's a bright guy, a nice guy. But oh, putting together a car company from scratch to build a volume production car. Oh, that's a big baby.

CSA Porsche?

Mitchell I used to say a Porsche looked like a potato. If one spun out, you didn't know which end was coming. Designed in the fields of Idaho.

But Tony Lapine, who worked for me, is now their chief designer. And they've done a good job on the new model, the 928. It's too high-assed, but for once they've got a car that looks like a designer worked on it. It was shocking for them to go to front engine and I made some comments about that at the London show. But then I drove it and it's a damn nice car.

CSA Mercedes?

Mitchell Those are the people I really criticize. Good engineering, finest craftsmanship . . . and all that. But just look at them! They used to have an ad that bragged about them having engineers, not designers. I told them, "Hell, you don't have to tell anyone that."

They now have some young designers who are in sympathy with what I'm saying. I think when I made some of my cracks about their design . . .

CSA What sort of cracks?

Mitchell Oh, like I couldn't figure out what their designers did all year long. Nothing changes. A new door handle is a big deal. It's a shame. With Cadillac's fine engineering, we think it's sacrilegious not to make it look as good as it is.

They had another ad that showed that old Gullwing coupe in the background in phantom, with one of their new sedans in the foreground. They ought to take another look at that old Gullwing. That was a pure, great design. I could go into their great museum in Germany with a pad of paper and design a beautiful sedan just by looking at their old classics. They took that beautiful grill and made it into a barrel. It's like they take a Ritz hotel and turn it into a Howard Johnson's. Their cars are just glued together nothings. No theme. It's a shame, such a well built car. Damn.

My guys at Opel in Germany know some of the young designers at Mercedes and they like what I'm saying. They want to make cars with nicer lines. They just don't have the freedom to do it.

CSA Firebird and Camaro?

Mitchell One of the great stories of great design in a high production car. Those cars are a decade old now. But there is no better looking car like it made anywhere. Not in Europe. Certainly not at Ford or Chrysler. It's a case of being a pure designer's car, not a committee car.

You go into any Pontiac dealer today and ask what his best seller is. Firebird. Ask any Chevrolet dealer. Camaro . . . and Corvettes if he can get them. And when these cars are downsized, don't think you won't see the same feel. GM is smart enough to know a winner. We never changed Cadillac so much that you couldn't tell it was a Cadillac. We're not going to make boxes out of the Camaro and Firebird, I'll guarantee that.

CSA How about GM's new "X" cars, the Citation, Phoenix, Omega and Skylark?

Mitchell I have a saying about designing a small car. It's like tailoring a dwarf. I'm from the era of the big car, where you make them wider, lower, sleeker. But I don't care who you are, designing a small car is a difficult job. The "X" cars are the last ones that I worked on while I was at GM. And when I went to the proving grounds to see the finished products, after having been retired for a year, they looked good. The boys have done a good job. I think they'll be very successful. They got the size down, but still kept style in. They even have a little Seville feeling in them.

You ever hear what I told Mercedes when they accused me of stealing Mercedes design for the Seville?

CSA Tell us.

Mitchell I told them, "Hell, I didn't copy Mercedes, I copied Rolls Royce. My father always said that if you're going to steal, rob a bank, not a grocery store." Rolls put that in their stockholders' report.

CSA Speaking of quotes, you've said that one way to get people to remember you was to spit on the table and wipe it up with your hand . . .

Mitchell Yes. Sidney Greenstreet said that in "The Hucksters."

At right, the first of the contemporary mid-engine Corvette prototypes.

"Designing a small car is like tailoring a dwarf."

WIDE 60 OVAL
Firestone

Mitchell loved clean body surfaces, but had nothing against a few attention attracting frills. Note the extremely clean Chevy II Super Nova show car at left, and the Super Spyder Corvair prototype at right.

CSA You've probably not done anything quite that extreme to win your way with the Corvette, but can you relate some of the "scenes" you've been involved in over the years?

Mitchell No, I'd rather not get into that. But I fought Roche on down. I told them the Corvette had greater owner loyalty than any other GM car including Cadillac. We needed it.

You know, it's something how the Corvette plays into so many other things that have happened. We did a number of four-place show cars in the fifties which I think influenced Ford to switch their Thunderbird to a four-seater. Now that car sold well and we sat on our hands with regard to the "personal luxury" car.

The immediate and obvious thought was to turn the Corvette into a four-place. That was no good. But people were going to Donner and Roche and saying, "Hey, we need an answer." The car that evolved was the Riviera. I had that done in a secret studio. Nobody knew about it. Oh, Gordon knew. He'd come down and look at it. I'd say, "What do you think it should look like?" He'd say it ought to be sheer . . . sharp. And that's the way it was made. I had the designers take the roof template and run that line right down the backlight into the deck. Ed Nichols supervised that room. We were trying to get a cross between Ferrari and Rolls Royce. The only thing Gordon and I disagreed about was that he wanted a straight line down the fenders and I wanted a lifting sweep. I got that in, and I got it back into the new Riviera. I'm sick of all these straight lines.

I wanted to call it the LaSalle. That's why it had those two grills, it was designed to be a Cadillac. But Cadillac didn't need it and didn't have the facilities to build it, so Buick, Olds and Pontiac sorta bid on it. Olds wanted to put a different engine in it and change it here and there. But I said, "You don't touch this car! Whoever gets this car builds it just the way it is." Buick did just that.

They did a marvelous job in their advertising. I told them that their ads shouldn't have any feel of Buick. They took it to the Gotham Hotel in Manhattan to photograph. The writers, the photographers and even the artist, Melbourne Brindle, went along. They really got the feel of the Riviera, a pure designer's car, into the advertising.

If you go to Europe for designs by Pininfarina, Farini, or anyone else, then go over and tell them what to do, they'll tell you to go sit in the corner. **They're** designing the car. That's the way it should be, and that's the way it was with the Riviera.

CSA Is the Corvette in this category?

Mitchell Absolutely. Nobody ever told us how we had to make it look. I said that was it, and that was it. I tried to do everything that way. That reminds me what my good friend Bill Lyons of Jaguar . . . there's one of the few men I knew who owned the plant, ran it, and designed the cars. I knew they'd screw up when he retired and they did. That new coupe has a Japanese taillight, and Italian front, and a padded roof. Looks like six guys did it in six different countries. I've got the last of the Jaguar XK-E V-12 roadsters. Oh, it's a beauty.

CSA You started to tell us what Bill Lyons said.

Mitchell He said the only thing a committee could design was a camel.

I know how Ford and Chrysler work. They're under product planners. To me, a product planner is a freak. If you can't be a designer, can't be an engineer, can't be a salesman, don't worry. You can always be a product planner. They're a nothing. If product planning was that good, you could go out here and hire someone to tell you how to make a good hot dog stand and you'd be a millionaire.

You can't do that. You have to have your individual thoughts and go out and say, "This is it." Hattie Carnegie didn't ask women what kind of hats they'd like to wear. The fashion designer doesn't stop people on the Champs Elysses in Paris and ask, "Say, would you like the hemlines a little lower next season?" THEY TELL THEM!

I'm the designer and I'm telling you to go out and sell it.

Salesmen are the designer's worst enemies. When I left General Motors, I had more contempt for salesmen than engineers. If something is selling, they don't want to change it. If it's new and selling, they won't sell anything else.

In industry today, the designer is the most unappreciated and underestimated employee of all. You can have salesmen, you can have finance, advertising, engineering, you can have all the schemes. But whether it's a can of soup or a Cadillac, if it doesn't have identity it won't make a bit of difference. This business of Iacocca buying a new ad agency for Chrysler. Hell, light bulbs don't sell anything. They've got to have a car.

When I was at General Motors, I was never held back. I told Mr. Donner once that if he ever put me under product planners, I'm gone. And they never did. You have to know and love an automobile to design one. I know how Ford works. Their cars have no soul. They're committee cars. Now, McAdam at Chrysler is, I think, one of the best designers around, but he's held back.

CSA Getting back to the one-liners, what's your impression of Ital Design?

Mitchell Giorgetto Giugiaro is one of the most talented and prolific designers around. But there again, he's got the folded cardboard design. Everything looks the same. No identity. He's doing too many too fast.

CSA The SS.

Mitchell The what?

CSA The Corvette SS from Sebring days.

"I know how Ford works. Their cars have no soul."

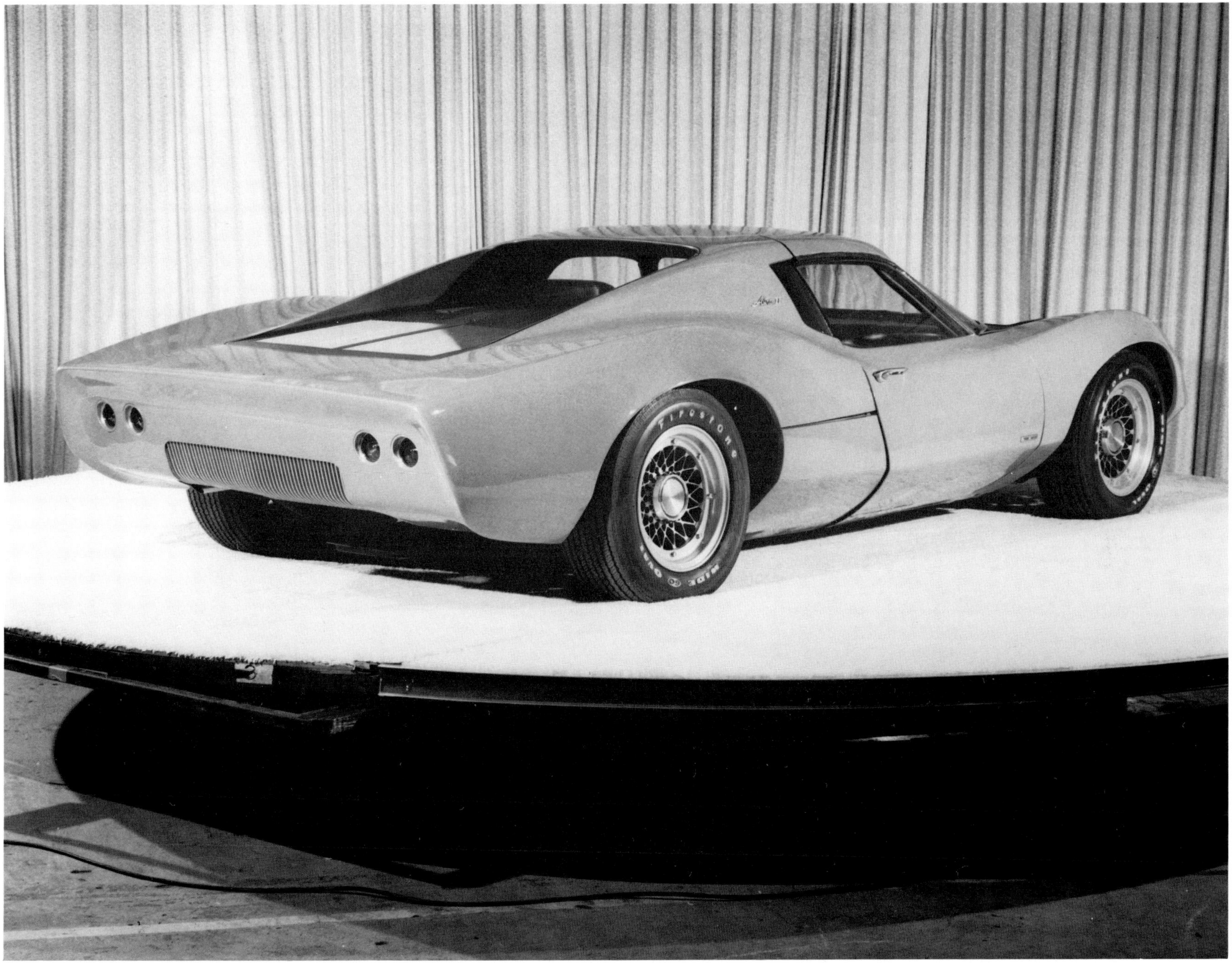
Firestone

EXPERIMENTAL
ASTRO III

Left: *Mitchell's love of aircraft surfaced clearly in the jet plane-influenced Astro III Corvette turbine car.*

"Nader doesn't know a car from a canoe."

Mitchell The what?

CSA The . . . oh, ok. New subject. The Avanti?

Mitchell I never liked that thing when it came out. Looked weird. Too narrow, I guess. But now, it's starting to look good to me. I was driving the other day with my wife, and she commented on how nice an Avanti looked that passed by. She was right, it looked really nice.

CSA Ralph Nader?

Mitchell Never had much to do with him personally. He reminds me of one of those people who doesn't have much to do and can always find trouble. He's a mess. I'd rather not say much more.

CSA Does he know cars?

Mitchell He doesn't know a car from a canoe.

CSA Market research?

Mitchell All they can tell you is where you've been, not where to go.

CSA Women and Corvettes?

Mitchell Just drive down the street and see how many gals you see driving Corvettes. It's a different world with this women's lib. My wife drives like a bat out of hell. My daughter Wendy could drive a Sting Ray when she was eleven years old. More and more women are racing professionally now.

CSA Government regulations?

Mitchell Pretty sad. The more you work with them so they understand your problems, the better off you are. The sad thing is that the emissions group doesn't care about mileage. The mileage group doesn't care about emissions. The safety group isn't concerned about insurance standings.

Feature this. If you make a bumper that won't give, you don't have a safe car. It has to be a system. But there's a government group that wants a car to hit a wall at speed and suffer no damage. They don't care that the driver's teeth just went out the windshield.

It's ridiculous. There're committees down there in Washington, each with its own axe to grind. And each doesn't care about the other. As soon as one finishes, another starts. I truly believe some of these people don't want us to succeed. They set nearly impossible standards, we meet them, and they're disappointed. It's not, "Hey, you did a great job." It's, "Hey, we should have made the standard tougher." I honestly believe some of them would just like to get rid of cars period.

I've helped make a movie on this subject. Shows crowded subways, girls waiting out in the rain for a bus or taxi, compared to the pleasure of driving your own automobile. Turn on the stereo, nobody bothers you . . . it's a different world. The automobile is one of man's great inventions. There isn't a commodity in the world that gives you what an automobile does.

CSA An extension of that might be that no other automobile delivers quite what a Corvette does. Did the success of the Corvette ever tempt you to push for another two-seater from within General Motors?

Mitchell Pontiac did one on their own while DeLorean was there. I personally wanted to see the Corvair Monza show cars go into production to offset the Mustang.

CSA Why didn't it happen?

Mitchell There's always the problem of whether you can sell enough to make it worthwhile. The Corvair had its own problems too. It came along right on the threshold of the horsepower boom. The Corvair's engine design was such that you just couldn't hop it up enough. And things like those rubber bands driving the fans didn't help either. The Corvair just couldn't be made to go like it looked.

CSA As you look back over your career at General Motors, is there a particular Corvette story or incident that still brings a smile to your face whenever you think of it?

Mitchell Well, I always wanted to take one of my Corvette bombs over to Europe and get it on some of those no-speed limit roads so I personally could beat the hell out of the Ferraris and Mercedes. I just wanted to see the drivers' faces.

I had four of the Can-Am aluminum 200 mph engines in my cars. One was in the Manta Ray. I worked through our people at Opel in Germany to get the Manta Ray to Europe as the pace car for the Formula One race at Monte Carlo.

Everybody was at Monte Carlo that year and I let them all drive the Manta Ray. Jackie Stewart, Mario

Andretti . . . even Princess Caroline. But I was worried about some of the possible press the car might get with that engine. You know, we were into the gas shortage, anti-performance thing. And the engine in that Manta Ray was anything but an economical non-performer. That engine was beautiful. All chromed . . . pipes coming right out the fenders. It made those Formula One cars sound like peanuts. Just to be safe, I had my guys lock the hood down so nobody could look in or take photos.

Well, after the Manta Ray had finished its Monte Carlo duties, we started on our way back to Germany. I was up front in the Manta Ray and my wife and some others followed in a Caprice and an Opel wagon. Oh, I was having the time of my life. I was driving like A. J. Foyt. 180 miles per hour . . . I was zooming by everybody. In the tunnels, I'd have to slow down to see where I was going. These guys in their BMWs, Ferraris and Mercedes wouldn't. They'd zoom by me, then we'd get out of the tunnel and I'd go by them again. I was in heaven, I'd never had the chance to drive like that on the highway. Of course, for those Europeans, it was just another Sunday afternoon drive.

We stopped for lunch, and my wife said, "For God's sake Bill, will you slow down? You're going to kill yourself!" I assured her everything was fine. While we were in that restaurant, or at toll booths,

Above: *Mitchell nabbed.*

people would just swarm around the Manta Ray. Europeans love cars. One other Ferrari driver said I passed him like he was tied to a wall.

We got back on the road and there was one long last shot of road before entering the ten-mile tunnel to Mont Blanc. I decided to really let go. Just when I put my foot into it, the engine froze. I switched off the ignition, stopped and got out, expecting to find oil everywhere. Nothing. Damn good thing it locked up before entering the tunnel. That would have been murder stranded in the middle of that.

CSA What had happened?

Mitchell You remember I told you that I had ordered the hood locked so nobody could peek at the engine? Well, through all that driving at Monte Carlo, and all my road racing through Europe, we hadn't put in one drop of oil. It went bone dry.

CSA What happened next?

Mitchell My wife and I went on while some of the other guys in our party arranged to trailer the Manta Ray back to Opel. We had to get back, because the people at Opel had a beautiful dinner banquet all set up for us in the evening.

At the banquet, we're all sitting at this huge table when all of a sudden two policemen come in and grab me. Just came in and lifted me right out of my seat! If I'd had a heart problem then, I'd have died on the spot.

They took me outside . . . lights are flashing, sirens blaring. They say something like, "We have cameras watching our highways. We know how you've been driving. You're going to be in jail a long time."

"I kept thinking, how am I going to explain this to my boss? How am I going to tell my kids?

Then they haul me over to this huge German in a black Mercedes. He says he's going to prosecute me. Says I've said enough bad things in my career about Mercedes that they can put me away for life.

At about this time, I caught a twinkle in Henry Haga's eyes. He runs Opel Design and had set the whole thing up. The big guy in the Mercedes was an actor and the policemen were all playing along. Damn near scared me to death. I've never been so embarrassed. I kept thinking, how am I going to explain this to my boss? How am I going to tell my kids. Daddy's not coming home. We really had a good laugh afterward, I'll tell you. But I needed about six drinks before I could start eating again.

CSA Can we safely assume that you haven't been speeding in Europe lately?

Mitchell I'm cured.

CSA In closing, did Harley Earl leave you with any pearls of wisdom that you might pass along?

Mitchell One thing does stick in my mind. When I came to GM from New York, I was kind of a hot-shot. I tended to look down my nose at people, sometimes for meaningless things. For instance, I had always loved clothes and always dressed well. I had a contemptuous feeling about the way Detroit people dressed.

During my second year as chief designer for Cadillac, I'd often come in on Sunday to acclimate myself to the technologies of the environment and the business. One Sunday I was in the studio and heard a noise. It was Mr. Earl.

We started talking and he said, "You know, Bill, there are a lot of people around here who can help you. Herman Jensen in the metal shop. Potonik in the drafting room. Ed Gale that runs the wood shop. They can all help you. They know more about this business than you're going to know for years. I know you have a feeling about Detroit people, but I want to tell you, the biggest SOB in the world is a nice guy if you go fishing with him."

After that I went bowling with these men. I drank whiskey and beer with them. I spent time with them, in the shop and out of it. They made me what I am.

Harley Earl was right. Think about it. There aren't many people in this world who don't have things to say and talents to offer. I had to have the respect and even the affection of the people who worked for me in order to succeed. Being vice president meant nothing if I didn't have people who could and would back me up. You must have relationships with people such that their talents are visible and available.

After that little conversation with Mr. Earl, I got to work on that shortcoming of mine. I think we'd all do well to heed Harley Earl on that one.

John Z. DeLorean

Chevy turnaround

Throughout the years, a few names have become inseparably linked with the development and success of the Corvette.

John Zachary DeLorean is not one of those names. But it could have been. Perhaps it should have been.

DeLorean was the youngest man to ever be Chevrolet's general manager. He held that position from 1969 through 1972. While he was there, he produced startling results that moved an ailing division to its present premier position. Chevrolet was hurting when DeLorean entered, but he turned it around. He and Semon Knudsen had done the same thing for Pontiac.

GM promoted him to Group Vice President in charge of North American auto and truck sales. Financially, GM awarded him with more than half a million dollars annually. The rumor mill in Detroit predicted that he would become GM's future president. And he was only forty-eight years old.

Seven months later, he resigned.

Why? What kind of man could turn his back on so much glitter? What kind of man could walk away from so much success?

Simple answer . . . a dedicated man.

John DeLorean has never fit comfortably into the mold of corporate executive. He went where he went because he produced results, not because his personal style delighted his superiors. Yet, he had a string of successful management coups that not even his biggest detractors could fault. So why leave?

He won't say, exactly. He hints at reasons. He says leaving the manager's slot at Chevrolet for the group executive's job was like going from baseball team manager to stadium owner. He missed the action, the sense of fulfillment.

But listen to the facts. When DeLorean was the manager of Pontiac, prior to coming to Chevrolet, he directed the development of a two-place sports car to invade the Corvette market. GM wouldn't let him build it.

After he came to Chevrolet, DeLorean oversaw the development of exciting Corvette prototypes, the mid-engine, and rotary models. He pushed hard for an all-new and lighter Corvette along the lines of the prototypes. GM said no, it wasn't needed.

DeLorean hatched another plan while at Chevrolet, this for another two-seater based on the Vega. In its experimental form, this car was called the XP-898. It employed dramatically innovative use of stressed plastic in its body structure. Dramatically innovative for the auto industry, that is, since the principles had already been proven in aviation and marine use. Sled tests at GM's proving grounds showed the XP-898 to be the most crash-worthy car GM had ever built. Word leaked that GM would indeed put such a car into production. Truth was, it was DeLorean who was pushing to get the XP-898 into production. But again, the answer was no.

After DeLorean left General Motors, he asked to buy the prototype mid-engine Corvette designed by Zora Duntov, and the rights to produce it. Though GM had discarded its thoughts of building a production version, DeLorean was turned down.

Now, John Z. DeLorean is building his own sports car. In many ways, it is a composite of cars he had tried to build while at General Motors. It will be aimed squarely at the Corvette market in size, cost, and performance.

Why did John DeLorean leave General Motors? There is that old adage about not keeping a good man down, but there must be more to it than that. Was DeLorean miffed at GM? With a half-million bucks a year? Be serious.

Was his ego hurt? Half a million can salve a lot of pride, if that is all there was to it. Does he plan to teach GM a lesson? Come on . . . DeLorean is more realistic than that.

Then why?

Get ready to learn something about a man. Then, just maybe, the final answer may develop. But there is no guarantee. One cannot easily categorize a maverick when it is merged with a genius.

DeLorean: The Man

Appropriately, John DeLorean was born in Detroit. He was the eldest of four sons of Zachary A. DeLorean, a life-long foundry worker at Ford Motor Company. He grew up amid the talk, the smell, and in the shadows of auto plants. He worked summers at Chrysler's Jefferson Avenue and Murray Body plants, assembling cars.

He earned an engineering degree from the Lawrence Institute of Technology in Detroit in 1948. Then came Chrysler Institute, a work-study cooperative engineering program, from which he received his master's degree in 1952. But he didn't stay with Chrysler. Too big. Already the conflict between John Z. and the big corporation was surfacing.

A reasonable fit was found at Packard. Its engineering department had an impeccable reputation, yet its size was on a completely different scale than those of the Big Three. Working under Forest McFarland, Packard's Research and Development Director, DeLorean learned quickly and well.

Packard's minuscule (by auto industry standards) ways required DeLorean to learn the "hands on" approach to engineering. After designing something, DeLorean would physically walk the part through the necessary steps for production. If someone couldn't make it properly, he'd show them how. This was probably the most formative period in the young engineer's career.

In 1954, he married Elizabeth Higgins. Two years later, he succeeded McFarland as research and development director at Packard. DeLorean was just thirty-one years old.

But it was no secret that Packard was dying. Again shunning the big auto companies, DeLorean instead chose to work for Thompson Products, in Cleveland, Ohio. The future was bright for him there, but he was no longer around automobiles. No problem. In a matter of months, the auto industry came after him.

GM comes calling

The industry came after him in the form of none other than General Motors, through the person of Oliver K. Kelley of GM's engineering staff. Kelley put DeLorean in contact with Semon Knudsen. Knudsen was the son of famed William Knudsen, a one-time Ford executive who switched to GM and eventually became its president. Later, the second generation Knudsen would reverse history by moving from GM to the presidency of Ford.

At the time DeLorean and Knudsen met, Knudsen was the head of the Pontiac Division. Knudsen was a rising star searching for star talent to help. To someone who doesn't care for big corporations, especially big auto corporations, GM held little attraction for DeLorean. But DeLorean and Knudsen hit it off. Both were real auto men, earthy engineering types who could not only conceptualize, but who could each literally tear into their projects themselves . . . and loved doing so. DeLorean grew up in a tough neighborhood, working on cars from his earliest memory. Knudsen grew up amid family prosperity, but he nevertheless knew cars. For his sixteenth birthday, his dad gave him a brand-new automobile . . . completely disassembled, with the admonishment, "You want to drive it, son, you put it together."

These two men developed instant rapport and Knudsen overcame John DeLorean's big-business phobia. In 1956, DeLorean was aboard at Pontiac as Director of Advanced Engineering.

As an auto engineer, DeLorean was excellent. Blessed with abundant energy — he once went seven years at GM without a Sunday off — DeLorean and Knudsen shoved Pontiac from the obscure status of old woman's car to the performance

text continues on page 170

The DeLorean family.

DMC

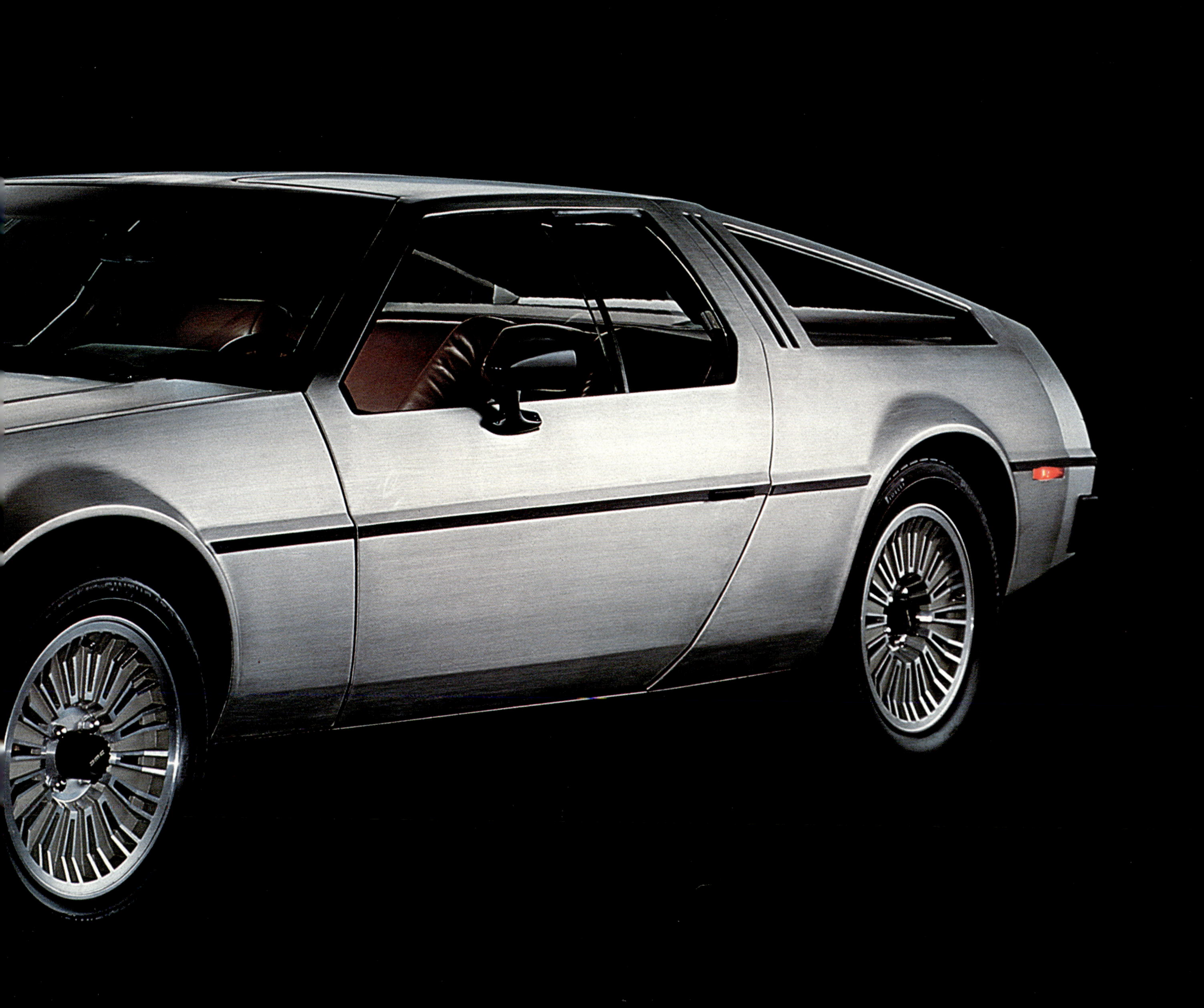

Left: *This is the prototype Pontiac two-seater which DeLorean wanted to market while at Pontiac. Officially the XP-833, it was called the Banshee, though this name was also applied to later Firebird-based show cars.*

The XP-833 was developed hot-on-the-heels of Ford's Mustang and was slated for 1967 production. DeLorean's people put together a very convincing presentation for GM's Board of Directors which detailed the success of the stylish Mustang, and warned that Ford was displaying a two-seat Cougar II at auto shows, surely a hint of Ford's future intentions. Anticipating Chevy's protests, the proposal pegged the XP-833's selling price at under $3000. Though it was also to have a fiberglass body, DeLorean and company maintained that the XP-833's cost alone would put it in a completely different market than the Corvette. It would be plus business for the corporation. The decision of the board was that the XP-833 would rob from the Corvette, and DeLorean was turned down.

The XP-833 was to be fitted with Pontiac's 230 CID overhead-cam six, an engine DeLorean helped design. So equipped, the curb weight was pegged at only 2186 pounds! Three-speed, four-speed, and automatic transmissions were to be available as well as an optional V-8.

William T. Collins now owns the XP-833 prototype. He was Pontiac's engineer for the project, then joined DeLorean and played an integral role in designing the DMC. He is now Director of Advanced Projects for American Motors.

Right: *The beautiful XP-898, another of DeLorean's pet projects while at GM. Based more on the Vega than the Corvette, this Chevy two-seater's unique plastic chassis construction planted the seeds in DeLorean's mind for the ERM chassis in the DMC-12.*

limelight. So brilliant was his performance, DeLorean quickly moved from Director of Advanced Engineering, to Assistant Chief Engineer, to Chief Engineer and finally in 1965, to General Manager of Pontiac. Between 1959 and 1965, **Motor Trend** magazine awarded its "Car of the Year" trophy to Pontiac three times. DeLorean was instrumental in the introduction of Pontiac's wildly successful "wide track" stance. In 1964, it was the GTO and the start of the performance boom.

DeLorean was as singularly responsible for the GTO as any individual could be in a corporate giant, and it proved that he was giving Pontiac much more than just engineering talent. He also had an uncanny marketing sense. His own personal life style permitted him to shake the traditional shackles of Detroit-bound vision. As his personal wealth grew, DeLorean's assets included much more than GM stock. They ultimately included a piece of a pro baseball team and farms in Idaho.

Thin and trim, DeLorean mixed easily with young people. He cruised their drive-ins and sized up their tastes. He saw their coming importance in the auto marketplace. He used words like "equal rights" and "environmental" before his peers knew what they meant. He was the highly fictionalized inspiration for swinging Adam Trenton, played by Rock Hudson in TV's version of Arthur Hailey's "Wheels."

In the days when white shirt and proper tie were mandatory at GM, DeLorean occasionally showed up after hours in turtleneck and bellbottoms. He was anything but inconspicuous, which historically isn't the right and proper path to follow at GM.

But while the top brass might have preferred a little less flamboyance in their boy-wonder, they couldn't ignore the bottom line. DeLorean was getting the job done. He delivered the goods. And because of that, a mere thirteen years after joining GM, he was promoted again to the general manager's position at Chevrolet. At forty-four, he was

XP
898
RADIAL T/A
B.F.GOODRICH

XP
898
RADIAL T/A
B.F.GOODRICH

the youngest man ever to take control of General Motors' largest division.

At Chevy, DeLorean continued to shine. He is credited with much of the planning behind the reworked Monte Carlo series which debuted in 1973, and became one of Chevy's most popular and profitable models. DeLorean directed his engineers to design in some new (for Detroit) steering and suspension geometry which gave the Monte Carlo excellent road feel for such a big car. After wondering why Mercedes cars "felt" so good, DeLorean discovered the answer was to put in 5° of caster in the front wheels. That had many advantages, with the single negative being increased steering effort. American car designers, long used to building heavy cars, had long since eliminated caster in favor of easier steering. But with power steering a foregone conclusion, DeLorean put it back in and the results were dramatic.

Rebound

Along with a continuing string of dazzling product innovations, DeLorean went to work on the Chevy dealer network, visiting dealers personally and simply doing whatever it took to get sales back on track. Sales did rebound and Chevy was off and

running. Chevy volume exceeded three million units in 1971, a first for a single nameplate. So solid was DeLorean's performance that he was again promoted in 1972 to the elite position of group vice president, in charge of all GM car and truck sales in North America. With almost twenty years still ahead of him before retirement, it was no wonder that speculation in Detroit pegged DeLorean as a sure future bet for the GM presidency.

But things weren't quite as they appeared. DeLorean's famed lifestyle, understandably exaggerated by a Detroit press which usually had woefully slim pickins for glamour news from GM's gray execs, was surely making him enemies. DeLorean's first marriage ended in divorce and, while single, he frequented the California scene. He was photographed in the company of some very lovely ladies. At age forty-four, he married twenty-year old Kelly Harmon, daughter of football great, Tom Harmon. Best man at their wedding was Semon Knudsen. Bridesmaid was Kelly's sister, who happened to be the wife of Ozzie and Harriet's Ricky Nelson. DeLorean was clearly not playing Detroit's social games according to the rules, and some wondered how long GM would tolerate it.

All was not smooth on the job, either. DeLorean's habit of speaking out didn't always endear him to GM's executive elite. When he was at Pontiac, DeLorean wanted to build a Corvette-like two-seater. But business at Pontiac was booming and Chevrolet's was going down the drain. Fearful of the wrath of Chevy dealers who would chafe at competition from within the corporation with their only self-selling model, GM turned DeLorean down.

The move to Chevrolet should have cured any leftover hard feelings about the scrubbed Pontiac two-seater. Afterall, it would be DeLorean who would control the Corvette's destiny. He left no doubts about the direction he sought for the Corvette. He was quoted as saying the Corvette was simply overweight. From Chevy's General Manager, very irreverent.

But the Corvette was a money maker. Chevrolet was spending less per car to advertise the Corvette than any other in the entire General Motors line. Yet, the Corvette turned in the highest profit margin of any car in the GM fleet. Long gone were the days of subsidizing the Corvette as an image booster. The Corvette was supporting itself very nicely, thank you, so leave it alone Mr. D.

But he didn't. The mid-engine Corvette prototypes were underway when DeLorean arrived, and he pushed to get them into production. Feeling pressure from Cole to put rotary power into something exotic, DeLorean directed Zora Arkus-Duntov to come up with a mid-engine rotary Corvette. Duntov, never a believer in anything without pistons, moaned that the rotary engines were too dinky to move a Corvette along properly. Snapped DeLorean, "You're supposed to be the great inventor . . . so go invent something!"

Duntov did. He came up with a mid-engine Corvette powered by not one or two, but FOUR rotors. Duntov made even himself a believer, as the four-rotor Corvette became his favorite of all. When he retired, Chevrolet Styling gave him an exquisitely detailed scale model of the four-rotor, and it's one of his great treasures.

But meanwhile, DeLorean was getting nowhere with his Corvette plans. Rebuffed time after time, he and his engineers came up with a new tact. It was called XP-898.

Here was a car that DeLorean could really sink his teeth into. An innovative vehicle, the XP-898 employed the first real breakthroughs in auto body fabrication in six decades. He wanted this one badly, but the story again was the same. Not needed in the GM line.

What was so special about the XP-898? To clear one common misconception, it was **not** a Corvette. The running gear was Vega, and the overall dimensions were approximately that of an Opel GT, though the XP-898 was five inches lower.

The thing that made the XP-898 so unique was its body/chassis construction. The best term to describe its construction would be "plastic sandwich." The sections for its underbody, nose section, firewall-dash, and floor-rear body were hand-laid plastic inner and outer panels, bonded together with polyurethane adhesive. The catch was that voids were left between the plastic panels. These were later filled with urethane foam forced in through

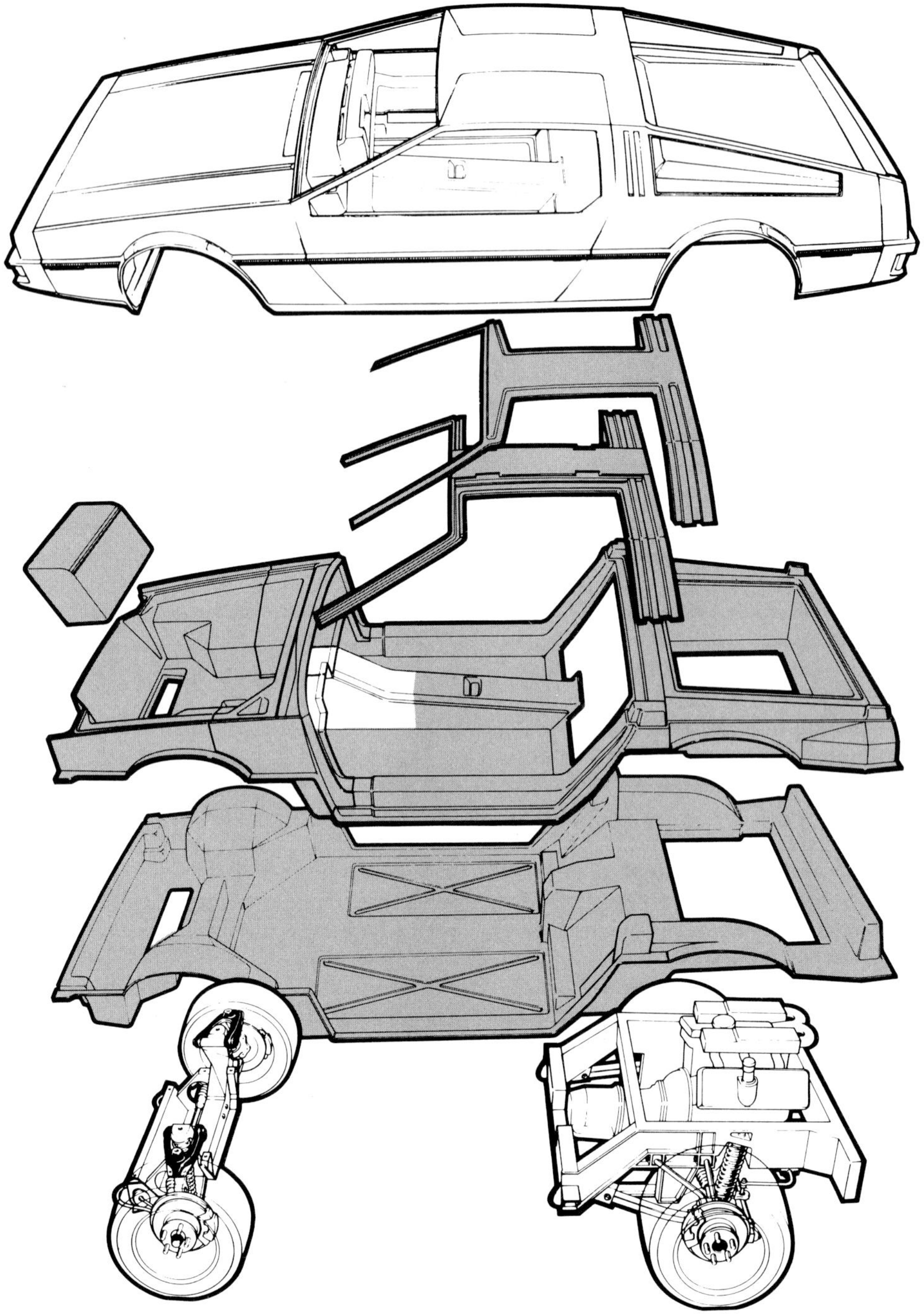

Left: *The body and chassis construction of the original DMC prototype is shown in this exploded rendering. The shaded portions are all designed to be ERM plastic. The front and rear suspension of the production DeLorean vehicle is now tied together by steel, a direct input of Lotus' Colin Chapman.*

Most crashworthy

access holes. The foam entered as a sort of liquid and gas, then hardened after seeking out every nook and cranny. The result was a very light structure with incredible strength. So strong that the XP-898 had no frame in the conventional sense. Sure, metal suspension components were used, but it was the plastic sandwich structures that were holding the car together.

DeLorean loved this car. Its construction techniques were ideally suited for modest production, economically speaking. Sled tests at GM's proving grounds proved the plastic sandwich structure to be the most crashworthy of any ever tested. At under 2300 pounds, the XP-898 was nearly three-quarters of a ton lighter than the Corvette and managed 0-60 mph times in the ten second range with its puny 111 hp Vega four-banger. DeLorean knew that the Corvette's plastic body and its immunity to rust was a big selling point. In the XP-898, DeLorean saw a car which had not only a body immune to rust, but most of its chassis as well. DeLorean felt the XP-898, or something like it, should go into production. Sandwich plastic for all of the GM line? Doubtful, but he thought this was simply too important a concept to just roll into another warehouse and forget. **Road and Track** magazine agreed with him. In their January, 1973, issue cover story on the XP-898, **R & T** urged its readers to send cards urging GM to put the XP-898 into production. **Road and Track** wasn't successful and neither was DeLorean.

How important the XP-898 episode was in DeLorean's decision to part company with General Motors isn't known. He won't say. But the XP-898 certainly figured strongly in his future efforts.

What he will say about leaving GM is that he couldn't adjust well to endless meetings at the group executive level. That he felt no sense of accomplishment. He's enjoyed his manager's position at Chevrolet as much as anything he'd ever done, but that was all past.

So a mere seven months after his big promotion, DeLorean hit the bricks to pursue "other interests." At first, there was no mention of DeLorean building his own car. He did try to buy the rights to produce the mid-engine Corvette prototype that he wanted to bring out while at Chevrolet. GM had turned thumbs down on the radical new Corvette as a production vehicle, and did likewise to DeLorean's request to be allowed to produce it himself.

For a year after his departure from GM in April, 1973, DeLorean served as the head of the National Alliance for Businessmen, an organization dedicated to finding jobs for disadvantaged individuals. He was by this time divorced from Kelly Harmon, and had remarried a top New York fashion model, Christina Ferrare. He wrote a book titled, **"On A Clear Day You Can See General Motors."** The book was to reflect his views of Detroit, but he later decided not to publish.

Because John Z. DeLorean knew then what he really wanted to do. The seeds that had been planted by the aborted Pontiac two-seater, the mid-engine Corvette prototypes, and finally the XP-898, had germinated. John DeLorean would build his own car. A car unlike any the world had ever seen.

DeLorean: The Car

John DeLorean's disappointment over GM's refusal to sell him the rights to the mid-engine Corvette prototype was short-lived. Thanks to the 1973-74 Arab oil embargo, DeLorean became aware that if there was one thing the world didn't need, it was another overweight, inefficient sports car. DeLorean's original thoughts had been to buy the mid-engine Corvette from GM, produce it, then later bring out a lighter, smaller two-seater. General Motors and the Arabs ruled out step one of the plan. On to step two.

Though not a stylist, DeLorean had a mental picture of the car he wanted to build. The car would in many ways be an extension of DeLorean himself, and its configuration would mirror many of the causes he had fought for. Having come this far, DeLorean was through compromising.

The new car would have aft engine placement. From the viewpoint of efficiency, DeLorean knew that the drive train and engine should be together, not connected by a driveshaft running the length of the car. Front engine-front drive is the worldwide trend now, and there are certain cooling, cost, and packaging advantages with this layout. But DeLorean wanted the engine in the rear for safety. Rear placement permits better weight distribution for better handling, plus it allows the frontal area to be designed for controlled crush in collisions.

Gullwing doors are usually associated with two cars, the Mercedes Gullwing and the Bricklin. One winner and one loser. There would be comparisons enough between his effort and Bricklin's without incorporating a conspicuous feature like gull doors, but DeLorean felt he had to have them. He knew his car would be very low, and he needed them for ease of entry. Also for safety. Yes, safety, because the gullwings allow a high side sill, the best way to build-in side impact protection.

DeLorean wanted to build a car that would last. An "ethical" car, as he puts it. It would have to be efficient. That meant lightness, and that means plastics. More than anything else, DeLorean's dream car would be a cross between the mid-engine Corvette prototypes and the experimental XP-898. It would use the experimental Corvette's aft engine placement, and would reflect its sex appeal. But it would draw from the XP-898's technology to trim weight to an absolute minimum, yet maintain formidable crashworthiness.

The car forming in DeLorean's mind would hit somewhere between the Corvette and Porsche 924 market. That was no accident. He wasn't on any campaign to embarrass General Motors. He knew better. But he also knew that the Corvette was immensely profitable for GM, that it was virtually without competition, and that supply never met demand. He wanted eventually to build different cars for different needs, but the two-place sports car was clearly the place to begin.

DeLorean started his project himself, moonlighting from his home north of Detroit during the year he served with the National Alliance of Businessmen. He lined up production rights to some of the plastic fabrication processes that interested him and made some preliminary inquiries into available powerplants. He caught Cole's rotary bug while at Chevrolet, and instinctively looked to the rotary as the logical engine for his car. He lined up a commitment from Comotor, a Citroën affiliate, to supply

Above: *The PRV (Peugeot, Renault, Volvo) engine used to power DeLorean's vehicle. Looks like it's built by Swiss watchmakers.*

30,000 rotaries a year. The plan was later changed to a Toyo Kogyo rotary instead, but both ideas fell through in the aftermath of the oil embargo.

In October, 1974, DeLorean's company was officially founded, and joined by William Collins, a chassis engineer from General Motors. DeLorean knew Collins well, since both had been at Pontiac. Collins had been Pontiac's Director of Advanced Engineering, Director of Production Engineering, and Project Manager for the GM '77 "B" and "C" body programs just before leaving in 1974. DeLorean had learned how to delegate authority well, and he gave Collins full responsibility to design and build the first prototype DeLorean vehicle.

World's premier stylist

Collins put together a "package" design, sketching out the dimensions of the new car. It would be wide and low, yet would have enough headroom for a six-foot-four occupant. That was exactly DeLorean's height, and Collins was just an inch shorter.

In December, 1974, Collins and DeLorean went to Italy's Turin auto show, and there interviewed four top Italian stylists for the job of designing the shape of the new DeLorean car. The four were Michelotti, Bertone, Pininfarina, and Giugiaro of Ital Design. By March, they'd decided on Giugiaro, probably the world's current premier stylist.

Collins has a passion for simplicity, a passion shared by DeLorean. When some of Giugiaro's early sketches showed the ever-present sloping front with pop-up headlights, both Collins and DeLorean said no. Flopping doors were just one more thing to malfunction and served no real purpose. This meant that Giugiaro had to lift the front of the design to accommodate headlight height laws, which turned out to be a very positive action. One of the few criticisms that Giugiaro has to endure is that all of his designs look alike. By forcing the headlight issue, Giugiaro was made to style a really unique car for DeLorean. It is unmistakably Giugiaro, yet it is unlike any other Ital Design effort.

Giugiaro styled blind rear quarters in early proposals which both Collins and DeLorean found unacceptable from the standpoint of safety. Collins was tuned into louvered slats from his recent GM

Left: *The production DMC-12 is quite different from these photos of prototype number one. The knee pad has been removed, and the stereo and heater/air conditioning controls on the console have been restyled.* **Right:** *DeLorean rejected louvers for the rear sails, preferring glass instead. Below is the original Citroën engine placed mid-ship with the rear-mounted radiator.*

days, but neither DeLorean nor Giugiaro liked them, so glass went in instead.

Six months after getting the assignment, Giugiaro completed the design of what was now called the DMC-12. Both Collins and DeLorean were delighted, as they should have been. Giugiaro did a magnificent job.

The next step was construction of a running prototype. This was handled by Mike Pocobello of Triad Industries in Detroit. No stranger to building exotic prototypes, Pocobello was formerly with Chevrolet R&D, and also served as chief engineer for a time on Jim Hall's Chaparral program. In addition to building the DMC-12 prototype, Pocobello also did the basic suspension work which, for the first car, included parallel wishbones and rack and pinion steering.

Meanwhile, Collins was busy on the construction techniques to be employed for the DMC-12's chassis. Here the XP-898 was to figure strongly.

The big difference between conventional plastic bodied cars and the XP-898 was that the XP-898 used plastic for structural components under stress. In cars like the Corvette, a plastic body is essentially draped over a load-bearing steel structure. Collins and DeLorean wanted to go the route of the XP-898. (Though this approach has since been modified, as will be pointed out.) To do so, a relatively new plastic forming process called **E**lastic **R**eservoir **M**olding will be used for some components.

ERM is sort of a cousin to the XP-898's sandwich idea, but there are differences. The XP-898's body panels were actually made up of outer and inner "skins" bonded together along mating edges. In a separate and later step, foam urethane was forced between the skins. The foam hardened and the panel assembly was complete.

The ERM process is a sandwich type too, but with a twist. Two layers of reinforcement material (the bread) are placed around a layer of flexible, but porous, foam core (the meat). The sandwich is placed into a mold which, under relatively low pressure and heat, forms the desired panel shape. While the shape is being formed, the sandwich is being compressed to about a tenth of its original thickness. The resin material impregnates the foam, resulting in a cellular-structured material of great strength, durability, and low weight.

But ERM is not without its problems. It is a brand new technology, and there are bugs to work out. The first DeLorean cars will have some ERM panels, but its use won't be exclusive. Other panels will probably be made with a process called Vacuum Resin Injection Molding, which is what Lotus uses, and maybe some by Sheet Molding Compound, the current science employed to make Corvette parts.

When the ERM process was first developed, there were some difficulties with paint appearance, and with impregnated color. But the process has been refined by DeLorean to the point that ERM is now extremely versatile. Color, even textures, can be impregnated into ERM panels, and paint appearance problems have been solved.

But DeLorean doesn't really care for paint anyway. It fouls the working environment and is next to impossible to apply with the level of consistent quality DeLorean envisions for his car. DeLorean grew up working in assembly plants, with paint dust settling in his hair. Enough of that. He had a better idea.

Stainless steel. Yep, the external surfaces of the DMC-12 consist of stainless steel trim panels. Each bolts on individually for ease of installation and repair.

This isn't as nuts as it sounds. Stainless steel has been used for auto bodies before. Allegheny Ludlum built a Ford body of the material way back in 1936 to demonstrate its feasibility. The auto companies didn't buy the idea, but that '36 stainless steel Ford still looks great today. True, stainless is difficult to weld, but that won't affect DeLorean's use of it for trim panels. Forget about welding these. If a panel gets scratched, spruce it up with sandpaper (no joke!) If it's more severely damaged, just unbolt it and put a new one on.

The more obvious solution to the trim panel problem would have been to opt for painted steel panels. If the "I don't want one because they all look alike" thinking becomes a sales deterrent, painted steel (or plastic, for that matter) could be substituted at any time without redesigning the car at all. But DeLorean plans to stick to stainless, despite its cost factor of nearly eight times regular steel.

Can they really afford stainless? Yes. By DeLorean's calculations, each car has about 100 pounds of stainless in the exterior skins. At going prices, regular steel is about ten cents a pound, and stainless is about eighty. This means the DMC-12 pays a $70 per car penalty to use stainless. But it doesn't have to be painted, and that offsets the extra cost. And, there's that beautiful selling point of a structure that doesn't rust.

Does it look good? Yes. It is different, it is unusual, but it is definitely beautiful. It doesn't shine, even in the strongest light. It shimmers. At dusk, it practically glows with a pink hue. It's . . . beautiful.

Power for the DMC will be an aluminum V-6, developed and shared by Peugeot, Renault, and Volvo. DeLorean will actually use the Renault version. Since it is completely certified for use in the United States, DeLorean may be able to avoid the 50,000 mile emissions test.

text continues on page 184

Stainless steel?

181

DeLorean Speaks

CSA You are credited with being instrumental in the development and marketing of the Pontiac GTO. The GTO is in turn credited with being the spark behind the muscle car boom. Much has changed in fifteen years, especially in the auto industry. What thoughts pass through your mind now when you see one of those first GTO's on the road?

DeLorean I still love and am very proud of the GTO; it was the first car to bring exciting performance to the average person . . . to the young people of America. Previously, only the well-to-do could afford exciting cars.

CSA Before you moved from Pontiac to Chevrolet, what were your thoughts about the Corvette? Did you ever consider introducing a Corvette-type model from within the Pontiac Division?

DeLorean We did develop a Pontiac two-seater, the prototype of which Bill Collins still has. GM management felt that Pontiac was going so well and Chevrolet was losing business so badly at the time, that the Chevrolet dealers would protest a sports car from Pontiac, the car line that was taking Chevy's business.

CSA While at Chevrolet, you've been quoted as saying something like, "The Corvette needs to go on a diet . . ." But it has also been reported that you ordered the mid-engine program stopped, and that you pushed for a high volume, steel-bodied Corvette replacement. What really happened behind the scenes relative to the Corvette during your Chevrolet tenure? Where did you personally want to aim the Corvette?

DeLorean Not true. I pushed hard for the mid-engine Corvette and, of course, built the double and four-rotor rotary Corvettes. The four-rotor was a very wild car.

CSA Is it true that you tried to purchase the mid-engine prototype Corvette production rights after leaving GM so that you could market a version of that car?

DeLorean Yes, I asked GM to sell me the rights, drawings, and prototype of the V-8 powered, mid-engine Corvette designed by Zora Duntov.

CSA Marketing people seem to agree that the Corvette buyer falls into a group distinct from "sports cars" such as Porsche, Datsun Z, or others. Do you think your car will develop its own individual following of loyalists, or will it draw from and share the affections of already dedicated groups?

DeLorean We are after a very different market than either Corvette or Porsche. This will become obvious as our advertising starts to hit.

CSA Yes, but the introduction of any two-place auto to the American market will invariably invite comparisons to the Corvette. Yet during the production of the Bricklin, executives of that company

"I pushed hard for the mid-engine Corvette . . ."

"We are like a little mouse in the ring with an elephant . . our job is to keep from getting stepped on."

"The Corvette is more important to America than it is to GM."

downplayed similarities between their product and the Corvette, maintaining that the cars were completely different and shouldn't be compared at all. Most enthusiasts concluded that comparisons were discouraged simply because the Bricklin didn't stack up well. Will you actively encourage or discourage a Corvette rivalry?

DeLorean I don't think it possible to avoid comparisons with both Corvette and Porsche. Obviously, we believe in our product, our concept, and our professional ability to bring it to market profitably. Corvette is a great car with a well deserved, well earned heritage going back over 25 years. You cannot expect to compete with such an image until you have earned your own stripes.

CSA Despite tremendous loyalty to older Corvettes, the percentage of repeat buyers of new Corvettes remains the lowest of any car in the GM line. GM says that's because the Corvette appeals to a very narrow age group, and that the buyer simply moves on to another GM product, probably a Monte Carlo or Grand Prix. Do you agree with that explanation? Do you think your car will have a similar narrow age appeal?

DeLorean All two-seaters have a much narrower appeal than four or five seat cars. That's why Ford left the two-seat Thunderbird for the five . . . even though that two-seater was, and still is, a winner.

CSA Chevrolet representatives have politely downplayed the significance and impact of your car on the Corvette market, citing the twenty-five year lead the Corvette has built up, in addition to the difficulty you'll have actually introducing and sustaining production of your car without the resources of a major corporation to fall back on. Yet, Chevrolet has recently announced tentative plans for a new Corvette assembly plant in Kentucky, coinciding with a probable all-new Corvette body in 1983. What do you think they really think about the possible impact of the DeLorean on a market that has been the Corvette's alone for so many years?

DeLorean There is no company or economic force in the world that can compete with or hurt GM. We are like a little mouse in the ring with a powerful elephant . . . our job is to keep from getting stepped on.

I don't think GM's accounting system is fine-tuned enough to measure any impact we would have on any of their markets. They have moved from 50% of the domestic market to upwards of 70%. And in all probability with their great economic power, they will pass 80% within a few years.

CSA By your perception, how important is the Corvette to Chevrolet and GM?

DeLorean I think the Corvette is more important to America than it is to GM. The Vette's profitability is hardly discernible in the $4,000,000 per working hour that GM makes.

CSA What do you think the single most important factor has been in the success of the Corvette? How will you use that knowledge to make your car succeed?

DeLorean The Corvette is a fine car, fun to drive, exciting to own, and a very good investment. When we go to market, we'd like to be as successful as Corvette.

CSA Is it true that you've written a book about some of the less desirable aspects of the auto industry in Detroit, but that you're reluctant to publish?

DeLorean The book I'm working on does not yet accurately express my viewpoints. When it does, I will print it.

CSA You're on the verge of an incredible achievement, the ultimate dream for someone who loves automobiles. Once you've met your auto production goals, what comes next? Are there bigger dreams yet uncovered within John DeLorean?

DeLorean We want to continue to expand our horizons and product line, always staying with our fundamental concept: We want to build cars for people who love and enjoy cars and driving.

Picking the engine was no easy task. After the rotary's glamour faded, DeLorean and Collins looked first to a Ford V-6. They settled temporarily on a Citroën four, mounted transversely. Basically, they took the engine and transaxle package from the front wheel drive Citroën CX and flipped it around, mounting it mid-ship in the DMC. This setup left plenty of room behind the engine to mount the radiator and its electric fans. And this setup is exactly what is used in the first prototype, which appears in CSA's photographs. But this was all to change.

DeLorean and Citroën were dissatisfied simultaneously, so Collins looked elsewhere. The final choice was the Peugeot-Renault-Volvo aluminum V-6, which was actually an early favorite. This is a very sweet engine, weighing 32 pounds less than the Citroën, but more powerful. It looks like it's made by Swiss watchmakers. As the saying goes, you gets what you pay for. The engine is very expensive.

But changing to the V-6 meant that Collins had to change the DMC engine configuration from a mid-engine, transverse four, to a rear-engine, conventional direction V-6. Visions of the Corvair? Not quite. First off, according to Collins, moving the engine to the rear only altered the car's weight distribution by two percent. That was because of the engine's lighter weight, and the necessary move of the radiator to the front.

When viewing the photos of the DMC-12 appearing on these pages, remember that these are of **prototype number one**. While it is very close in visual appearance to the final production form, nearly every part of it has or will undergo some change. Think of these photos as historical book markers in the development of the DeLorean automobile, but certainly not as accurate portrayals of the finished production vehicle. Think of the prototype DMC in the same way that you would think of the first Motorama Corvette. Changes had to be made before production could begin. And changes will be made during production for quite some time, just as in the Corvette's case.

Bill Collins has left the DeLorean project now. He's with American Motors in the position of Director of Product Planning. The final development of the

DMC 12

DMC's suspension and chassis was completed by none other than Colin Chapman of Lotus fame. Though DeLorean's projected annual volume of 30,000 units will exceed any single model Lotus has ever produced, Chapman is undoubtedly the best qualified engineer anywhere when it comes to building very special cars in less than Detroit volumes.

Chapman's input has already been felt. The all-plastic chassis concept has been modified, partially based on Chapman's not altogether great experience with a similar concept in his 1961 Lotus Elite. Chapman has tied the front and rear suspensions of the DMC together with steel, but the use of plastic in the car will remain extensive. Chapman also fine-tuned (completely reworked would be more accurate) the suspension to the highest degree. So well has the DeLorean-Chapman effort worked out, that the firms are planning to establish a joint engineering center in England. If all goes as planned, the joint firm will sell its engineering expertise to other companies. They plan to be to auto engineering what Ital Design is to auto styling.

Speaking of Ital Design, the exterior of the DMC also went through an update at the hands of Giugiaro. This was nothing too extensive, but again necessary before putting the car into production. The interior has changed, too. The knee pad, which drew both raves and criticisms from auto people, is gone. In fact, the whole interior is different, though similar.

The gullwing doors remain, and they're beautifully done. Ever mindful of the problems Bricklin had with his heavy electrically operated units, the DMC's doors are perfectly counterbalanced and operate manually with ease. They actually open higher in the production version than shown in the prototype's photos, because of an error in design clearance in the first car. On the production DMC, the top surface of the doors will open almost perpendicular to the roof.

The DMC has unique side window treatment. Consistent with his "keep it simple" approach, Collins chose to fix the forward section of glass, and have the rear section slide manually. A roll-down window is out since there just isn't room. Not only that, but roll-down mechanisms add weight and the key to this door's ease of operation is its lightness. Plus, rolling the window down changes the door's center of gravity, and that fouls the delicate counterbalancing. The sliding window will stay, but there is thought being given to adding power to "roll" the window forward. Also, the moving window pane will get a little wider, and will pop out flush with the fixed window in the closed position. This is not the case with the first prototype DMC.

Other little, but important, changes were made to the production design also. Moving the engine to the rearward location forced the radiator to be moved to the front. This eats into the front storage area which is quite generous in the prototype. But it also permits a storage area to be created behind the seats, accessible from the inside of the car. DeLorean's people feel this is a good trade-off. As it was before, there was nowhere to stow anything inside the car, assuming the passenger seat was occupied. That would have meant constantly popping the front lid. Neither will that lid have to be lifted to get to the fuel filler, as is the case in the prototype. Now the filler spout is accessible through its own little lid on the left front fender.

The DeLorean looks like a front-engine, rear-drive layout from the inside, because it has what appears to be a transmission tunnel between the seats. Actually, that's to house a central support member, something like Chevy's experimental XP-819 Corvette. Also like the XP-819, the DMC puts a fuel cell in there. For impact protection, there's no better place.

Corvette lessons

It cannot be emphasized enough that the DeLorean motor car has undergone tremendous change from its initial concept to the production version. The comparison to the Corvette as it started is a valid one. The Corvette used a proven powerplant in a radical new body. So does the DeLorean. The Corvette started as a one-off prototype which drew raves from the public and pleas to GM to put it into production. The story is much the same for the DMC, except that the pleas have been more like hopes that DeLorean could really pull it off. And the Corvette underwent changes practically from car to car as Chevrolet learned to build it. DeLorean must pay the same dues.

Above: *Artist conception of the DeLorean auto plant in Northern Ireland, near Belfast. Construction began on October 2, 1978.*

DeLorean: The Company

If you ask John DeLorean what the most difficult part of his whole project has been, chances are he'll say the economics. The amount of money required to put a car into production today is staggering. By most people's figuring, it hasn't been done successfully in this country since 1925, when Walter P. Chrysler said goodbye to GM and built his own company. DeLorean delights in comparing himself to Chrysler, who was also an engineer with a solid automotive background. Malcolm Bricklin, by contrast, delighted in telling everyone how little he knew about cars. He didn't really need to. It showed.

John DeLorean is reasonably wealthy by most standards. But his own money which he sunk into the project to get it rolling wasn't nearly enough. Around 1975, the total bill was thought to be around 90 million. By 1980, it had grown to 150 million, maybe more.

Talk about risks. As DeLorean points out, there is no way to effectively measure the market for a new car. You build it and try to sell it, then you find out. Sure, you can run market tests and determine that some percentage of people say they'd like to have one. Five years later when you offer it to them,

DMC

things may have changed. If your car bombs, a lot of people are out a lot of money.

So it's no surprise that people don't stand in line to invest in new auto companies. DeLorean found that out the hard way. Much of the delay in bringing the DMC to the marketplace has been due to financial elements. But thanks to sources of capital as diverse as Johnny Carson and the government of Northern Ireland, it's happening.

Carson put in a half-million, but DeLorean hit an Irish Sweepstakes of sorts when Ireland got involved. DeLorean's initial thinking was to build his cars in the United States, but quickly found that wasn't going to work. He discovered that areas outside the continental United States would fork over big money to lure him and the jobs he would create. Now why states in the US wouldn't compete for DeLorean's business the way they did for Volkswagen (Pennsylvania won) and Honda (Ohio) is a bit perplexing. Must have something to do with that "established business" business.

Anyway, once it was evident that DeLorean was serious about all this, a lot of places were interested. For a long while, Puerto Rico looked like a sure bet. The problem was that "long while." It took months to get anything done. At the last minute, Ireland jumped into the bidding with its deal for a plant in Northern Ireland near Belfast. The Irish were serious, too, and within 45 days the deal was sealed. The Irish government agreed to kick in well over 100 million in return for a royalty payback on each car built, and seats on the DeLorean company's board of directors.

This was one very expensive proposition for the Irish. Their critics were quick to point out that the government would be spending over $50,000 for each of the eventual 2000 jobs DeLorean would create. But nobody needs to be told that Northern Ireland is a country of social unrest. The government feels the solution is in putting people to work, as unemployment in the hot spots is typically high.

But what of building cars in such hot spots? It doesn't bother DeLorean. In fact, it pleases him that his company may help heal a divided people. And for what it's worth, Irish industry has been quite free of the terrorism common to Irish life. Whatever political differences exist, rival groups all seem to want to improve the economic lot of their members.

DeLorean has attracted real talent to help in his venture. In addition to Collins, and now Colin Chapman doing the engineering, in 1975 he enlisted C. R. Brown, famous for establishing Mazda in the United States, to handle marketing. Eugene Cafiero, Chrysler's vice-chairman until the arrival of Lee Iacocca, has recently joined DeLorean. Some of the most talented automotive people around have come aboard. DeLorean clearly has the guns to get the job done.

He's also getting the dealers to sell his cars. Despite DeLorean's stringent requirements of a $25,000 cash stock purchase, substantial purchase agreements, and a revolving letter of credit, DeLorean has had good success in signing up 400 domestic dealers that he plans to have.

It's interesting to note how car dealers view the DMC and its potential market impact. DeLorean wanted to know, so the J. D. Power Company was contracted to survey dealers attending the 1978 National Automobile Dealers Association convention held in San Francisco.

Some of the dealers questioned had already signed up to sell DeLoreans, some had not. Three-fourths of those who had, felt that the DMC filled an unanswered void in the US marketplace. Of those dealers not handling the DeLorean car, two-thirds felt similarly. Those of both groups who felt that the DMC did compete with a US car felt that the car was the Corvette. Porsche was second.

As to what car DMC's prospective buyers were already buying, 76% of the DeLorean dealers felt it was Corvette. Next was Mercedes, then Porsche, then Datsun Z.

Isn't it interesting how the Corvette keeps figuring into all this? The DMC is the product of a company wholly independent of General Motors. Yet think of John DeLorean's past. His attempt to build a Corvette-like car while at Pontiac. His aspirations for the Corvette while at Chevrolet. His attempt to buy the Duntov-designed mid-engine Corvette after leaving GM. See how it all fits?

Past, Present & Future

GM
MARK OF EXCELLENCE
ENGINE COOLING SYSTEM
ORIGINAL FACTORY FILL COOLANT PROVIDES FREEZING PROTECTION TO -20°F.
PROTECTION MUST BE MAINTAINED AT LEAST TO 0°F. FOR PROPER TEMPERATURE LIGHT OPERATION.
SEE OWNER'S MANUAL FOR RECOMMENDED COOLING SYSTEM DRAIN PROCEDURE.
CAUTION: If you siphon coolant from the radiator, do not use mouth to start siphoning action. The coolant solution is POISONOUS and can cause death or serious illness if swallowed.
PRINTED IN U.S.A. 8-16-72 PT. NO. 337450
THIS ENGINE IS EQUIPPED TO REDUCE EXHAUST EMISSIONS
THE FOLLOWING ADJUSTMENTS ARE NECESSARY TO MAINTAIN THE EFFECTIVENESS OF THE SYSTEM
(With engine at operating temperature, choke open, air cleaner installed, air conditioning on.)
1. Set mixture screw(s) for max. idle rpm and adjust speed screw to obtain 700 RPM IN NEUTRAL.
2. Set ignition timing at 4° BTC (Plug vacuum advance line — this step only.)
3. Adjust mixture screw in to obtain a 20 rpm drop (lean roll.)
4. Adjust mixture screw out 1/4 turn.
5. Repeat steps 3 and 4 for second mixture screw (if so equipped.)
6. Readjust speed screw if necessary to specified idle rpm.
See Service Manual for Additional Tune-Up Instruction.
T
PRINTED IN U.S.A.
PART NO. 3932350
Delco Remy
IGNITION COIL FOR TRANSISTOR IGNITION
HARRISON
ALUMINUM RADIATOR
IMPORTANT - PROPER MAINTENANCE REQUIRES THAT THIS COOLING SYSTEM BE PROTECTED AGAINST CORROSION AS DESCRIBED IN THE OWNER'S GUIDE. TO AVOID RADIATOR DAMAGE, USE ONLY THOSE ANTI-FREEZE ADDITIVES AND CLEANERS SPECIFICALLY RECOMMENDED FOR ALUMINUM RADIATORS BY THEIR MARKETERS OR WHICH MEET THE REQUIREMENTS OF G.M. SPECIFICATIONS. SUITABLE PRODUCTS ARE AVAILABLE FROM YOUR GENERAL MOTORS DEALER. DO NOT USE INHIBITORS LABELED AS "ACID NEUTRALIZERS".
WARNING
ENGINE COOLANT ONLY
334117
TIRE PRESSURE
AP
TIRE SIZE: F70 X 15-4 PLY RATING
STANDARD: UP TO VEHICLE LOAD LIMIT
TIRE COOL HOT
FRONT 24 30
REAR 24 30
VEHICLE LOAD LIMIT—450 LBS.
VEHICLE CAPACITY—2 SEATS
(2 PASSENGERS) + 150 LBS. LUGGAGE
See Owner's Manual for Additional Information
PART NO. 3934888
PRINTED IN U.S.A.
WARNING: VEHICLE MUST OPERATE ON A FUEL HAVING A MINIMUM OF 103 RESEARCH OCTANE AND 95 MOTOR OCTANE OR ENGINE DAMAGE MAY RESULT
USE LIMITED SLIP DIFF. LUBRICANT ONLY
TURBO-JET 454
425 HORSEPOWER
AC CRANKCASE BREATHER AC
WASH IN KEROSENE AND RE-OIL EVERY 3000 MILES — OFTENER UNDER SEVERE CONDITIONS
AC SPARK PLUG — FLINT, MICH.
DO NOT CONNECT RADIO BY-PASS CONDENSER TO THIS FIELD TERMINAL
GM AC
Keep your GM car all GM
For maximum performance and economy, specify General Motors parts identified by one of these trademarks.
CR 6485887
AC
GF-90
FLOW
CAUTION
THIS COOLANT SYSTEM PROTECTED TO -20° FAHRENHEIT BY GM PERMANENT TYPE ANTIFREEZE
TURBO-JET 427
3 x 2
435 HORSEPOWER
Delco Remy
PRIMARY AMPLIFIER FOR MAGNETIC IMPULSE TRANSISTOR IGNITION
GENERAL MOTORS CORP.
HARRISON
LOCKPORT N.Y.
ALUMINUM RADIATOR
USE ONLY ANTI-FREEZES AND OTHER ADDITIVES SPECIFICALLY RECOMMENDED BY THEIR MANUFACTURER FOR USE WITH ALUMINUM SEE OWNERS MANUAL FOR SERVICE INFORMATION.
PART NO.
340
HORSEPOWER
PRINTED IN U.S.A.

Everything about

Corvette Labels

Corvettes can make no exclusive claim to the use of labels as owner-informative devices. Just where the practice of using labels (a term used loosely here to include also decals, tags, stickers, cards and other message-conveying materials) originated is anyone's guess. But thanks to its prodigious range of engine options, its variety of equipment, and its frequent use as a launch pad for new innovations, the Corvette seems to have attracted far more than its fair share.

A close look at the maze of things stuck onto Corvettes, from the radiator in front, to the gas filler in the rear, is interesting for two reasons. First, much can be learned about Corvettes by studying the information presented through the labels. The way the labels are worded, their purposes, and their appearance tell much about the Corvette's evolution from the six cylinder Blue Flame of the early years, to the beautiful highway cruisers of today. For this reason, reviewing the labels of all Corvettes can be fascinating to all owners, regardless of their own personal preferences.

More importantly correct Corvette restoration requires an accurate understanding and proper use of labels. With just a few exceptions, labels used on Corvettes have not stood the test of time well. Many are paper and are subject to the effects of weather, engine heat, or just time. The more durable foil and plastic labels deteriorate eventually, no matter how carefully preserved. Worse, even those labels that have held up well are often destroyed or severely damaged during the restoration process. For instance, the metal or foil labels used for Harrison radiators are durable, but won't stand up to a radiator boil-out and refurbishing. Knowing what labels are required, knowing where to get them and how to use them, are indispensable for a good Corvette restoration.

Back in 1972, before Corvette restoration became the "in" thing, a gentleman named Murrell F. (Dob) Dobbins faced the problem of locating various labels to put the finishing touches to his 1967 model Corvette. A longtime Corvette buff, Dobbins knew what labels he needed, but not where to get them. The longer the search went on, the more difficult it became. In time, it became apparent that selling labels was something General Motors wasn't very interested in. Oh, a few could be purchased at Chevy parts counters, but for the most part, GM viewed labels as items to be put on during assembly, not sold later as replacement parts. Generally speaking, they just aren't necessary for the upkeep of an automobile, Corvettes included. And the more Dobbins looked, the more he realized that nobody else had much interest in providing Corvette labels either.

So Dobbins went about becoming his own source. He bought what was available through regular channels, and sought out the rest where he could. What wasn't available, he contracted to have reproduced. The rest of the story is as you might expect. Soon friends and even strangers approached him to get labels for their cars, too. It didn't take much analysis on Dob's part to figure out that this was a little corner of the Corvette market that no one else had staked out, so he might as well be the one.

In time, M. F. Dobbins became the master source of labels for the Corvette enthusiast. He now has available probably 95% of all the labels used for Corvettes from 1953 to the current year. He purchases what he can from General Motors for inventory. If it's simply not available anywhere, he'll contract to have it reproduced himself.

Along the way, Dobbins has by sheer osmosis, absorbed an awfully lot of knowledge about Corvette labels. In short, he's become a leading authority on the subject. There may be people who know a bit more about a particular year, but few can match Dob's knowledge of the entire range. So when it came to selecting someone to supply labels and expertise for an article of this type, Dob was CSA's obvious choice.

Articles about Corvette labels have been done before. Dobbin's own book, **The Vette Vues Fact Book of the 1963-1967 Sting Ray,** has excellent coverage of the first five years of Sting Ray label usage. CSA's goal here is to present a really comprehensive look at the entire Corvette label spectrum. There are a couple of ways to organize such a presentation. The first would be chronological by model year. "The 1962 Corvette had a such and such label located on the rocker cover . . ." That technique has the advantage of being convenient for someone checking for a particular model, but the disadvantage of being somewhat difficult to follow when similar labels are used for several model years.

Another organization method would be to segregate labels by their purpose. There are labels which inform, such as the starting procedure label on the sunvisors of 1974 and 1975 Corvettes. There are labels which warn of danger, such as those affixed to air conditioning components cautioning of high refrigerant fluid pressures. There are labels which advertise or boast, like the "GM Mark of Excellence" aluminum stickers put on doors of '67 models, and the "Tonawanda No. 1 Team" valve cover labels. And there are those which simply adorn, like the "LT-1" hood labels.

A third way to segregate labels is by their location. Thus, categories would be divided into such group locations as air cleaner, valve cover, or radiator. The technique chosen to present this section actually combines all three choices. Overall divisions are roughly by location, but a chronological listing of years is presented within each location discussion. The purpose of each label is usually evident, but additional information relating to a label's intent is presented where appropriate. A "catch-all" category finishes off the article and includes all those labels which don't conveniently fit elsewhere.

Unfortunately, the nature of the inks, foil stocks, size, and fabrication techniques, prevent a genuinely accurate reproduction on this text's paper of all labels in their original form. Throughout the pictorial presentation, notes are included to indicate the coloration and material stock of each label, and the percentage of reduction of this text's representation relative to the original.

M. F. Dobbins

Valve Covers

Valve covers have historically been Chevrolet's favorite location for advertising an engine's nickname, displacement, or horsepower. Such was the case with most Corvettes through the 1967. It started with the very first Corvettes made in Flint, the 1953 models.

The '53 Corvette's six cylinder valve cover was painted blue. This cover was a uniquely modified version of the passenger car's cover, and was attached by two central studs. To the valve covers were affixed water-activated decals (a decal or "decalcomania" is a water-activated label). On the right side (passenger side) appeared the words "Blue Flame" preceded by a small arrow pointed at the "B". The word "Special" was affixed to the left side (driver's side) of the valve cover, followed by a slightly skewed lightning bolt. The lightning bolt and all lettering were white, but the "Blue Flame" portion had red "speed" lines scattered through and between the lettering.

In 1954, the Corvette's valve cover changed (along with the Chevy passenger car) to a more smoothly shaped unit held down by four stovebolts around the periphery. The labels were again water activated decals, but changed in style. The "Blue Flame" and preceding small arrow were reduced in size from 1953, but were still put on the right hand side of the valve cover. This was followed by a "150" outlined by an arrow. Everything was again white, with red speed lines through the "Blue Flame" lettering. No decals were used on the left side of valve covers during 1954 Corvette production. Most valve covers of 1954 were painted blue, as in 1953, but some also appeared chromed. A running camshaft design change during 1954 lifted the horsepower of the Blue Flame Six from 150 to 155, but this was not reflected in a decal change as the "150" continued to be used throughout the year. Also, some enthusiasts have assumed that the chrome valve covers which appeared during 1954 (and had no decals) were used for the higher horsepower engines. That may have been the intent, but it wasn't the result. The use of chrome valve covers in 1954 was random and did not coincide with engine horsepower, or anything else that has been determined.

The few 1955 model Corvettes built with six cylinder engines had the same valve cover decal treatment as the '54 models. No valve cover decals were used at all on the '55 V-8 models, which had chrome plated, stamped steel covers.

Decals weren't used on the painted steel valve covers of the base engines of 1956 or 1957 Corvettes, but it is generally believed that all optional engines had simple numerical decals indicating horsepower. Since the optional engines all had cast aluminum valve covers, Chevrolet selected "Chevy orange" as the decal color. The only engine option in 1956 was the dual-four carb package rated at 245 horsepower. This engine continued through 1961 with the same rating and same decals.

The 1957 Corvette had additional engines available at 250 horsepower (fuel injected), 270 horsepower (2x4 with special cam), and 283 horsepower (fuel injected with special cam). All received appropriate horsepower labels. The 270 horsepower engine carried through to 1961, but the fuel injected versions got power boosts. The 283 of 1957 became 290 horsepower in 1958 and 1959, then 315 for 1960 and 1961. The 250 horse fuel engine of 1957 continued at the same power rating through the 1959 model, then jumped to 275 horsepower in 1960 and 1961.

Decals for the base engine Corvettes of this period started appearing in 1958. Because the red decals used on the aluminum valve covers became visually lost on the orange-painted covers of the base engines, Chevy switched to gold, but only for the base engines. From 1958 through

Above: *1953 valve cover decals.* **Below:** *1954 valve cover decals. The lettering is white with red "speed" streaks. Shown 70% of actual size.*

1961, base Corvette engine horsepower remained at 230. Note that on Corvette V-8 engines built through the 1961 model year using valve cover decals, only one decal was used. It was always placed on the right hand valve cover.

1963 was the year of the big body and chassis change for the Corvette, but the step-up in engine displacement from 283 to 327 cubic inches occurred one model year earlier, in 1962. With the new engines came new valve cover decals.

To get away from two differently colored decals, Chevrolet came up with one that looked good on either cast aluminum or orange-painted surfaces. The new color scheme was metallic gold and black. Chevrolet also re-designed the painted steel valve covers for the lower horsepower engines. The new design eliminated the "Chevrolet" script previously used. In its place was a centrally located, rectangular recess into which was glued a label proclaiming, "Chevrolet 327 Turbo-Fire." This label was made of metal for the 1962 and early 1963 cars. Late in 1963, it was made of vinyl and remained vinyl through 1966. A small (3″x1″) water-activated decal was placed about a half inch below the recess on the smooth valve cover surface. Where previous horsepower decals simply contained three numbers, the new style had the numbers and the word "horsepower" spelled out. Both the recess label and the horsepower decal were done in the metallic gold and black motif. Painted valve covers were used on the base 250 horsepower engine from 1962 through 1965, on the 300 horse engine available from 1962 through 1965 as an option, and on the same 300 engine which became the base powerplant in 1966.

The high horsepower, 327 cubic-inch displacement engines of the period had cast aluminum valve covers without the rectangular recesses, so they didn't get the "Chevrolet 327 Turbo-Fire" label, but similar gold and black horsepower decals were placed a half-inch below the last fin. Both the 340 and 365 horsepower motors of 1962 and 1963 have this treatment on their cast aluminum valve covers. The same is true of 1964 and 1965, though the horsepower ratings of these engines grew to 365 and 375 respectively. In 1965 and 1966, a 350 horsepower, 327 cubic-inch engine also joined the lineup and got similar valve cover decal treatment.

In 1967, strange things happened. On the base engine, 300 horsepower Corvettes, the same valve covers used prior to 1962 with the "Chevrolet" script were reintroduced. A red, white and blue paper label stating, "Flint No. 1 Team", was stuck onto the right side valve cover. The rear of the left side valve cover had a small yellow tag with a black number, probably an inspection indentifier. Engine size and horsepower labels for the small blocks moved to the air cleaners in 1967, so all such information was gone from valve covers.

Big block Corvettes came along in 1965, but not much use of their valve covers was made for decals. In the 1965, 396 cubic inch engine mill, no decals appeared on the valve covers at all. The same was true for the '66 model's 427 engines. The 1967 big blocks received a small, shiny "Built

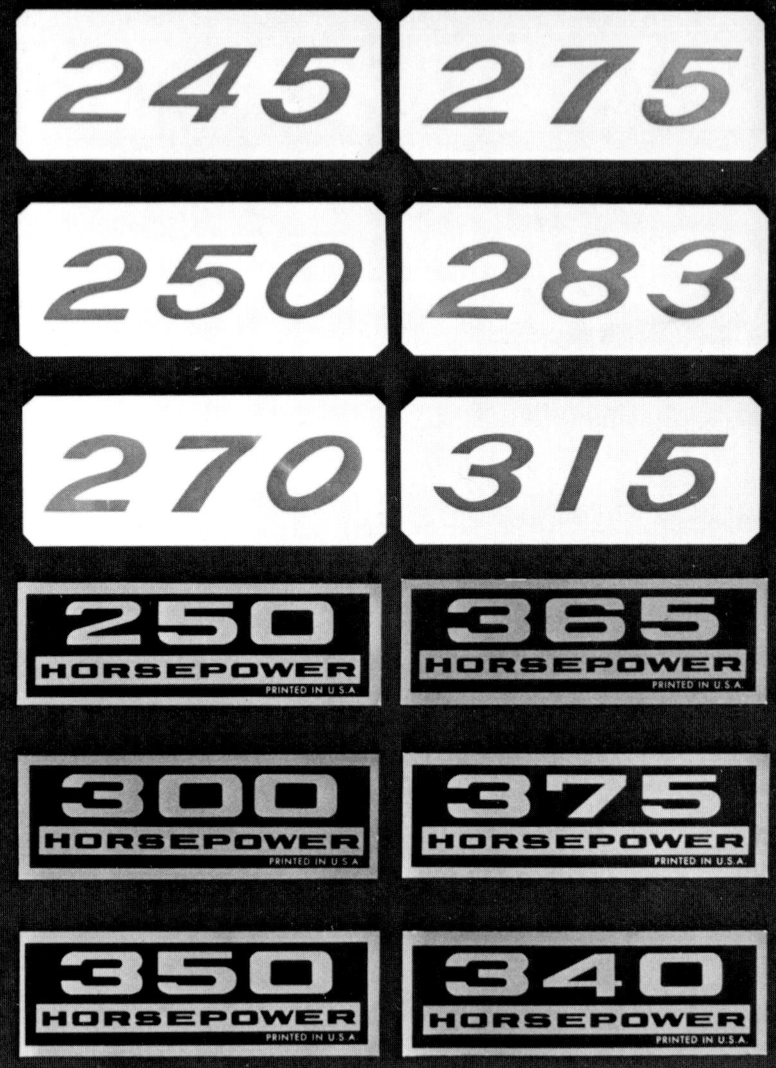

Valve cover decals used for Corvette V-8 engines (except 1955) through 1966. The top six are Chevy orange on clear. Others are black on metallic gold. Shown 58% of actual size.

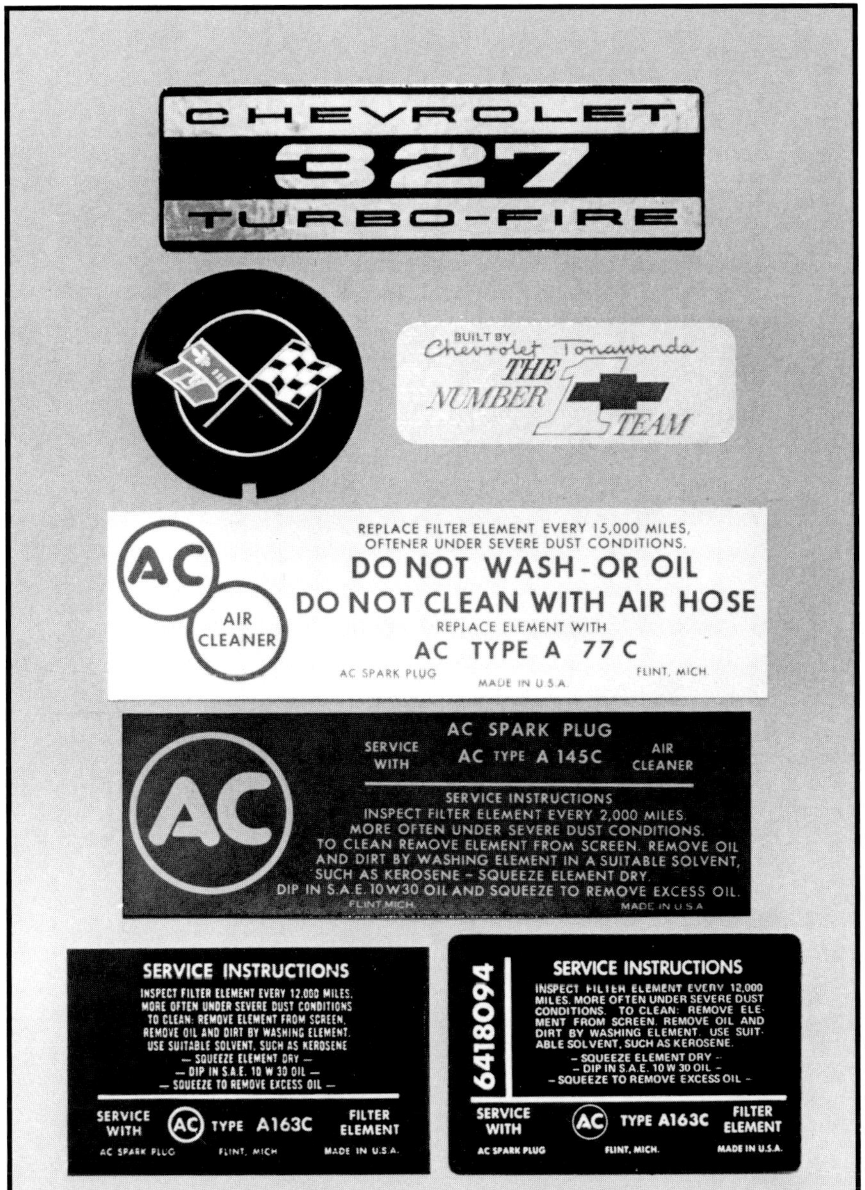

Above: *Valve cover labels. Top is gold on black. Flag emblem is orange and silver on black. Tonawanda label is blue and red on silver.* **Below:** *Air cleaner instruction labels. Top horizontal is orange lettering on clear. Bottom horizontal is yellow on clear. Bottom labels are white on black. Shown 55% of actual size.*

by Chevrolet Tonawanda THE NUMBER 1 TEAM'' sticker on the right hand valve cover only. This continued through 1970 for all big blocks.

With the exception of a crossed-flag insignia, which barely qualifies as a label, the use of labels on valve covers petered out on Corvettes around 1970. The reasons are fairly obvious. Corvette engine compartments were becoming cluttered with a maze of paraphernalia required by not only a sharp increase in preference for highly optioned Corvettes, but by an ever-increasing degree of plumbing required to meet federal emission standards. It was getting difficult to see the valve covers, let alone labels attached. So Chevrolet moved engine information labels up where they could be seen, to the top surface of the air cleaners.

Air Cleaners

It doesn't take a great deal of savvy to understand what to do with an air cleaner element. It either gets pitched out and replaced with a new one, or it gets cleaned. Other than the appropriate instructions in owner's manuals, Chevrolet hasn't seen the necessity to go into much detail about air cleaner instructions via the label route. On later models, Chevrolet did use the top of the air cleaner for engine information, since the air cleaner offered a nice, unobstructed viewing surface.

Exceptions to the use of air cleaner decals did occur for fuel injected Corvettes, for two reasons. First, fuel injection was a strange looking critter to someone used to seeing carburetors. Especially with the '63 and later units, it wasn't all that evident to the novice that there even was an air cleaner in that big black tube. More importantly, fuel injection is valuable and somewhat sensitive equipment. Chevy felt the need to inform owners clearly that the units needed a clean, unobstructed air source.

The '57 Corvette with fuel injection had an air cleaner element, which was disposable, attached close to the injection unit. The filtering unit was exposed, and replacement time made itself pretty well known. No decal was used. But the 1958 through 1962 Corvettes had fender-mounted air cleaners for fuel units, and it was with these units that Chevy saw the necessity of using decals on the cleaner to specify proper care. For the 1958 through 1961 models, this took the form of an orange decal placed right on top of the air cleaner. It specified that the filter element should be replaced every 15,000 miles, "oftener" under severe dust conditions. It cautioned not to attempt to clean by washing, oiling, or air blasting. A type A-77C filter (AC, natch) was the recommended replacement.

The filter element of the fuel injected '62 model Corvettes changed, so the decal did, too. Instead of orange, it was yellow. And the instructions were completely different, since the '62 element was a re-usable type that was to be inspected every 2,000 miles, cleaned in a "suitable solvent" such as kerosene, and oiled with 10W30 motor oil. It was placed on the air cleaner, next to the fender bracket. The decal was close in size to that used the previous four model years.

Air cleaner horsepower and displacement labels for Corvette "small" block V-8 engines, used from 1967 through 1971. All are orange on silver. Shown 55% of actual size.

Air cleaner horsepower and displacement labels. Flag label centers above one horsepower band. Flag labels are orange, white, and black on silver. Curved bands are orange on silver. Shown 70% of actual size.

The air cleaner and element changed again in 1963, and Chevy started using a small black vinyl label with white lettering. Its instructions were similar to that of 1962, since the element was again the re-usable type. The same label was used for 1963 and 1964 fuel injected Corvettes, but was revised slightly in 1965. Considering that '65 was fuel injection's last year, it's strange that Chevy would bother to change the decal, since the instructions and replacement element (AC type A163C) remained the same. The only changes to the '65 decal were rounded corners, more legible type style with instructions spread over six lines instead of five, and the addition of a part number.

1967 marked the start of the use of labels on the top of the carburetor air cleaners of small block Corvettes to designate engine displacement and horsepower. The two 327 cubic inch displacement engines which had horsepower ratings of 300 and 350, had red labels on silver adhesive paper stock. The type was in three curved lines reading "327" on the first line, TURBO-FIRE on the second line, and either 300 or 350 HORSEPOWER on the third. The 1968 small block engines had the same power ratings, and used the very same labels. In 1969, Corvette engine displacement for the small blocks increased to 350 cubic inches. For both 1969 and 1970, similar air cleaner decals were used as for '67 and '68, with the appropriate changes in displacement and horsepower. Both '69 and '70 had small block engines with 300 and 350 horsepower, and 1970 also saw the introduction of the LT-1, rated at 370 horses. The LT-1 of 1970 was the highest rated, non-fuel injected small block ever available in a Corvette, and it lasted only a year in its high-horsepower form.

For the 1971 model year, General Motors detuned its engines to permit using regular and no-lead fuels, allowing fuel companies to start phasing in the unleaded gas needed for catalytic converters, which everyone knew were coming in a few years. The '71 base engine became 270 horsepower, and the LT-1 dropped to 330, thanks to lower compression.

In 1972, horsepower ratings dropped again, this time a result of the technique used to determine power, not because of any major engine change. Still, a rating of 255 horsepower, compared to the rating of 370 for the engine just two years earlier, was something Chevy chose not to brag about. Starting in 1972, displacement and power ratings disappeared from Corvette air cleaners.

The "big block" engines of the 1965 through 1971 period also used air cleaner labels to proclaim displacement and power ratings. These labels were also of the paper-foil adhesive-backed type, but styles varied. The 1965 big engine had a red, white, black, grey, and silver label which incorporated the Corvette crossed-flag emblem and the numerals, "396". Below this label was placed a curved band in red and silver, which stated, "TURBO-JET 425 HP". The 425 horsepower engine of 1966 got the same labels, except that the "396" became "427" to reflect the increase in displacement. Variations of the same labels were also used for the 390 horsepower versions of the 427 engines for 1966, '67, '68, and 1969.

Air cleaner horsepower and displacement labels for "big" blocks with triple carburetors (1967-1969). Both are orange, white, and black on silver. Shown 63% of actual size.

Air cleaner horsepower and displacement labels for "454" engine Corvettes. Black and white on silver. Shown 73% of actual size.

The big blocks of the 1967 through 1969 period which used triple carbs were treated to unique labels. These combined the crossed flag emblem with a lower section that read, "TURBO-JET 427 3x2 435 HORSEPOWER" (or 400 HORSEPOWER). The colors were red, white, black, silver, and grey. These were again the foil paper, adhesive-backed type.

1970 through 1974 Corvettes had as options the largest engines ever, displacement wise. The big block was opened up to 454 cubes. Power ratings in 1970 were 460 and 390 horsepower, and each got label treatment similar to '65-69 Corvette big engines, with obvious numerical corrections. Horsepower ratings dropped in 1971 to 425 and 365 respectfully, and each engine got an all-new larger silver, white, and black air cleaner label which indicated displacement and power.

Starting in 1971, all engines (except the '71 and '72 LT-1) started receiving a small paper label on the air cleaner which advised the owner to "Keep your GM car all GM". These labels were printed in red, white, and varying shades of blue. There are at least six different versions used. All show GM, Delco, and "AC" trademarks and all (except 1971) list the correct air filter replacement number. The labels changed each year as far as part number, but not necessarily other information. The labels used in 1972, for instance, contain the same information as those used in 1973. But the 1972 labels are slightly smaller, have a different part number, and use a brighter shade of blue ink. 1974 through 1976 labels look exactly the same, but the part number for each is different. If the label on your Corvette is intact, get every bit of information from it before ordering a replacement. Then compare the replacement to the original. It seems a minor point, but Corvette people are in a world of their own when it comes to accuracy and originality.

Jacking Instructions

Jacking instructions for Corvettes have always been paper labels, placed in locations conspicuous when retrieving either the jack or the spare tire.

Chevrolet made good use of the jack instructions label developed for the first Corvettes. The label was pasted to the top side of the plywood spare tire cover, and showed sketches of the 1953-1955 Corvette hubcap. Despite the sketch, and the instructions to "set parking brake, move selector lever to park position . . .", which obviously applied to the automatic transmission installed in all 1953 and 1954 Corvettes, the label continued to be used for all Corvettes through the 1960 model.

A completely new label was designed for the 1961 and 1962 models. The problem of instructions for manual transmissions was solved by recommending leaving the gearshift in reverse for jacking rear wheels, and in "first" when jacking the front wheels. The label was much larger, with illustrations of front and rear jacking techniques, tire stowage details, and

Air cleaner "Keep your GM car all GM" labels, used starting in 1971. Starting from top, years shown are '71, '72 (350 & 454), '73, '74, '75, and '76. Blue and red lettering on white. Shown 57% of actual size.

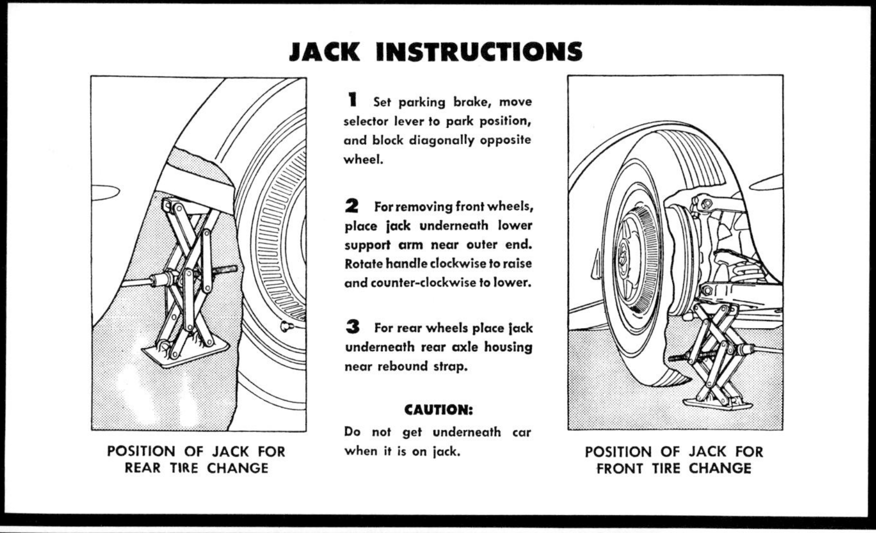

JACK INSTRUCTIONS

1 Set parking brake, move selector lever to park position, and block diagonally opposite wheel.

2 For removing front wheels, place jack underneath lower support arm near outer end. Rotate handle clockwise to raise and counter-clockwise to lower.

3 For rear wheels place jack underneath rear axle housing near rebound strap.

CAUTION:
Do not get underneath car when it is on jack.

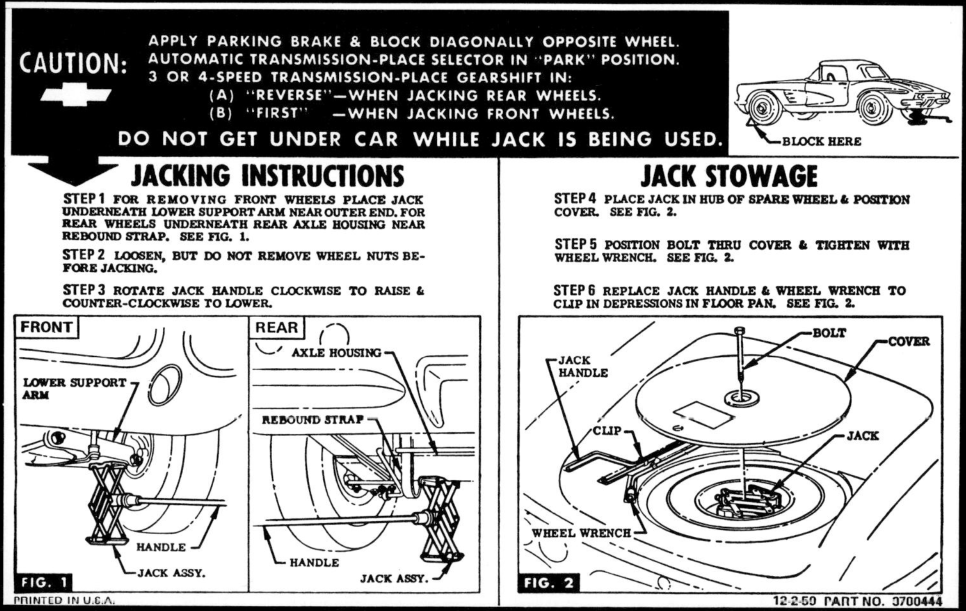

CAUTION: APPLY PARKING BRAKE & BLOCK DIAGONALLY OPPOSITE WHEEL.
AUTOMATIC TRANSMISSION-PLACE SELECTOR IN "PARK" POSITION.
3 OR 4-SPEED TRANSMISSION-PLACE GEARSHIFT IN:
(A) "REVERSE"—WHEN JACKING REAR WHEELS.
(B) "FIRST" —WHEN JACKING FRONT WHEELS.
DO NOT GET UNDER CAR WHILE JACK IS BEING USED.

JACKING INSTRUCTIONS

STEP 1 FOR REMOVING FRONT WHEELS PLACE JACK UNDERNEATH LOWER SUPPORT ARM NEAR OUTER END. FOR REAR WHEELS UNDERNEATH REAR AXLE HOUSING NEAR REBOUND STRAP. SEE FIG. 1.

STEP 2 LOOSEN, BUT DO NOT REMOVE WHEEL NUTS BEFORE JACKING.

STEP 3 ROTATE JACK HANDLE CLOCKWISE TO RAISE & COUNTER-CLOCKWISE TO LOWER.

JACK STOWAGE

STEP 4 PLACE JACK IN HUB OF SPARE WHEEL & POSITION COVER. SEE FIG. 2.

STEP 5 POSITION BOLT THRU COVER & TIGHTEN WITH WHEEL WRENCH. SEE FIG. 2.

STEP 6 REPLACE JACK HANDLE & WHEEL WRENCH TO CLIP IN DEPRESSIONS IN FLOOR PAN. SEE FIG. 2.

PRINTED IN U.S.A.

12-2-50 PART NO. 3700444

Above: *1953-1960 jacking instructions label.* **Below:** *1961-1962 jacking instructions label. Black lettering on white. Shown 52% of actual size.*

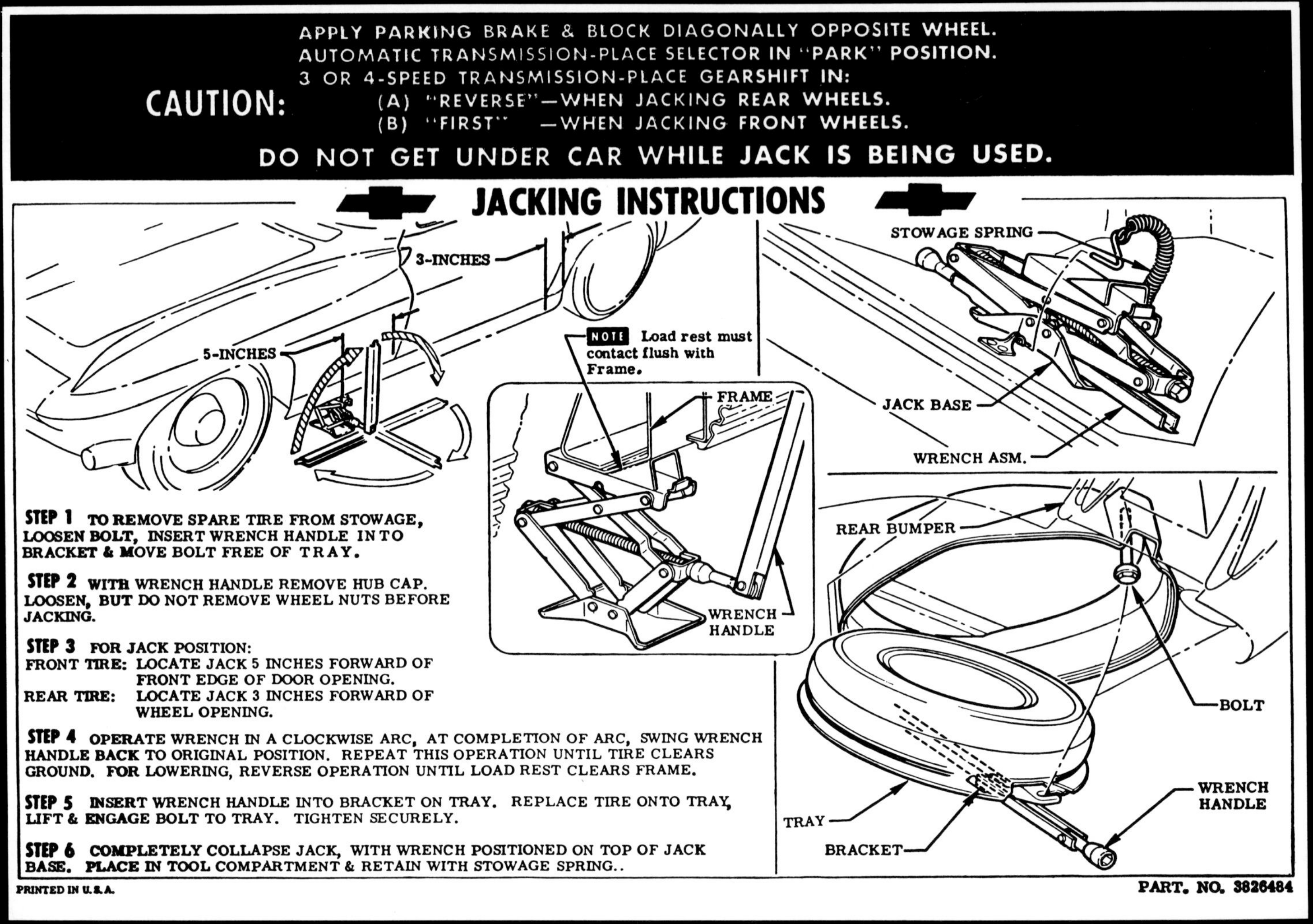
CAUTION: APPLY PARKING BRAKE & BLOCK DIAGONALLY OPPOSITE WHEEL.
AUTOMATIC TRANSMISSION-PLACE SELECTOR IN "PARK" POSITION.
3 OR 4-SPEED TRANSMISSION-PLACE GEARSHIFT IN:
(A) "REVERSE"—WHEN JACKING REAR WHEELS.
(B) "FIRST" —WHEN JACKING FRONT WHEELS.

DO NOT GET UNDER CAR WHILE JACK IS BEING USED.

JACKING INSTRUCTIONS

STEP 1 TO REMOVE SPARE TIRE FROM STOWAGE, LOOSEN BOLT, INSERT WRENCH HANDLE INTO BRACKET & MOVE BOLT FREE OF TRAY.

STEP 2 WITH WRENCH HANDLE REMOVE HUB CAP. LOOSEN, BUT DO NOT REMOVE WHEEL NUTS BEFORE JACKING.

STEP 3 FOR JACK POSITION:
FRONT TIRE: LOCATE JACK 5 INCHES FORWARD OF FRONT EDGE OF DOOR OPENING.
REAR TIRE: LOCATE JACK 3 INCHES FORWARD OF WHEEL OPENING.

STEP 4 OPERATE WRENCH IN A CLOCKWISE ARC, AT COMPLETION OF ARC, SWING WRENCH HANDLE BACK TO ORIGINAL POSITION. REPEAT THIS OPERATION UNTIL TIRE CLEARS GROUND. FOR LOWERING, REVERSE OPERATION UNTIL LOAD REST CLEARS FRAME.

STEP 5 INSERT WRENCH HANDLE INTO BRACKET ON TRAY. REPLACE TIRE ONTO TRAY, LIFT & ENGAGE BOLT TO TRAY. TIGHTEN SECURELY.

STEP 6 COMPLETELY COLLAPSE JACK, WITH WRENCH POSITIONED ON TOP OF JACK BASE. PLACE IN TOOL COMPARTMENT & RETAIN WITH STOWAGE SPRING..

PRINTED IN U.S.A. PART. NO. 3826484

1963-1966 jacking instructions label for Corvettes not equipped with optional knock-off wheels. Black lettering on white. Shown 75% of actual size.

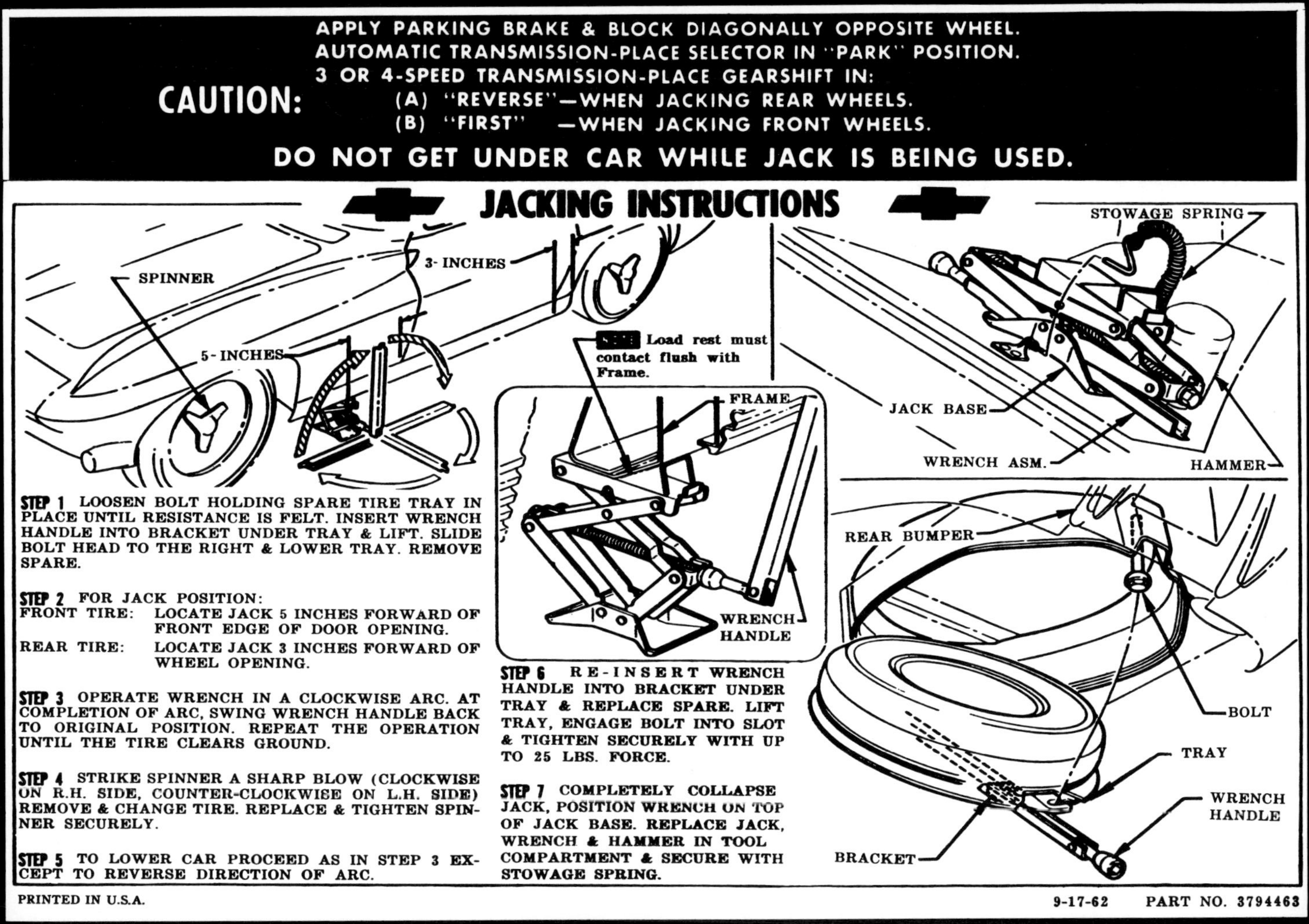

1963-1966 jacking instructions label for Corvettes equipped with optional knock-off wheels. Black lettering on white. Shown 75% of actual size.

a sample situation sketch showing a '61 model jacked at the right rear and blocked at the left front.

1962 was the last year for a rear-access trunk in Corvettes. In 1963, the spare tire was moved to a special hinged tray, below the rear of the car. The tray is held in place by a sliding bolt arrangement, the bolt head conveniently being the same size as the wheel lug bolts so that the lug wrench can be used to loosen the retaining bolt. Access requires working on one's knees, or even flat on the back, and many a Corvette owner has had unpleasant comments about the difficulty of getting at the spare tire.

The new spare location in 1963 required a completely new instructions label. The label was pasted to the inside of the carpet-covered masonite storage compartment behind the seats (except in 36.5 gallon fuel tank cars), which housed the jack and lug wrench. The same label was used from 1963 through 1966, except that Corvettes with knock-off aluminum wheels had a modified version. The knock-off wheel label was the same size and contained the same sketches, except that one sketch had the knock-off spinners roughed in and the lead hammer used to remove the wheels shown in place of the jack. In addition to the obvious instruction required for "striking the spinner a sharp blow . . . ", the knock-off label had far more detailed things to say about removing the spare and replacing it. Remember that contrary to the current practice of supplying only four aluminum wheels with new Corvettes, the option price in 1963 through 1967 included all five. The knock-off label for 1963-1966 went so far as to specify proper torque for the spare tire retaining cover bolt. Chevrolet wanted them to stay put. In Corvettes equipped with the 36.5 gallon fuel tank, the jacking instructions label was placed in the rear corner, top left side of the tank cover.

Safety standards required the knock-off wheel of the 1963-1966 period to be changed in 1967 to a design without spinners. This completely new wheel was a bolt-on style, with a center cap to hide lug nuts. This new wheel option required a new jacking instruction label, though the old label would have sufficed for '67 Corvettes with the newly-standard rally wheel treatment. Despite that, Chevrolet decided to re-do the label completely, again. For 1967, they came up with a much smaller (less than half size) label than used for previous Sting Rays. The new label was worded to cover either type of wheel installed, "WITH ALUMINUM WHEELS, USE SCREW DRIVER TO REMOVE COVER ASM", and the previously elaborate instructions for putting the spare back in place were left out completely. Chevrolet must have figured that if you were smart enough to get the spare out, you'd figure out how to get it back in.

Bolt-on aluminum wheels were gone as an option in 1968, and this year brought on a completely new body style. The chassis of the 1968 Corvette was virtually the same as the previous five years, and the spare remained in the same location, as it has through current models. A new jacking instructions label was again designed for 1968, and the label remained unchanged through 1972. Someone in Chevrolet must have been preach-

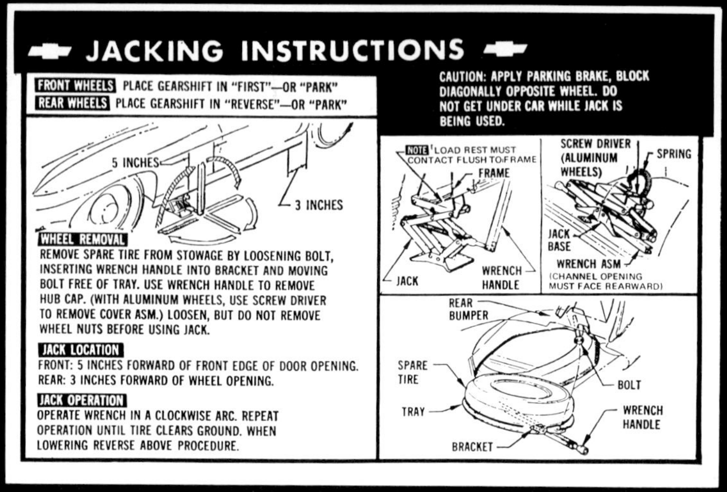

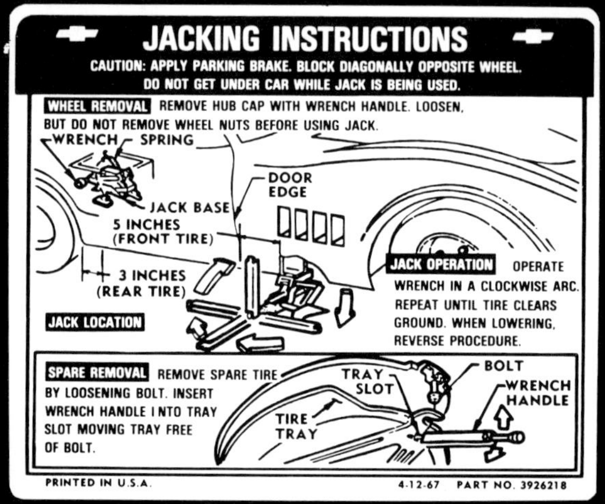

Above: *Jacking instructions label for 1967.* **Below:** *Jacking instructions label for 1968-1972. Black lettering on white. Shown 57% of actual size.*

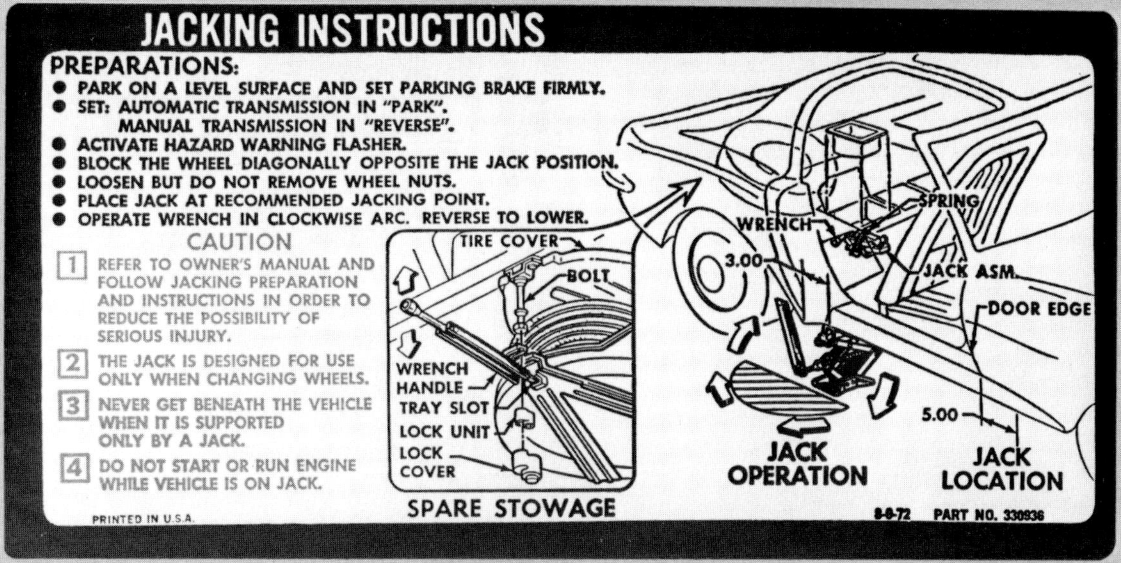

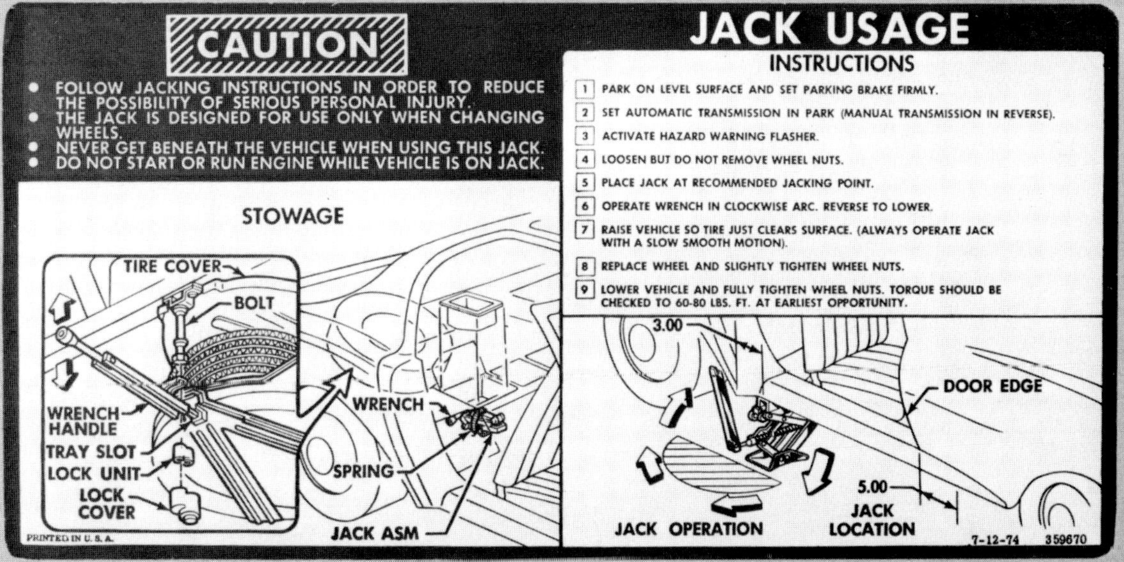

Above: *1973-1974 jacking instructions label.* **Below:** *1975-1978 jacking instructions label. Black lettering on white, except for "caution" which is red on top label and yellow on bottom. Shown 57% of actual size.*

ing either paper savings, or simplicity, because this label got even smaller than 1967's, and instructions were at an absolute minimum. Gone were the details about what gear to leave the Corvette in while jacking, and it took real concentration to figure the tire tray illustration out. Heaven have mercy on he or she who was doing this for the first time!

The jacking label made a complete about-face in 1973. The label grew to more than double-size. All previous jacking instruction labels had been black ink on white paper stock, but four "Cautions" were added to the '73 label in red ink:

(1) REFER TO OWNER'S MANUAL AND FOLLOW JACKING PREPARATION AND INSTRUCTIONS IN ORDER TO REDUCE THE POSSIBILITY OF SERIOUS INJURY.

(2) THE JACK IS DESIGNED FOR USE ONLY WHEN CHANGING WHEELS.

(3) NEVER GET BENEATH THE VEHICLE WHEN IT IS SUPPORTED ONLY BY A JACK.

(4) DO NOT START OR RUN ENGINE WHILE VEHICLE IS ON JACK.

The instructions concerning proper transmission gear while jacking returned. For the first time, mention was made of engaging the four-way flasher system while changing tires, even though the flashers had been standard on Corvettes since the 1967 model. Only two sketches were used, but they were well detailed. Since the jack was hidden under an insert tray in one of three compartments behind the seats, this was included in the illustration.

In 1975, the label was updated again, resulting in probably the clearest and most complete jacking instructions label ever. Illustrations were similar, but sharper. The cautions were reworded slightly and printed in yellow instead of red. Instructions were expanded, but listed in an easy-to-follow group of nine numbered statements. Unlike every other jacking label used for Corvettes, the title of this label was "Jack Usage".

The return to detailed, comprehensive jacking labels on later model Corvettes parallels a national concern for safety. In the case of the Corvette specifically, it probably also reflects an awareness on the part of Chevrolet that its later Corvettes were appealing to and being purchased by a much more diverse group of people whose mechanical know-how could no longer be taken for granted.

Radiator and Cooling System

Though there is some question as to the consistency of usage, GM assembly drawings indicate that labels started to be applied to the radiators of Corvettes starting with the 1956 model. The first label used was a simple and small, green on white paper caution that read, "THIS COOLANT SYSTEM PROTECTED TO −20° FAHRENHEIT BY GM PERMANENT TYPE ANTIFREEZE."

In 1958, a larger label replaced the '56-57 one. It was again green on white, but the message changed. The new label stated that the engine

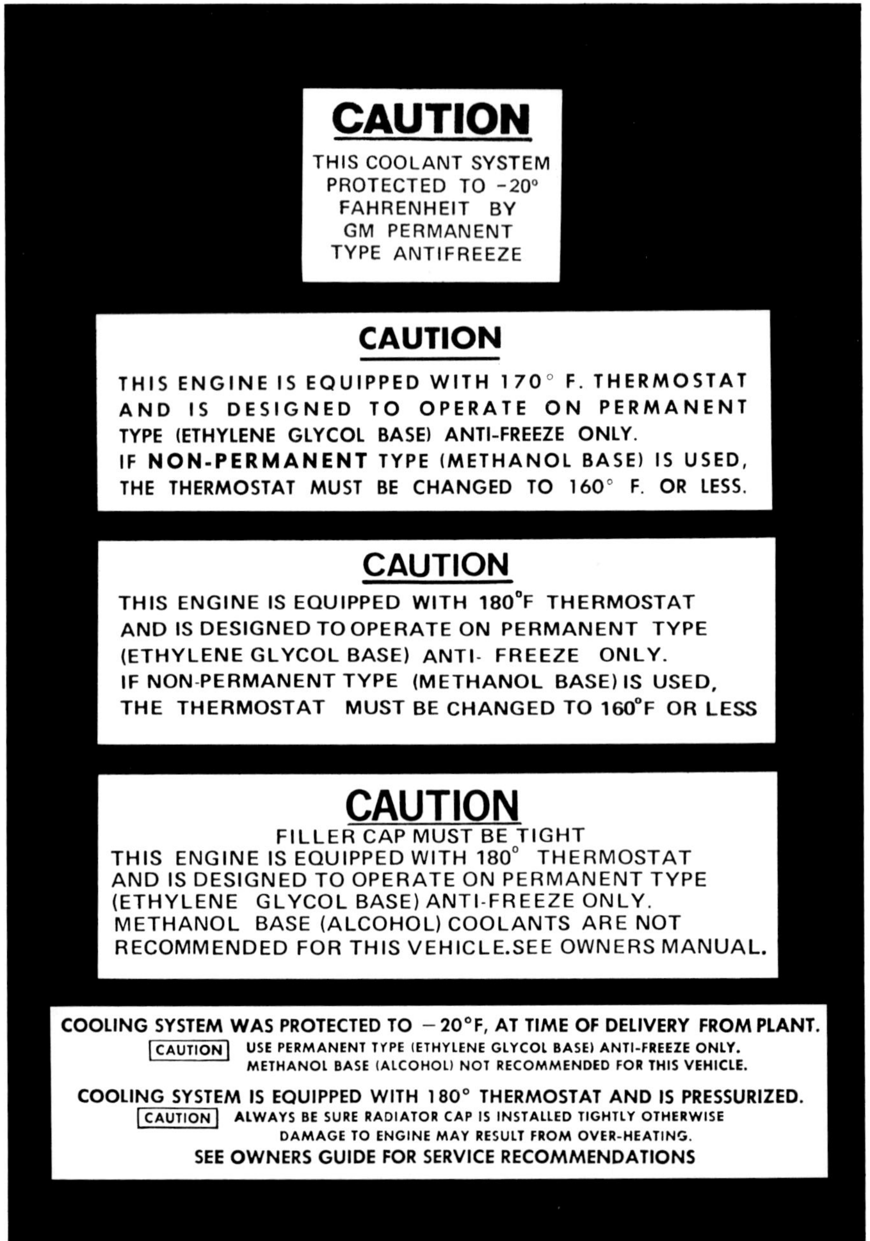

CAUTION
THIS COOLANT SYSTEM PROTECTED TO −20° FAHRENHEIT BY GM PERMANENT TYPE ANTIFREEZE

CAUTION
THIS ENGINE IS EQUIPPED WITH 170° F. THERMOSTAT AND IS DESIGNED TO OPERATE ON PERMANENT TYPE (ETHYLENE GLYCOL BASE) ANTI-FREEZE ONLY.
IF **NON-PERMANENT** TYPE (METHANOL BASE) IS USED, THE THERMOSTAT MUST BE CHANGED TO 160° F. OR LESS.

CAUTION
THIS ENGINE IS EQUIPPED WITH 180°F THERMOSTAT AND IS DESIGNED TO OPERATE ON PERMANENT TYPE (ETHYLENE GLYCOL BASE) ANTI- FREEZE ONLY.
IF NON-PERMANENT TYPE (METHANOL BASE) IS USED, THE THERMOSTAT MUST BE CHANGED TO 160°F OR LESS

CAUTION
FILLER CAP MUST BE TIGHT
THIS ENGINE IS EQUIPPED WITH 180° THERMOSTAT AND IS DESIGNED TO OPERATE ON PERMANENT TYPE (ETHYLENE GLYCOL BASE) ANTI-FREEZE ONLY.
METHANOL BASE (ALCOHOL) COOLANTS ARE NOT RECOMMENDED FOR THIS VEHICLE.SEE OWNERS MANUAL.

COOLING SYSTEM WAS PROTECTED TO −20°F, AT TIME OF DELIVERY FROM PLANT.
CAUTION USE PERMANENT TYPE (ETHYLENE GLYCOL BASE) ANTI-FREEZE ONLY. METHANOL BASE (ALCOHOL) NOT RECOMMENDED FOR THIS VEHICLE.
COOLING SYSTEM IS EQUIPPED WITH 180° THERMOSTAT AND IS PRESSURIZED.
CAUTION ALWAYS BE SURE RADIATOR CAP IS INSTALLED TIGHTLY OTHERWISE DAMAGE TO ENGINE MAY RESULT FROM OVER-HEATING.
SEE OWNERS GUIDE FOR SERVICE RECOMMENDATIONS

Radiator caution labels. See text for correct applications. Lettering is green on white. Shown 70% of actual size.

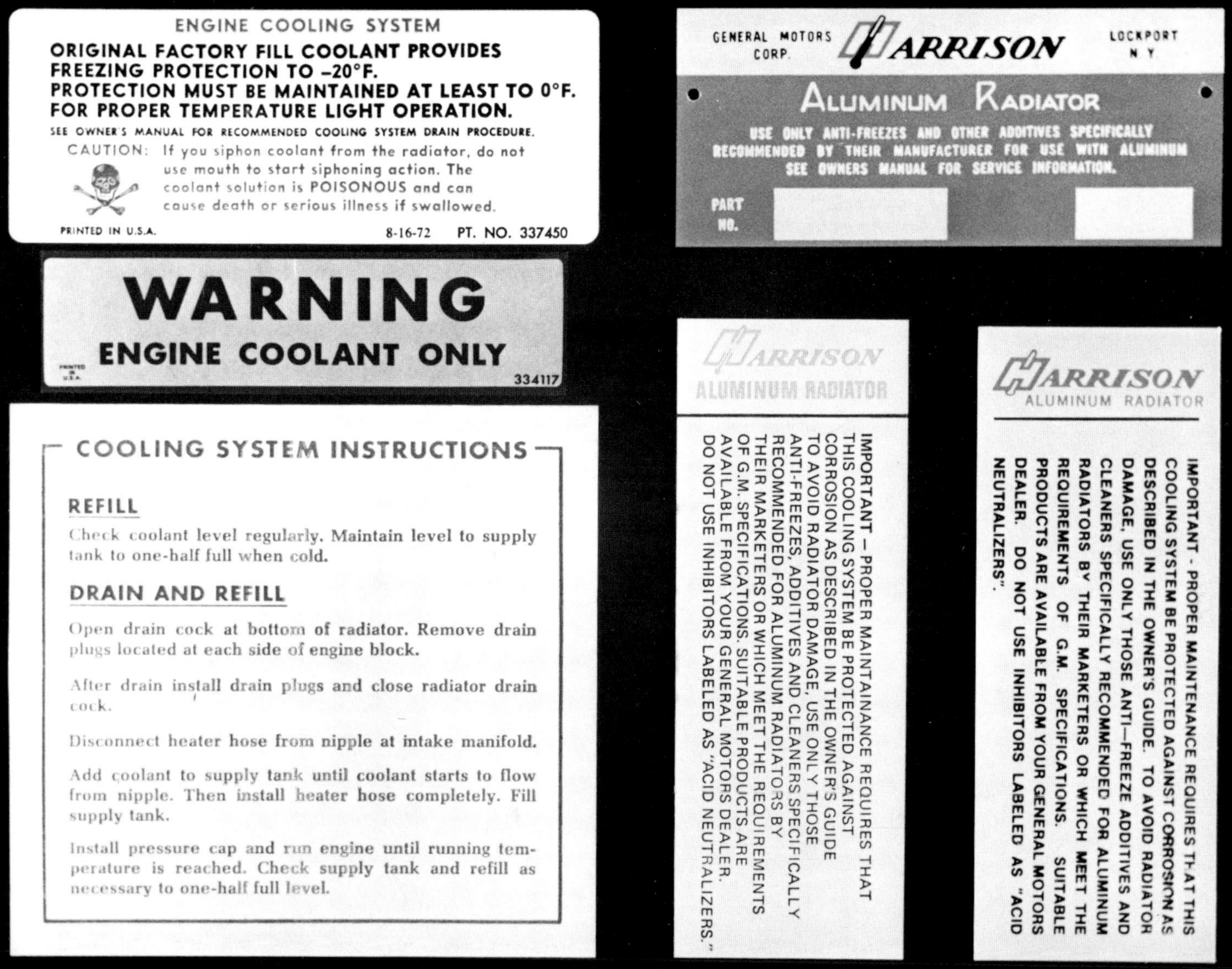

Radiator instruction, caution, and ID labels. ***Above left:*** *red and black on white. Left center, black on orange.* ***Below left:*** *green on white. Labels to right are blue and black on silver. Shown 70% of actual size.*

was equipped with a 170° thermostat and was designed to operate on permanent type (ethylene glycol base) anti-freeze only. If non-permanent type were used, the label recommended changing the thermostat to 160° or less. This same label was used from 1958 through 1962, but the location changed. The 1958 through 1960 models, and the '61 with integral expansion tank radiator, had the label on top of the radiator just to the right of center. The 1961 models with supply tanks and all '62 Corvettes had the label on the top left side of the radiator.

Starting with the 1960 high horsepower small blocks (270 hp, 315 hp), Chevy began using aluminum radiators in Corvettes. Those '60 models with aluminum radiators, and the early '61's, had the integrated overflow tank built right into the top of the radiator. On these models, an aluminum plate with blue and black printing was screwed to the expansion tank or the radiator. This tag also appeared on early '62 models. All the other '61 and newer small block Corvettes had aluminum radiators with fender-mounted expansion tanks. These received a silver foil radiator label (adhesive backed) through 1968, except for late '62 and early '63, when an adhesive-backed plate was used. To keep things really confusing, the little green tag that appeared on '56 and '57 radiators surfaced again, this time below the expansion tank neck of '61 and '62 Corvettes so equipped.

New green on white paper caution labels started to be used on the '63 model, but the first version was revised quickly and was used only for '63 Corvettes built before December, 1962. The early version still had the comment about switching the thermostat to a lower temperature type if non-permanent type (methanol base) anti-freeze was used. On the revised '63 label, Chevrolet flat-out told owners not to use anything but permanent anti-freeze. This label was used through the remainder of the '63 model run and into 1964 (up until April of 1964 in fact), when it changed again. Additions included a new warning about possible engine damage from over-heating due to an improperly tightened radiator cap, and a notation that the system was factory-protected to −20°F. This label continued in use through 1965 and possibly into 1966.

The three green and white radiator/cooling system labels for the '63 through '65 models were not placed in the same locations. The first, that one appearing on just early '63 cars, went on the side of the supply tank, facing the rear of the car. Its replacement, the one used for the remainder of 1963 and part of 1964, went on the top left side of the radiator. Some 1963 cars are known to have both labels from the factory. The third was put on the right side of the radiator shroud, reading from bottom to top in about the one-two o'clock position.

With the exception of the 396 and L-88, big block radiators were made of copper, so they did not use the Harrison aluminum radiator labels. The 396 cubic inch '65 models did have a large, green on white paper label affixed to their fender walls which explained the correct procedure for draining and refilling the radiator. The '66 and '67 big block models did not use radiator expansion tanks, and did not have the big green tags.

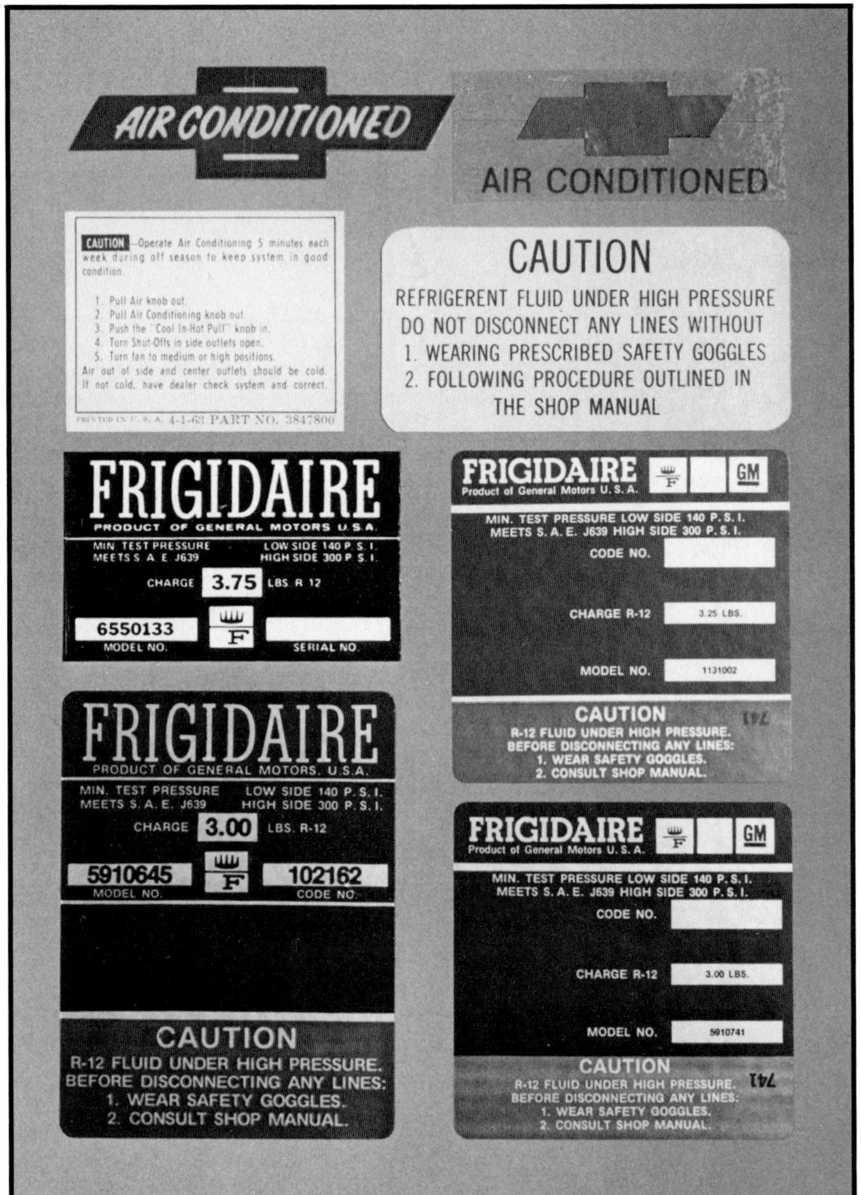

Air conditioning labels. Top left, white lettering on blue. Top right is blue on clear. Top left "caution" label is red on white. Top right "caution" is orange on clear. "Frigidaire" labels are silver lettering on black, except for caution sections which are silver on green. Shown 58% of actual size.

Harrison air conditioning labels. All are blue and black on silver. Shown 58% of actual size.

The '65 big block also had the long green on white "caution" label on its radiator shroud used the same year on small block equipped cars.

Use of labels for later model Corvettes has been somewhat sporadic. The '73 Corvettes had a unique red and black on white paper label that had a caution, complete with skull and crossbones, concerning not using your mouth to siphon coolant from the radiator. The '74 through '77 models had a "WARNING . . . ENGINE COOLANT ONLY" sticker on the plastic expansion tanks to keep unknowing station attendants from pouring oil or power steering fluid in. 1963 and newer Corvettes often have small numeral decals on the cooling system components which are presumably inspection numbers.

Air Conditioning

The first year for factory-installed air conditioning in Corvettes was 1963, and that's when the label story starts, too. The '63 equipped with air had a unique red on white caution label inside the glove box. This label instructed the owner to run the air conditioning unit five minutes each week during the off season to keep the system in "good" condition. No such label appeared on any later model Corvettes.

The '63 through '66 Corvettes equipped with air had blue Chevrolet "bow tie" emblems with "air conditioning" spelled out. The '63 through '65 version had the lettering within the bow tie, but for '66 the lettering was below. These labels were placed on the rear corner of the passenger-side of the rear window of coupes, and on the passenger-side roll-up window of convertibles.

Several labels were used within the engine compartment for air conditioned Corvettes. The '63 to '65 models had a black on silver foil "Frigidaire" label placed on the back end of the compressor. They were put on so that they could be read from the "mechanic's angle" front of the car. Another label used for the same models was an orange decal cautioning of high pressure lines. This went on the pulley end of the compressor top. A third label used was made of sheet aluminum and was stuck to the exchanger box with adhesive. This "Harrison" air conditioning label identified model, year, and serial numbers of the unit. During 1964 production, the material of the label changed from sheet aluminum to thinner foil stock. But the appearance of the label and the information on it was similar, though '65 through '67 versions of the label did not include the serial numbers.

In 1966, the "Frigidaire" and "caution" labels used the previous years were combined in one new label. The Frigidaire ID portion was again black on silver, but the caution part became green. This label continued In this exact form through the 1969 model. Similar labels, reduced in size, appeared on later Corvettes, also. The "Harrison" air conditioning heat exchanger label also continued on Corvettes to current years, but each finished label is unique to the year since each model year is designated.

Above: *Paint warning label.* **Center and Below.** *Tire pressure labels. Top label is red and white. Others are black lettering on white, except for "hot" ratings on round labels which are red. Shown 85% of actual size.*

HOW TO SELECT THE PROPER GASOLINE FOR
PERFORMANCE • ECONOMY • ECOLOGY

This vehicle is designed to operate on unleaded or low-lead fuels of at least 91 Research Octane. These fuels will minimize spark plug fouling and emission system deterioration. Leaded regular fuels containing more than 0.5 grams of lead per gallon normally should not be used. The engine **does not require premium fuel. Therefore, its use would be an unnecessary additional expense.**

If the service station gas pump has a symbol similar to the sample below, preferably use unleaded or low-lead gasoline with a symbol number of 2. A higher number is satisfactory but not required.

LOW LEAD 2 — Ask your gasoline dealer for information on the fuel you are using both as to lead content and octane rating. — UNLEADED 2

PRINTED IN U.S.A. PT. NO. 339203

ENGINE STARTING PROCEDURE

FASTEN YOUR SEAT BELTS

On passenger cars, seat belts must be buckled after outboard front seat occupants are seated before starter will operate. Shoulder belts lock only during a sudden stop or impact. Buzzer and light will operate if front belts are unbuckled when vehicle is underway. Engine may be restarted if driver stays seated.

If Starter Will Not Operate, Check The Following:

1. Remove any objects from unoccupied front seat positions.
2. Rebuckle belts.
3. If starter still will not operate, use the following emergency start provision:
   - Set parking brake firmly. Move shift lever to "park" ("reverse" for manual transmission).
   - Leave ignition key in run (on) position.
   - Open hood and press button marked "start" mounted on orange support. See Owner's Manual for location.
   - Close hood, enter car, buckle belts and follow starting procedure.

MANUAL TRANSMISSION MODELS

1. Apply parking brake and shift transmission to neutral.
2. Depress the clutch pedal to floor throughout the starting procedure. A starter interlock prevents starter operation unless the clutch pedal is fully depressed.
3. Operate accelerator pedal and starter as outlined under Engine Starting Conditions.

CAUTION
Extended running of engine (5 minutes or more) without depressing accelerator pedal could cause damage to engine or exhaust system due to overheating.

AUTOMATIC TRANSMISSION MODELS

1. Apply the parking brake.
2. Place transmission selector in "P" or "N" ("P" preferred).
   A starter safety switch prevents starter operation while the transmission selector is in any drive position. (If it is necessary to re-start the engine with the car moving, place the selector lever in "N").
3. Depress accelerator pedal and activate starter as outlined under Engine Starting Conditions.

READ OWNER'S MANUAL FOR OPERATING INSTRUCTIONS

PRINTED IN U.S.A. 7-13-73 PART NO. 345532

ENGINE STARTING CONDITIONS

- Cold Engine—Fully depress accelerator pedal and slowly release. With foot off the pedal, crank the engine by turning the ignition key to the Start position—release when engine starts. If engine starts, but fails to run, repeat this procedure. When engine is running smoothly (approximately 30 seconds), the idle speed may be reduced by slightly depressing the accelerator pedal and then slowly releasing.
- Warm Engine—Depress accelerator pedal about halfway and hold while cranking the engine.
- Extremely Cold Weather (Below 0°F) Or After Car Has Been Standing Idle Several Days—Fully depress and release accelerator pedal two or three times before cranking the engine. With foot off the accelerator pedal, crank the engine by turning the key to Start position and release when engine starts.
- Warm Up—Always let the engine idle for 20 to 30 seconds after starting and drive at moderate speeds for several miles, especially during cold weather.

IF ENGINE IS FLOODED

Depress accelerator pedal and hold to floor while starting until engine is cleared of excess fuel and is running smoothly. Never pump the accelerator pedal.

VEHICLE SAFETY MAINTENANCE SCHEDULE (Refer to Owner's Manual for Details) — Services to be Performed at Mileage Intervals Indicated by ●

CHECK OFF EACH ITEM UNDER MILEAGE AS SERVICE IS PERFORMED.	6000	12000	18000	24000	30000	36000	42000	48000	54000
Brakes and Power Steering—Check all lines and hoses.	●	●	●	●	●	●	●	●	●
—Check condition of brake linings and parking brake adjustment.		●		●		●		●	
Chassis —Lube and check all fluid levels.*	●	●	●	●	●	●	●	●	●
—Check condition of front and rear suspension and steering system.	●	●	●	●	●	●	●	●	●
Exhaust System—Check condition of system and underbody.	●	●	●	●	●	●	●	●	●
Tires and Wheels—Check condition. (Check tire pressure at least monthly.)	●	●	●	●	●	●	●	●	●
Engine —Change oil.* Check condition of all belts.	●	●	●	●	●	●	●	●	●
—Replace oil filter (at 1st oil change and then every 2nd Change).	●		●		●		●		●
—Change coolant every two years.				●				●	
Throttle Linkage—Check operation and condition.		●		●		●		●	
Emission Control Systems—Service.	See Emission Control Systems Booklet								
Headlights—Aim.		●		●		●		●	
Transmission (Automatic)—Change fluid and service filter.				●				●	

*SERVICE EVERY 4 MOS. OR 6,000 MILES, WHICHEVER OCCURS FIRST. SEE OWNER'S MANUAL FOR ADDITIONAL VEHICLE MAINTENANCE REQUIREMENTS.

CONTINUE SERVICES AT LIKE INTERVALS

325131 PRINTED IN U.S.A.

GM
MARK OF EXCELLENCE

Catalytic Converter INFORMATION

Your new General Motors vehicle is designed to meet strict exhaust emission requirements and to provide good fuel economy, with a minimum of scheduled maintenance. The exhaust system on the vehicle is equipped with a catalytic converter, which is an important component for controlling exhaust emissions.

- Keep your engine in proper operating condition to help prevent loss of fuel economy and emission control, and damage to the catalytic converter. If engine malfunction should occur, involving misfire or noticeable loss of performance, have your engine serviced promptly. Continued operation with a severe malfunction could cause the converter and exhaust system to overheat and lead to damage to the converter, the vehicle and nearby property. Please refer to Owner's Manual.
- As with any vehicle, do not park or operate this vehicle in areas where combustible materials such as grass or leaves can come into contact with a hot exhaust system, possibly causing these materials to ignite.
- Do not push or tow this vehicle to start, since under some conditions damage to the catalytic converter, the vehicle and nearby property may result.

DO YOUR PART FOR CLEAN AIR

PRINTED IN USA 557269

Instructions labels and "GM Excellence" label. Instruction labels are black lettering on white. GM label is blue on silver. Shown 54% of actual size.

Glove Box, Door, And Sun Visor

It was in 1958 that Corvettes made the complete change to acrylic lacquer for exterior finishes. Starting in 1958, and continuing through 1961, Chevrolet put a warning label into the lid of the glove box to inform owners that the new lacquer being used was not compatible with enamels or other lacquers. However, early in 1958 production, this red and white label was put on the top of the fan shroud. Also, a few 1957 models were painted silver, and that particular silver was acrylic lacquer. These models had the same red and white paint warning label, but it was placed on the firewall, above the heater.

1966 was the first year that Chevrolet informed Corvette owners of recommended tire pressures through labels. This was done with an adhesive-backed, round label placed on the inside surface of the glove box door. The 1967 model's label contained the exact same information (24 pounds of air pressure in all tires cold, 30 hot), but for some reason a new part number was assigned to it. For 1968 through 1972 Corvettes, another tire pressure label was designed, this time a bit larger, but with the same recommendations.

Tire pressure labels moved to the door posts starting in 1973. The label for 1973 to 1975 Corvettes is square, as are following years. The '73-'75 recommends 20 pounds of pressure for both front and rear tires at cold temperatures. This changed in 1976 to a recommendation of 26 pounds rear and 20 pounds front.

A really unusual label appeared on the doors of 1967 Corvettes, and on all other General Motors cars of the era. GM management had decided a drive for improved quality was in order, and one of the visual outgrowths of that program was the adoption of a "GM Mark of Excellence" trademark. This neat logo started showing up everywhere, including a bright blue and silver stick-on label for Corvette doors. The logo continued for years, but the door stickers just lasted one model year.

Another one year item was a gasoline recommendation label applied to the center storage compartment of 1973 models. This little paper sticker advised owners that 91 Research Octane fuel was all that was needed, and buying better was an "unnecessary additional expense."

Sun visors haven't been the most popular place for labels, but the Corvette has seen a couple of instances of its use for that purpose. The first was in 1971 when a black and white fiberglass "maintenance" schedule was placed on the inside surface of the driver's visor. The same schedule was used the following year, but the label for it was paper and it was moved to the center of the storage compartment.

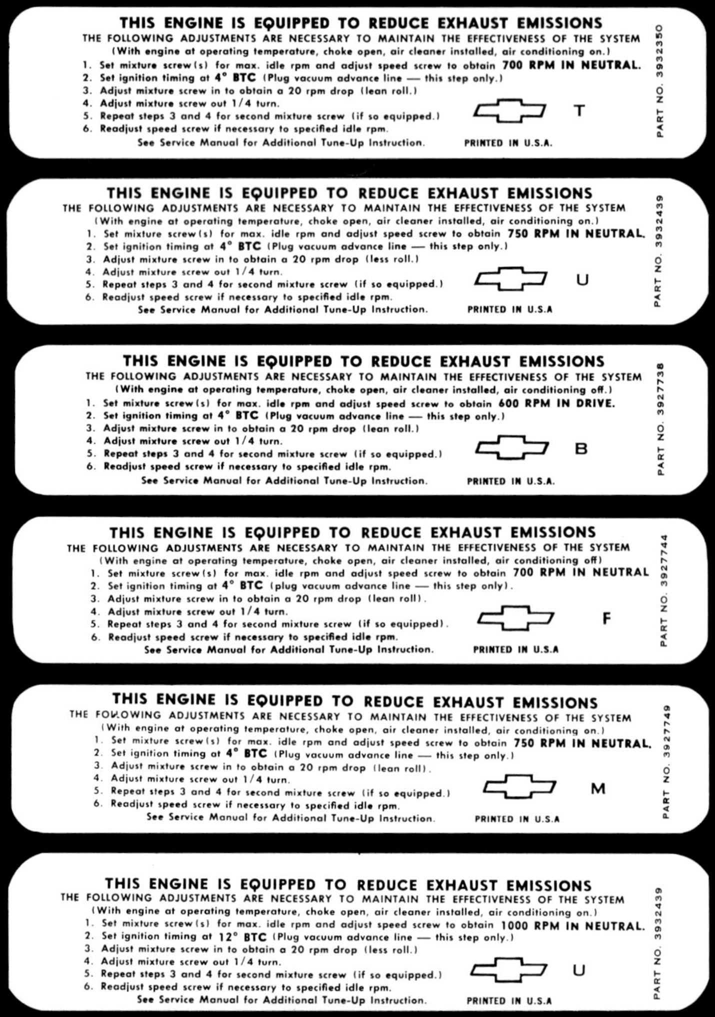

Emission information labels. All shown are 1968, as follows from top: 300 HP, 350 HP, 300-390-400 HP/Auto, 390 HP/Man, 400-435 HP/Man, 430 HP (L-88). Black on white with red highlight lettering. Shown 58% of actual size.

Emission information labels. Top three shown are 1969, lower two are 1970. From top, 300-350 HP, 390-400 HP, 435 & L-88, 300 HP, 350 HP. Black on white with red highlight lettering. Shown 58% of actual size.

A second use of the visor for labels came in 1976 when a catalytic converter information label was affixed to the passenger visor. This label had the usual business about keeping the engine in good tune, but also stated, "As with any vehicle, do not park or operate this vehicle in areas where combustible materials such as grass or leaves can come in contact with a hot exhaust system, possibly causing these materials to ignite." What GM was hinting at, but not coming right out and saying, was that converters got very hot. They got so hot that they could catch dried leaves and such on fire if you parked over them. In fact, many national and state parks prohibit catalytic converter-equipped cars to park in certain areas for fear of starting forest fires.

In 1974 and 1975, an engine starting procedure label was placed on the sun visor. This was the era of the infamous "interlock" seat belt system which required the driver and passenger (or a package in the passenger seat of over a few pounds) to be buckled up before the car would start. There was a by-pass button under the hood to be used if the system fouled, and the confusion of it all led Chevrolet to go with a detailed explanation via the visor label.

Emissions

The 1968 model year brought with it the beginning vestiges of emissions control equipment. Appropriate labels for the engine compartment came with this equipment. They told of its presence and how to tune-up the engine in spite of it. The first year (1968) the labels were long and narrow and printed in red and black on white adhesive paper stock. They were placed on the top left side of the radiator. A different label was used for each engine (one was used for the 390 hp and 400 hp), and the 300 hp engine with automatic had a different label than the 300 hp with manual transmission, because the timing and RPM settings were different. Each label had its own separate part number and letter suffix on the right hand side.

From 1969 on, the labels were placed on the firewall above the brake master cylinder. Placement on the radiator may not have been good because of road dirt, heat, and antifreeze.

The 1969 and 1970 labels were printed in the same colors and on the same stock as the 1968 labels, but each year had a different layout for the information.

In 1971 a few changes occurred in the emission labels. They were made larger to accommodate more information and printed in black only on white stock. In order to withstand abuse better, the labels were laminated with clear plastic. The labels have basically remained the same, except for a reduction in size in 1974, up to the present time. Since 1978 was the silver anniversary of the Corvette, the labels were printed in black on silver, a subtle touch of commemoration.

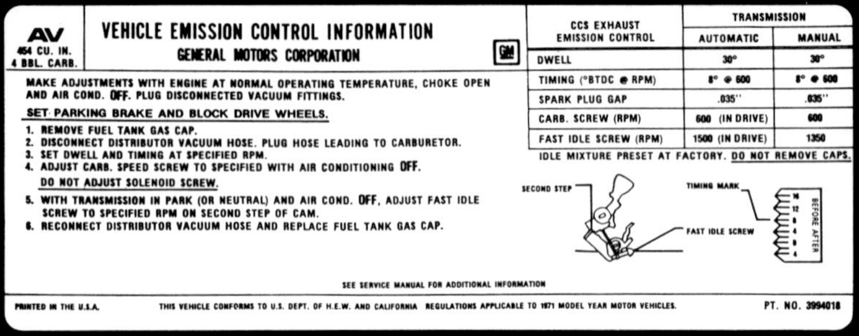

AV
454 CU. IN.
4 BBL. CARB.

VEHICLE EMISSION CONTROL INFORMATION
GENERAL MOTORS CORPORATION

MAKE ADJUSTMENTS WITH ENGINE AT NORMAL OPERATING TEMPERATURE, CHOKE OPEN AND AIR COND. OFF. PLUG DISCONNECTED VACUUM FITTINGS.

SET PARKING BRAKE AND BLOCK DRIVE WHEELS.

1. REMOVE FUEL TANK GAS CAP.
2. DISCONNECT DISTRIBUTOR VACUUM HOSE. PLUG HOSE LEADING TO CARBURETOR.
3. SET DWELL AND TIMING AT SPECIFIED RPM.
4. ADJUST CARB. SPEED SCREW TO SPECIFIED WITH AIR CONDITIONING OFF. DO NOT ADJUST SOLENOID SCREW.
5. WITH TRANSMISSION IN PARK (OR NEUTRAL) AND AIR COND. OFF, ADJUST FAST IDLE SCREW TO SPECIFIED RPM ON SECOND STEP OF CAM.
6. RECONNECT DISTRIBUTOR VACUUM HOSE AND REPLACE FUEL TANK GAS CAP.

CCS EXHAUST EMISSION CONTROL	TRANSMISSION	
	AUTOMATIC	MANUAL
DWELL	30°	30°
TIMING (°BTDC @ RPM)	8° @ 600	8° @ 600
SPARK PLUG GAP	.035''	.035''
CARB. SCREW (RPM)	600 (IN DRIVE)	600
FAST IDLE SCREW (RPM)	1500 (IN DRIVE)	1350

IDLE MIXTURE PRESET AT FACTORY. DO NOT REMOVE CAPS.

SEE SERVICE MANUAL FOR ADDITIONAL INFORMATION

PRINTED IN THE U.S.A. THIS VEHICLE CONFORMS TO U.S. DEPT. OF H.E.W. AND CALIFORNIA REGULATIONS APPLICABLE TO 1971 MODEL YEAR MOTOR VEHICLES. PT. NO. 3994018

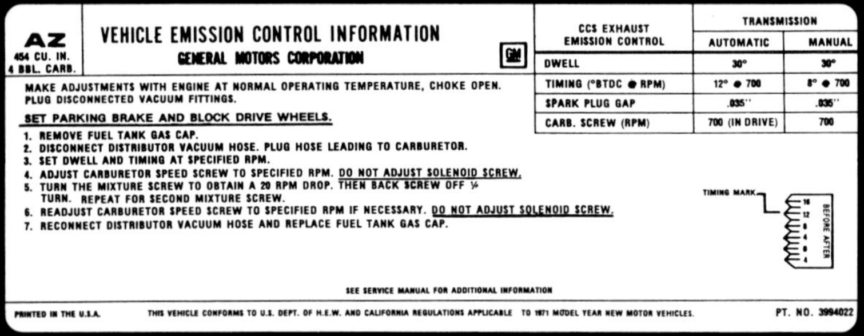

AZ
454 CU. IN.
4 BBL. CARB.

VEHICLE EMISSION CONTROL INFORMATION
GENERAL MOTORS CORPORATION

MAKE ADJUSTMENTS WITH ENGINE AT NORMAL OPERATING TEMPERATURE, CHOKE OPEN. PLUG DISCONNECTED VACUUM FITTINGS.

SET PARKING BRAKE AND BLOCK DRIVE WHEELS.

1. REMOVE FUEL TANK GAS CAP.
2. DISCONNECT DISTRIBUTOR VACUUM HOSE. PLUG HOSE LEADING TO CARBURETOR.
3. SET DWELL AND TIMING AT SPECIFIED RPM.
4. ADJUST CARBURETOR SPEED SCREW TO SPECIFIED RPM. DO NOT ADJUST SOLENOID SCREW.
5. TURN THE MIXTURE SCREW TO OBTAIN A 20 RPM DROP. THEN BACK SCREW OFF ¼ TURN. REPEAT FOR SECOND MIXTURE SCREW.
6. READJUST CARBURETOR SPEED SCREW TO SPECIFIED RPM IF NECESSARY. DO NOT ADJUST SOLENOID SCREW.
7. RECONNECT DISTRIBUTOR VACUUM HOSE AND REPLACE FUEL TANK GAS CAP.

CCS EXHAUST EMISSION CONTROL	TRANSMISSION	
	AUTOMATIC	MANUAL
DWELL	30°	30°
TIMING (°BTDC @ RPM)	12° @ 700	8° @ 700
SPARK PLUG GAP	.035''	.035''
CARB. SCREW (RPM)	700 (IN DRIVE)	700

SEE SERVICE MANUAL FOR ADDITIONAL INFORMATION

PRINTED IN THE U.S.A. THIS VEHICLE CONFORMS TO U.S. DEPT. OF H.E.W. AND CALIFORNIA REGULATIONS APPLICABLE TO 1971 MODEL YEAR NEW MOTOR VEHICLES. PT. NO. 3994022

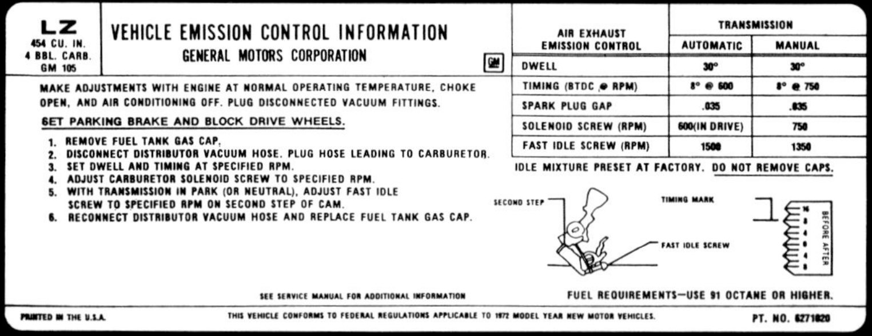

LZ
454 CU. IN.
4 BBL. CARB.
GM 105

VEHICLE EMISSION CONTROL INFORMATION
GENERAL MOTORS CORPORATION

MAKE ADJUSTMENTS WITH ENGINE AT NORMAL OPERATING TEMPERATURE, CHOKE OPEN, AND AIR CONDITIONING OFF. PLUG DISCONNECTED VACUUM FITTINGS.

SET PARKING BRAKE AND BLOCK DRIVE WHEELS.

1. REMOVE FUEL TANK GAS CAP.
2. DISCONNECT DISTRIBUTOR VACUUM HOSE. PLUG HOSE LEADING TO CARBURETOR.
3. SET DWELL AND TIMING AT SPECIFIED RPM.
4. ADJUST CARBURETOR SOLENOID SCREW TO SPECIFIED RPM.
5. WITH TRANSMISSION IN PARK (OR NEUTRAL), ADJUST FAST IDLE SCREW TO SPECIFIED RPM ON SECOND STEP OF CAM.
6. RECONNECT DISTRIBUTOR VACUUM HOSE AND REPLACE FUEL TANK GAS CAP.

AIR EXHAUST EMISSION CONTROL	TRANSMISSION	
	AUTOMATIC	MANUAL
DWELL	30°	30°
TIMING (BTDC @ RPM)	8° @ 600	8° @ 750
SPARK PLUG GAP	.035	.035
SOLENOID SCREW (RPM)	600(IN DRIVE)	750
FAST IDLE SCREW (RPM)	1500	1350

IDLE MIXTURE PRESET AT FACTORY. DO NOT REMOVE CAPS.

SEE SERVICE MANUAL FOR ADDITIONAL INFORMATION

FUEL REQUIREMENTS—USE 91 OCTANE OR HIGHER.

PRINTED IN THE U.S.A. THIS VEHICLE CONFORMS TO FEDERAL REGULATIONS APPLICABLE TO 1972 MODEL YEAR NEW MOTOR VEHICLES. PT. NO. 6271820

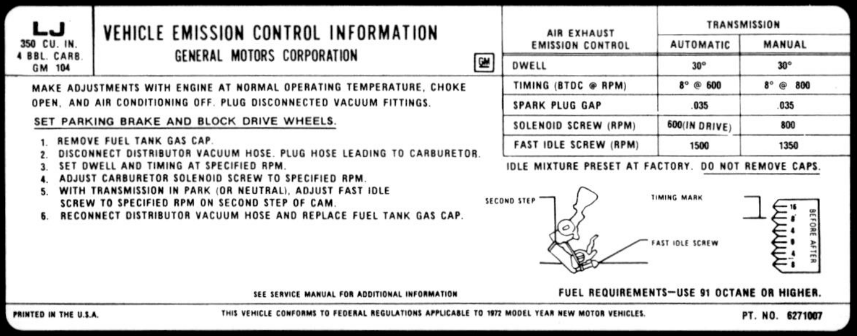

LJ
350 CU. IN.
4 BBL. CARB.
GM 104

VEHICLE EMISSION CONTROL INFORMATION
GENERAL MOTORS CORPORATION

MAKE ADJUSTMENTS WITH ENGINE AT NORMAL OPERATING TEMPERATURE, CHOKE OPEN, AND AIR CONDITIONING OFF. PLUG DISCONNECTED VACUUM FITTINGS.

SET PARKING BRAKE AND BLOCK DRIVE WHEELS.

1. REMOVE FUEL TANK GAS CAP.
2. DISCONNECT DISTRIBUTOR VACUUM HOSE. PLUG HOSE LEADING TO CARBURETOR.
3. SET DWELL AND TIMING AT SPECIFIED RPM.
4. ADJUST CARBURETOR SOLENOID SCREW TO SPECIFIED RPM.
5. WITH TRANSMISSION IN PARK (OR NEUTRAL), ADJUST FAST IDLE SCREW TO SPECIFIED RPM ON SECOND STEP OF CAM.
6. RECONNECT DISTRIBUTOR VACUUM HOSE AND REPLACE FUEL TANK GAS CAP.

AIR EXHAUST EMISSION CONTROL	TRANSMISSION	
	AUTOMATIC	MANUAL
DWELL	30°	30°
TIMING (BTDC @ RPM)	8° @ 600	8° @ 800
SPARK PLUG GAP	.035	.035
SOLENOID SCREW (RPM)	600(IN DRIVE)	800
FAST IDLE SCREW (RPM)	1500	1350

IDLE MIXTURE PRESET AT FACTORY. DO NOT REMOVE CAPS.

SEE SERVICE MANUAL FOR ADDITIONAL INFORMATION

FUEL REQUIREMENTS—USE 91 OCTANE OR HIGHER.

PRINTED IN THE U.S.A. THIS VEHICLE CONFORMS TO FEDERAL REGULATIONS APPLICABLE TO 1972 MODEL YEAR NEW MOTOR VEHICLES. PT. NO. 6271007

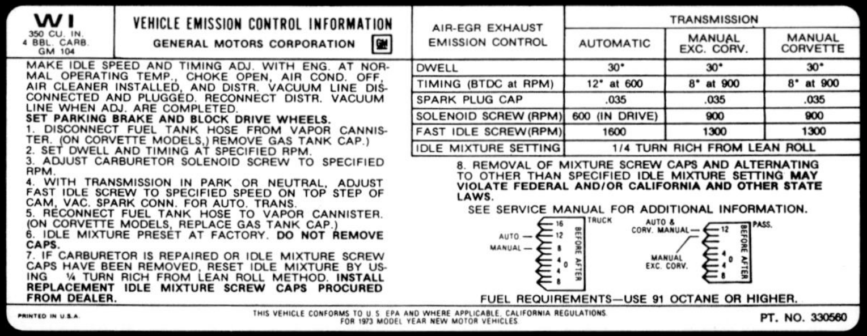

WI
350 CU. IN.
4 BBL. CARB.
GM 104

VEHICLE EMISSION CONTROL INFORMATION
GENERAL MOTORS CORPORATION

MAKE IDLE SPEED AND TIMING ADJ. WITH ENG. AT NORMAL OPERATING TEMP., CHOKE OPEN, AIR COND. OFF, AIR CLEANER INSTALLED, AND DISTR. VACUUM LINE DISCONNECTED AND PLUGGED. RECONNECT DISTR. VACUUM LINE WHEN ADJ. ARE COMPLETED.

SET PARKING BRAKE AND BLOCK DRIVE WHEELS.

1. DISCONNECT FUEL TANK HOSE FROM VAPOR CANNISTER. (ON CORVETTE MODELS,) REMOVE GAS TANK CAP.)
2. SET DWELL AND TIMING AT SPECIFIED RPM.
3. ADJUST CARBURETOR SOLENOID SCREW TO SPECIFIED RPM.
4. WITH TRANSMISSION IN PARK OR NEUTRAL, ADJUST FAST IDLE SCREW TO SPECIFIED SPEED ON TOP STEP OF CAM, VAC. SPARK CONN. FOR AUTO. TRANS.
5. RECONNECT FUEL TANK HOSE TO VAPOR CANNISTER. (ON CORVETTE MODELS, REPLACE GAS TANK CAP.)
6. IDLE MIXTURE PRESET AT FACTORY. **DO NOT REMOVE CAPS.**
7. IF CARBURETOR IS REPAIRED OR IDLE MIXTURE SCREW CAPS HAVE BEEN REMOVED, RESET IDLE MIXTURE BY USING ¼ TURN RICH FROM LEAN ROLL METHOD. **INSTALL REPLACEMENT IDLE MIXTURE SCREW CAPS PROCURED FROM DEALER.**

AIR-EGR EXHAUST EMISSION CONTROL	TRANSMISSION		
	AUTOMATIC	MANUAL EXC. CORV.	MANUAL CORVETTE
DWELL	30°	30°	30°
TIMING (BTDC at RPM)	12° at 600	8° at 900	8° at 900
SPARK PLUG CAP	.035	.035	.035
SOLENOID SCREW (RPM)	600 (IN DRIVE)	900	900
FAST IDLE SCREW(RPM)	1600	1300	1300
IDLE MIXTURE SETTING	1/4 TURN RICH FROM LEAN ROLL		

8. REMOVAL OF MIXTURE SCREW CAPS AND ALTERNATING TO OTHER THAN SPECIFIED IDLE MIXTURE SETTING **MAY VIOLATE FEDERAL AND/OR CALIFORNIA AND OTHER STATE LAWS.**

SEE SERVICE MANUAL FOR ADDITIONAL INFORMATION.

FUEL REQUIREMENTS—USE 91 OCTANE OR HIGHER.

PRINTED IN U.S.A. THIS VEHICLE CONFORMS TO U.S. EPA AND WHERE APPLICABLE, CALIFORNIA REGULATIONS FOR 1973 MODEL YEAR NEW MOTOR VEHICLES. PT. NO. 330560

Emission information labels. Top and top left are 1971, bottom left and top right are 1972, bottom right is 1973. Each label's application is coded at top left of label. Black lettering on white. Shown 60% of actual size.

ZB
350-400 CU. IN.
4 BBL. CARB.
GM 104-4

VEHICLE EMISSION CONTROL INFORMATION

GENERAL MOTORS CORPORATION GM

MAKE IDLE SPEED AND TIMING ADJUSTMENTS WITH ENGINE AT NORMAL OPERATING TEMP., CHOKE OPEN, AIR COND. OFF, AIR CLEANER INSTALLED, AND DISTR. VACUUM LINE DISCONNECTED AND PLUGGED. RECONNECT DISTR. VACUUM LINE WHEN ADJUSTMENTS ARE COMPLETED.
SET PARKING BRAKE AND BLOCK DRIVE WHEELS.

1. DISCONNECT FUEL TANK HOSE FROM VAPOR CANISTER. (ON CORV. MODELS, REM. GAS TANK CAP.)
2. ADJUST CARBURETOR SOLENOID SCREW TO SPECIFIED RPM.
3. SET DWELL AND TIMING AT SPECIFIED RPM. RESET IDLE SPEED IF NECESSARY. SEE SERVICE MANUAL FOR PROCEDURES. IDLE MIXTURE SPECIFICATIONS ARE SHOWN AT RIGHT.
5. REMOVAL OF MIXTURE SCREW CAPS AND/OR ALTERING IDLE MIXTURE TO OTHER THAN SPECIFICATIONS MAY VIOLATE FEDERAL AND OTHER STATE LAWS.
6. CONNECT VACUUM LINE AT DISTRIBUTOR. DISCONNECT AND PLUG VACUUM LINE TO EGR VALVE. WITH TRANSMISSION IN PARK OR NEUTRAL, ADJUST FAST IDLE SCREW TO SPECIFIED SPEED ON TOP STEP OF CAM. UNPLUG AND RECONNECT VACUUM LINE TO EGR VALVE.
7. RECONNECT FUEL TANK TO VAPOR CANISTER. (ON CORVETTE MODELS, REPLACE GAS TANK CAP.)

	TRANSMISSION	
	AUTOMATIC	MANUAL
EXH. EMISSION CO SYSTEM	CCS-EGR	AIR-EGR
DWELL	30°	30°
TIMING (°BTC @ RPM)	8° @ 600	8° @ 900
SOLENOID SCREW (RPM)	600 (DR)	900 (N)
FAST IDLE SCREW (RPM)	1600 (N)	1300 (N)
LEAN DROP IDLE MIX. (RPM)	650-600 (DR)	950-900 (N)
MAX. IDLE CO (% @ RPM)	0.5 @ 600 (DR)	0.5 @ 900 (N)

SEE SERVICE MANUAL FOR ADDITIONAL INFORMATION
FUEL REQUIREMENTS—USE 91 OCTANE OR HIGHER.

PRINTED IN U.S.A. THIS VEHICLE CONFORMS TO U.S.E.P.A. REGULATIONS APPLICABLE TO 1974 MODEL YEAR NEW MOTOR VEHICLES. PT. NO. 346209

ZH
454 CU. IN.
4 BBL. CARB.
GM 105

VEHICLE EMISSION CONTROL INFORMATION

GENERAL MOTORS CORPORATION GM

MAKE IDLE SPEED AND TIMING ADJUSTMENTS WITH ENGINE AT NORMAL OPERATING TEMP., CHOKE OPEN, AIR COND. OFF, AIR CLEANER INSTALLED, AND DISTR. VACUUM LINE DISCONNECTED AND PLUGGED. RECONNECT DISTR. VACUUM LINE WHEN ADJUSTMENTS ARE COMPLETED.
SET PARKING BRAKE AND BLOCK DRIVE WHEELS.

1. DISCONNECT FUEL TANK HOSE FROM VAPOR CANISTER. (ON CORV. MODELS, REM. GAS TANK CAP.)
2. ADJUST CARBURETOR SOLENOID SCREW TO SPECIFIED RPM.
3. SET DWELL AND TIMING AT SPECIFIED RPM. RESET IDLE SPEED IF NECESSARY. SEE SERVICE MANUAL FOR PROCEDURES. IDLE MIXTURE SPECIFICATIONS ARE SHOWN AT RIGHT.
5. REMOVAL OF MIXTURE SCREW CAPS AND/OR ALTERING IDLE MIXTURE TO OTHER THAN SPECIFICATIONS MAY VIOLATE FEDERAL AND OTHER STATE LAWS.
6. CONNECT VACUUM LINE AT DISTRIBUTOR. DISCONNECT AND PLUG VACUUM LINE TO EGR VALVE. WITH TRANSMISSION IN PARK OR NEUTRAL, ADJUST FAST IDLE SCREW TO SPECIFIED SPEED ON TOP STEP OF CAM. UNPLUG AND RECONNECT VACUUM LINE TO EGR VALVE.
7. RECONNECT FUEL TANK TO VAPOR CANISTER. (ON CORVETTE MODELS, REPLACE GAS TANK CAP.)

AIR-EGR EXHAUST EMISSION CONTROL	TRANSMISSION	
	AUTOMATIC	MANUAL
DWELL	30°	30°
TIMING (°BTC @ RPM)	10° @ 600	10° @ 800
SOLENOID SCREW (RPM)	600 (DR)	800 (N)
FAST IDLE SCREW (RPM)	1600 (N)	1500 (N)
LEAN DROP IDLE MIX. (RPM)	630-600 (DR)	850-800 (N)
MAX. IDLE CO (% @ RPM)	0.5 @ 600 (DR)	0.5 @ 800 (N)

SEE SERVICE MANUAL FOR ADDITIONAL INFORMATION
FUEL REQUIREMENTS—USE 91 OCTANE OR HIGHER.

PRINTED IN U.S.A. THIS VEHICLE CONFORMS TO U.S.E.P.A. REGULATIONS APPLICABLE TO 1974 MODEL YEAR NEW MOTOR VEHICLES. PT. NO. 346213

ZF
350 CU. IN.
HI PERF.
GM 104-4

VEHICLE EMISSION CONTROL INFORMATION

GENERAL MOTORS CORPORATION GM

MAKE IDLE SPEED AND TIMING ADJUSTMENTS WITH ENGINE AT NORMAL OPERATING TEMP., CHOKE OPEN, AIR COND. OFF, AIR CLEANER INSTALLED, AND DISTR. VACUUM LINE DISCONNECTED AND PLUGGED. RECONNECT DISTR. VACUUM LINE WHEN ADJUSTMENTS ARE COMPLETED.
SET PARKING BRAKE AND BLOCK DRIVE WHEELS.

1. DISCONNECT FUEL TANK HOSE FROM VAPOR CANISTER. (ON CORVETTE MODELS, REMOVE GAS TANK CAP.)
2. ADJUST CARBURETOR SOLENOID SCREW TO SPECIFIED RPM.
3. SET DWELL AND TIMING AT SPECIFIED RPM. RESET IDLE SPEED IF NECESSARY.
4. IDLE MIXTURE HAS BEEN SET AT THE FACTORY. IF IDLE MIXTURE ADJUSTMENT IS NECESSARY, SEE SERVICE MANUAL FOR PROCEDURES. IDLE MIXTURE SPECIFICATIONS ARE SHOWN AT RIGHT.
5. REMOVAL OF MIXTURE SCREW CAPS AND/OR ALTERING IDLE MIXTURE TO OTHER THAN SPECIFICATIONS MAY VIOLATE FEDERAL AND/OR CALIFORNIA AND OTHER STATE LAWS.
6. CONNECT VACUUM LINE AT DISTRIBUTOR. DISCONNECT AND PLUG VACUUM LINE TO EGR VALVE. WITH TRANSMISSION IN PARK OR NEUTRAL, ADJUST FAST IDLE SCREW TO SPECIFIED SPEED ON TOP STEP OF CAM. UNPLUG AND RECONNECT VACUUM LINE TO EGR VALVE.
7. RECONNECT FUEL TANK HOSE TO VAPOR CANISTER. (ON CORVETTE MODELS, REPLACE GAS TANK CAP.)

AIR-EGR EXHAUST EMISSION CONTROL	TRANSMISSION	
	AUTOMATIC	MANUAL
DWELL	30°	30°
TIMING (°BTC @ RPM)	8° @ 700	8° @ 900
SOLENOID SCREW (RPM)	700 (DR)	900 (N)
FAST IDLE SCREW (RPM)	1600 (N)	1300 (N)
LEAN DROP IDLE MIXTURE (RPM)	730-700 (DR)	950-900 (N)
MAX. IDLE CO (% @ RPM)	0.5 @ 700 (DR)	0.5 @ 900 (N)

SEE SERVICE MANUAL FOR ADDITIONAL INFORMATION
FUEL REQUIREMENTS—USE 91 OCTANE OR HIGHER.

PRINTED IN U.S.A. THIS VEHICLE CONFORMS TO U.S. E.P.A. AND, WHERE APPLICABLE, CALIFORNIA REGULATIONS FOR 1974 MODEL YEAR NEW MOTOR VEHICLES. PT. NO. 346212

Emission information labels. All shown are 1974 model. Top is for base engine, middle for "454" and bottom for L-82 (incl California). Black lettering on white. Shown 85% of actual size.

AS — 350-400 CU. IN. 4 BBL. CARB. GM 10K43A

VEHICLE EMISSION CONTROL INFORMATION
GENERAL MOTORS CORPORATION

AIR-EGR-EFE-OC EXHAUST EMISSION CONTROL	TRANSMISSION: AUTOMATIC CORVETTE	AUTOMATIC EXC. CORVETTE	MANUAL
TIMING (°BTC @ RPM)	6° @ 600	8° @ 600	6° @ 800
SPARK PLUG GAP (IN.)	0.060	0.060	0.060
CURB IDLE SPEED (RPM)	600 (DR)	600 (DR)	800(N)
FAST IDLE SPEED (RPM)	1600 (N)	1600 (N)	1600(N)

MAKE ALL ADJUSTMENTS WITH ENGINE AT NORMAL OPERATING TEMPERATURE, CHOKE FULL OPEN, AIR CLEANER INSTALLED, AND AIR CONDITIONING OFF.

SET PARKING BRAKE AND BLOCK DRIVE WHEELS.

1. DISCONNECT AND PLUG VACUUM HOSE AT DISTRIBUTOR. SET IGNITION TIMING AT SPECIFIED RPM. UNPLUG AND RECONNECT VACUUM HOSE AT DISTRIBUTOR.
2. ADJUST CARBURETOR SPEED SCREW TO OBTAIN SPECIFIED CURB IDLE RPM.
3. DISCONNECT AND PLUG VACUUM HOSE AT EGR VALVE. WITH TRANSMISSION IN PARK OR NEUTRAL, ADJUST IDLE SCREW TO SPECIFIED SPEED ON HIGH STEP OF CAM. UNPLUG AND RECONNECT VACUUM HOSE TO EGR VALVE.

NOTE: IDLE MIXTURE SCREWS ARE PRESET AND CAPPED AT FACTORY — **DO NOT BREAK CAPS**—ADJUSTMENT DURING TUNE UP IS **NOT** RECOMMENDED.

FOP MAJOR REPAIR, ADJUSTING MIXTURE SETTING BY OTHER THAN APPROVED SERVICE MANUAL PROCEDURE MAY VIOLATE FEDERAL AND/OR CALIFORNIA OR OTHER STATE LAWS.

SEE SERVICE MANUAL FOR ADDITIONAL INFORMATION.

PRINTED IN U.S.A. THIS VEHICLE CONFORMS TO U.S.E.P.A. REGULATIONS APPLICABLE TO 1975 MODEL YEAR NEW MOTOR VEHICLES, WITH THE EXCEPTION OF THE CARBON MONOXIDE STANDARD FOR CALIFORNIA. PT. NO. 360420

XZ — 350-400 CU. IN. 4 BBL. CARB. 11K4

VEHICLE EMISSION CONTROL INFORMATION
GENERAL MOTORS CORPORATION

CATALYST AIR-EGR-EFE EXHAUST EMISSION CONTROL

	TRANSMISSION: AUTOMATIC 350 CU. IN.	AUTOMATIC 400 CU. IN.	MANUAL 350 CU. IN.
TIMING (°BTC @ RPM)	6° @ 600	8° @ 600	6° @ 900
SPARK PLUG GAP (IN.)	0.045	0.045	0.045
CURB IDLE SPEED (RPM)	600 (DR)	600 (DR)	900 (N)
FAST IDLE SPEED (RPM)	1600(P)OR(N)	1600 (P)OR(N)	1600 (N)

MAKE ALL ADJUSTMENTS WITH ENGINE AT NORMAL OPERATING TEMPERATURE, CHOKE FULL OPEN, AIR CLEANER INSTALLED, AND AIR CONDITIONING OFF.

SET PARKING BRAKE AND BLOCK DRIVE WHEELS.

1. DISCONNECT AND PLUG VACUUM HOSE AT DISTRIBUTOR. SET IGNITION TIMING AT SPECIFIED RPM. UNPLUG AND RECONNECT VACUUM HOSE AT DISTRIBUTOR.
2. ADJUST CARBURETOR SPEED SCREW TO OBTAIN SPECIFIED CURB IDLE RPM.
3. DISCONNECT AND PLUG VACUUM HOSE AT EGR VALVE. WITH TRANSMISSION IN PARK OR NEUTRAL, ADJUST FAST IDLE SCREW TO SPECIFIED SPEED ON HIGH STEP OF CAM. UNPLUG AND RECONNECT VACUUM HOSE TO EGR VALVE.

NOTE: IDLE MIXTURE SCREWS ARE PRESET AND CAPPED AT FACTORY — DO NOT BREAK CAPS — ADJUSTMENT DURING TUNE UP IS NOT RECOMMENDED.

FOR MAJOR REPAIR, ADJUSTING MIXTURE SETTING BY OTHER THAN APPROVED SERVICE MANUAL PROCEDURE MAY VIOLATE FEDERAL AND/OR CALIFORNIA OR OTHER STATE LAWS.

SEE SERVICE MANUAL FOR ADDITIONAL INFORMATION.

PRINTED IN U.S.A. THIS VEHICLE CONFORMS TO U.S. E.P.A., AND WHERE APPLICABLE CALIFORNIA, REGULATIONS APPLICABLE TO 1976 MODEL YEAR NEW MOTOR VEHICLES. PT. NO. 458580

AZ — 350 CU. IN. 4 BBL. CARB 710J4S

VEHICLE EMISSION CONTROL INFORMATION
GENERAL MOTORS CORPORATION

CATALYST AIR-EGR-EFE LOW ALTITUDE CERTIFICATION

	TRANSMISSION: AUTOMATIC
TIMING (° BTC @ RPM)	8° @ 500
SPARK PLUG GAP (IN.)	0.045
CURB IDLE SPEED (RPM)	500 (DR)
FAST IDLE SPEED (RPM)	1600 (P) OR (N)
SOLENOID ASM. ADJUSTMENT WITH AIR COND. (RPM)	650 (DR)

MAKE ALL ADJUSTMENTS WITH ENGINE AT NORMAL OPERATING TEMPERATURE, CHOKE FULL OPEN, AIR CLEANER INSTALLED, AND AIR CONDITIONING OFF, EXCEPT WHERE NOTED.

SET PARKING BRAKE AND BLOCK DRIVE WHEELS.

1. DISCONNECT AND PLUG VACUUM HOSE AT DISTRIBUTOR. SET IGNITION TIMING AT SPECIFIED RPM. UNPLUG AND RECONNECT VACUUM HOSE AT DISTRIBUTOR.
2. ADJUST CARBURETOR SPEED SCREW TO OBTAIN SPECIFIED CURB IDLE SPEED.
3. WITH AIR COND.: DISCONNECT ELECTRICAL LEAD FROM AIR COND. COMPRESSOR. WITH AIR COND. SWITCH ON AND SOLENOID FULLY EXTENDED, ADJUST SOLENOID SCREW TO SPECIFIED RPM. RECONNECT COMPRESSOR LEAD. TURN AIR COND. SWITCH OFF.
4. DISCONNECT AND PLUG VACUUM HOSE AT EGR VALVE. WITH TRANSMISSION IN PARK OR NEUTRAL, ADJUST FAST IDLE SCREW TO SPECIFIED SPEED ON HIGH STEP OF CAM. UNPLUG AND RECONNECT VACUUM HOSE TO EGR VALVE.

NOTE: IDLE MIXTURE SCREWS ARE PRESET AND CAPPED AT FACTORY — DO NOT BREAK CAPS — ADJUSTMENT DURING TUNE UP IS NOT RECOMMENDED.

FOR MAJOR REPAIR, ADJUSTING MIXTURE SETTING BY OTHER THAN APPROVED SERVICE MANUAL PROCEDURE MAY VIOLATE FEDERAL AND/OR CALIFORNIA OR OTHER STATE LAWS.

SEE SERVICE MANUAL AND MAINTENANCE SCHEDULE I FOR ADDITIONAL INFORMATION.

PRINTED IN U.S.A. THIS VEHICLE CONFORMS TO U.S. E.P.A., AND WHERE APPLICABLE CALIFORNIA, REGULATIONS APPLICABLE TO 1977 MODEL YEAR NEW MOTOR VEHICLES. PT. NO. 460126

XY — 350 CU. IN. HI PERF. 4 BBL. 10J4

VEHICLE EMISSION CONTROL INFORMATION
GENERAL MOTORS CORPORATION

CATALYST AIR-EGR-EFE EXHAUST EMISSION CONTROL

	TRANSMISSION: AUTOMATIC	MANUAL
TIMING (°BTC @ RPM)	12° @ 700	12° @ 1000
SPARK PLUG GAP (IN.)	0.045	0.045
SOLENOID ASM. ADJUSTMENT AUTO. TRANS. WITH AIR COND.	700 (DR)	—
CURB IDLE SPEED (RPM)	700(DR)	1000 (N)
FAST IDLE SPEED (RPM)	1600 (N) OR (P)	1600(N)

MAKE ALL ADJUSTMENTS WITH ENGINE AT NORMAL OPERATING TEMPERATURE, CHOKE FULL OPEN, AIR CLEANER INSTALLED, AND AIR CONDITIONING OFF, EXCEPT WHERE NOTED.

SET PARKING BRAKE AND BLOCK DRIVE WHEELS.

1. DISCONNECT AND PLUG VACUUM HOSE AT DISTRIBUTOR. SET IGNITION TIMING AT SPECIFIED RPM. UNPLUG AND RECONNECT VACUUM HOSE AT DISTRIBUTOR.
2. ADJUST CARBURETOR SPEED SCREW TO OBTAIN SPECIFIED CURB IDLE RPM. WITH AIR CONDITIONING OFF IF SO EQUIPPED.
3. ON AUTOMATICS WITH AIR COND., WITH AIR COND. ON AND SOLENOID FULLY EXTENDED ADJUST SOLENOID SCREW TO SPECIFIED RPM.
4. DISCONNECT AND PLUG VACUUM HOSE AT EGR VALVE. WITH TRANSMISSION IN PARK OR NEUTRAL, ADJUST FAST IDLE SCREW TO SPECIFIED SPEED ON HIGH STEP OF CAM. UNPLUG AND RECONNECT VACUUM HOSE TO EGR VALVE.

NOTE: IDLE MIXTURE SCREWS ARE PRESET AND CAPPED AT FACTORY — DO NOT BREAK CAPS — ADJUSTMENT DURING TUNE UP IS NOT RECOMMENDED.

FOR MAJOR REPAIR, ADJUSTING MIXTURE SETTING BY OTHER THAN APPROVED SERVICE MANUAL PROCEDURE MAY VIOLATE FEDERAL AND/OR CALIFORNIA OR OTHER STATE LAWS.

SEE SERVICE MANUAL FOR ADDITIONAL INFORMATION

PRINTED IN U.S.A. THIS VEHICLE CONFORMS TO U.S. EPA REGULATIONS APPLICABLE TO 1976 MODEL YEAR NEW MOTOR VEHICLES. WITH THE EXCEPTION OF THE CARBON MONOXIDE STANDARD FOR CALIFORNIA. PT. NO. 458579

CA — 350 CU. IN. HI PERF. 4 BBL. 710J4S

VEHICLE EMISSION CONTROL INFORMATION
GENERAL MOTORS CORPORATION

CATALYST AIR-EGR-EFE LOW ALTITUDE CERTIFICATION

	TRANSMISSION: AUTOMATIC	MANUAL
TIMING (° BTC @ RPM)	12° @ 700	12° @ 800
SPARK PLUG GAP (IN.)	0.045	0.045
SOLENOID ASM. ADJUSTMENT WITH AIR COND. (RPM)	800 (DR)	—
CURB IDLE SPEED (RPM)	700 (DR)	800 (N)
FAST IDLE SPEED (RPM)	1600 (P) OR (N)	1300 (N)

MAKE ALL ADJUSTMENTS WITH ENGINE AT NORMAL OPERATING TEMPERATURE, CHOKE FULL OPEN, AIR CLEANER INSTALLED, AND AIR CONDITIONING OFF, EXCEPT WHERE NOTED.

SET PARKING BRAKE AND BLOCK DRIVE WHEELS.

1. DISCONNECT AND PLUG VACUUM HOSE AT DISTRIBUTOR. SET IGNITION TIMING AT SPECIFIED RPM. UNPLUG AND RECONNECT VACUUM HOSE AT DISTRIBUTOR.
2. ADJUST CARBURETOR SPEED SCREW TO OBTAIN SPECIFIED CURB IDLE SPEED.
3. ON AUTOMATICS WITH AIR COND.: DISCONNECT ELECTRICAL LEAD FROM AIR COND. COMPRESSOR. WITH AIR COND. SWITCH ON AND SOLENOID FULLY EXTENDED, ADJUST SOLENOID SCREW TO SPECIFIED RPM. RECONNECT COMPRESSOR LEAD. TURN AIR COND. SWITCH OFF.
4. DISCONNECT AND PLUG VACUUM HOSE AT EGR VALVE. WITH TRANSMISSION IN PARK OR NEUTRAL, ADJUST FAST IDLE SCREW TO SPECIFIED SPEED ON HIGH STEP OF CAM. UNPLUG AND RECONNECT VACUUM HOSE TO EGR VALVE.

NOTE: IDLE MIXTURE SCREWS ARE PRESET AND CAPPED AT FACTORY — DO NOT BREAK CAPS — ADJUSTMENT DURING TUNE UP IS NOT RECOMMENDED.

FOR MAJOR REPAIR, ADJUSTING MIXTURE SETTING BY OTHER THAN APPROVED SERVICE MANUAL PROCEDURE MAY VIOLATE FEDERAL AND/OR CALIFORNIA OR OTHER STATE LAWS.

SEE SERVICE MANUAL AND MAINTENANCE SCHEDULE I FOR ADDITIONAL INFORMATION.

PRINTED IN U.S.A. THIS VEHICLE CONFORMS TO U.S. E.P.A. REGULATIONS APPLICABLE TO 1977 MODEL YEAR NEW MOTOR VEHICLES. PT. NO. 460127

CB — 350 CU. IN. 4 BBL. CARB. 710J4S

VEHICLE EMISSION CONTROL INFORMATION
GENERAL MOTORS CORPORATION

CATALYST AIR-EGR-EFE HIGH ALTITUDE CERTIFICATION

	TRANSMISSION: AUTOMATIC
TIMING (° BTC @ RPM)	8° @ 600
SPARK PLUG GAP (IN.)	0.045
CURB IDLE SPEED (RPM)	600 (DR)
FAST IDLE SPEED (RPM)	1600 (P) OR (N)
SOLENOID ASM. ADJUSTMENT WITH AIR COND. (RPM)	650 (DR)

MAKE ALL ADJUSTMENTS WITH ENGINE AT NORMAL OPERATING TEMPERATURE, CHOKE FULL OPEN, AIR CLEANER INSTALLED, AND AIR CONDITIONING OFF, EXCEPT WHERE NOTED.

SET PARKING BRAKE AND BLOCK DRIVE WHEELS.

1. DISCONNECT AND PLUG VACUUM HOSE AT DISTRIBUTOR. SET IGNITION TIMING AT SPECIFIED RPM. UNPLUG AND RECONNECT VACUUM HOSE AT DISTRIBUTOR.
2. ADJUST CARBURETOR SPEED SCREW TO OBTAIN SPECIFIED CURB IDLE SPEED.
3. WITH AIR COND.: DISCONNECT ELECTRICAL LEAD FROM AIR COND. COMPRESSOR. WITH AIR COND. SWITCH ON AND SOLENOID FULLY EXTENDED, ADJUST SOLENOID SCREW TO SPECIFIED RPM. RECONNECT COMPRESSOR LEAD. TURN AIR COND. SWITCH OFF.
4. DISCONNECT AND PLUG VACUUM HOSE AT EGR VALVE. WITH TRANSMISSION IN PARK OR NEUTRAL, ADJUST FAST IDLE SCREW TO SPECIFIED SPEED ON HIGH STEP OF CAM. UNPLUG AND RECONNECT VACUUM HOSE TO EGR VALVE.

NOTE: IDLE MIXTURE SCREWS ARE PRESET AND CAPPED AT FACTORY — DO NOT BREAK CAPS — ADJUSTMENT DURING TUNE UP IS NOT RECOMMENDED.

FOR MAJOR REPAIR, ADJUSTING MIXTURE SETTING BY OTHER THAN APPROVED SERVICE MANUAL PROCEDURE MAY VIOLATE FEDERAL AND/OR CALIFORNIA OR OTHER STATE LAWS.

SEE SERVICE MANUAL AND MAINTENANCE SCHEDULE I FOR ADDITIONAL INFORMATION.

PRINTED IN U.S.A. THIS VEHICLE CONFORMS TO U.S. E.P.A. REGULATIONS APPLICABLE TO 1977 MODEL YEAR NEW MOTOR VEHICLES. PT. NO. 460128

AY — 350 CU. IN. 4 BBL. CARB. 710J4

VEHICLE EMISSION CONTROL INFORMATION
GENERAL MOTORS CORPORATION

CATALYST EGR-EFE LOW ALTITUDE CERTIFICATION

	TRANSMISSION: AUTOMATIC	MANUAL
TIMING (° BTC @ RPM)	8° @ 500	8° @ 700
SPARK PLUG GAP (IN.)	0.045	0.045
SOLENOID ASM. ADJUSTMENT WITH AIR COND. (RPM)	650 (DR)	—
CURB IDLE SPEED (RPM)	500 (DR)	700 (N)
FAST IDLE SPEED (RPM)	1600 (P) OR (N)	1300 (N)

MAKE ALL ADJUSTMENTS WITH ENGINE AT NORMAL OPERATING TEMPERATURE, CHOKE FULL OPEN, AIR CLEANER INSTALLED, AND AIR CONDITIONING OFF, EXCEPT WHERE NOTED.

SET PARKING BRAKE AND BLOCK DRIVE WHEELS.

1. DISCONNECT AND PLUG VACUUM HOSE AT DISTRIBUTOR. SET IGNITION TIMING AT SPECIFIED RPM. UNPLUG AND RECONNECT VACUUM HOSE AT DISTRIBUTOR.
2. ADJUST CARBURETOR SPEED SCREW TO OBTAIN SPECIFIED CURB IDLE SPEED.
3. ON AUTOMATICS WITH AIR COND.: DISCONNECT ELECTRICAL LEAD FROM AIR COND. COMPRESSOR. WITH AIR COND. SWITCH ON AND SOLENOID FULLY EXTENDED, ADJUST SOLENOID SCREW TO SPECIFIED RPM. RECONNECT COMPRESSOR LEAD. TURN AIR COND. SWITCH OFF.
4. DISCONNECT AND PLUG VACUUM HOSE AT EGR VALVE. WITH TRANSMISSION IN PARK OR NEUTRAL, ADJUST FAST IDLE SCREW TO SPECIFIED SPEED ON HIGH STEP OF CAM. UNPLUG AND RECONNECT VACUUM HOSE TO EGR VALVE.

NOTE: IDLE MIXTURE SCREWS ARE PRESET AND CAPPED AT FACTORY — DO NOT BREAK CAPS — ADJUSTMENT DURING TUNE UP IS NOT RECOMMENDED.

FOR MAJOR REPAIR, ADJUSTING MIXTURE SETTING BY OTHER THAN APPROVED SERVICE MANUAL PROCEDURE MAY VIOLATE FEDERAL AND/OR CALIFORNIA OR OTHER STATE LAWS.

SEE SERVICE MANUAL AND MAINTENANCE SCHEDULE I FOR ADDITIONAL INFORMATION.

PRINTED IN U.S.A. THIS VEHICLE CONFORMS TO U.S. E.P.A. REGULATIONS APPLICABLE TO 1977 MODEL YEAR NEW MOTOR VEHICLES. PT. NO. 460125

Emission information labels. Top is 1975, top left two are 1976, remainder are 1977. Each label's application is coded at top left of label. Black lettering on white. Shown 65% of actual size.

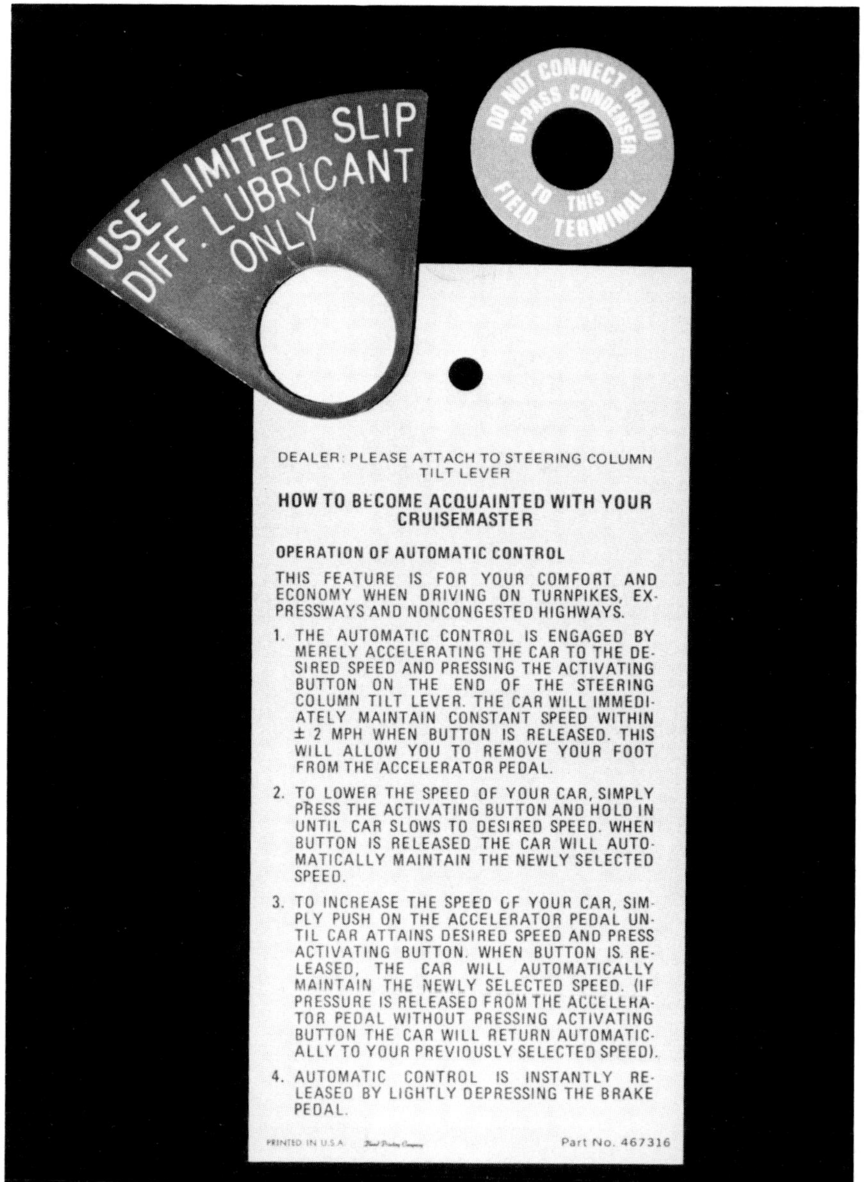

Special labels. Top left is plastic limited slip tag, top right is generator field terminal tag, large label is for '77 models with cruise control. Top two are white lettering on orange, bottom is black lettering on pale green. Shown 70% of actual size.

Odd Balls

There are a number of labels which deserve mentioning, but which do not fall into large generalized groups.

A red and white caution label appeared on Corvettes from 1957 through 1972 equipped with positraction. The purpose of the label was to warn that with limited slip differential, "a rear wheel may drive if in contact with ground even though opposite wheel is raised. Do not run engine with vehicle on jack unless transmission is in neutral or park." Since the message was geared to times when the car was jacked, the label was always put where it would be likely seen if the jack was reached for. On '57 through '62 Corvettes, this meant on the spare tire cover. On the later models, it was placed inside the lid of the behind-seat compartment. One style of caution label was probably used for 1957 and 1958 and another style was used between 1959 and 1971. A similar label with subtle wording changes appeared in 1972.

Though not exactly a label, a red plastic tag with white indented lettering was attached at the filler plug of positraction units. This started with the '65 and continues through current models. The replacement tag says, "USE LIMITED SLIP DIFF. LUBRICANT ONLY." The original said "USE POSITRACTION DIFF. LUBRICANT ONLY."

Another label of interest is a round cardboard tag which spun freely about the field pole of the generator of Corvettes built from 1953 through 1962. It cautioned against connecting the radio by-pass condenser to the field terminal. Use of the tag was terminated in 1963 by the switch to alternators.

1953, 1954, and 1955 six-cylinder Corvettes had a glass solvent jar for the windshield washer to which was attached a label which read, "Automatic windshield washer—GM accessories—in freezing weather add GM solvent—fill with water to ¾ level."

1954 and 1955 Corvettes had a large instruction sheet glued to the inside of the top compartment lid on the driver's side for raising and lowering the folding top. If ever a top needed such instructions, this was it. The label was complete with nine illustrations and twelve raising instructions. Chevrolet deleted the use of the sheet coinciding with the introduction of the '56 model Corvette and its much-easier-to-operate top.

All 1955, 1956, and hydraulic lifter engines of '58 through '61 had a beautiful little black on metallic gold decal on the oil filler cap. The cap was the breathing type with a mesh insert, and the decal advised washing in kerosene and re-oiling every 3000 miles or "oftener" in severe conditions.

Two labels appeared on or near the steering columns of Corvettes over the years. In 1969, the year the ignition switch moved from the dash to the steering column, a black label with white lettering was placed on the column and advised "THIS IS A ROTATING INTERLOCK. DO NOT MANIPULATE. DAMAGE MAY RESULT."

CAUTION

THIS VEHICLE EQUIPPED WITH LIMITED SLIP DIFFERENTIAL. REAR WHEEL MAY DRIVE IF IN CONTACT WITH GROUND EVEN THOUGH OPPOSITE WHEEL IS RAISED. DO NOT RUN ENGINE WITH VEHICLE ON JACK UNLESS TRANSMISSION IS IN NEUTRAL OR PARK. SEE OWNER'S MANUAL.

PRINTED IN U. S. A. 7-22-58 PART NO. 3745926

Positraction caution label. This appeared on '57 through '72 Corvettes. Orange lettering on white. Shown 100% of actual size.

Positraction caution label. This appeared first on '72 model Corvettes. Orange lettering on white. Shown 100% of actual size.

INSTRUCTIONS FOR RAISING AND LOWERING FOLDING TOP

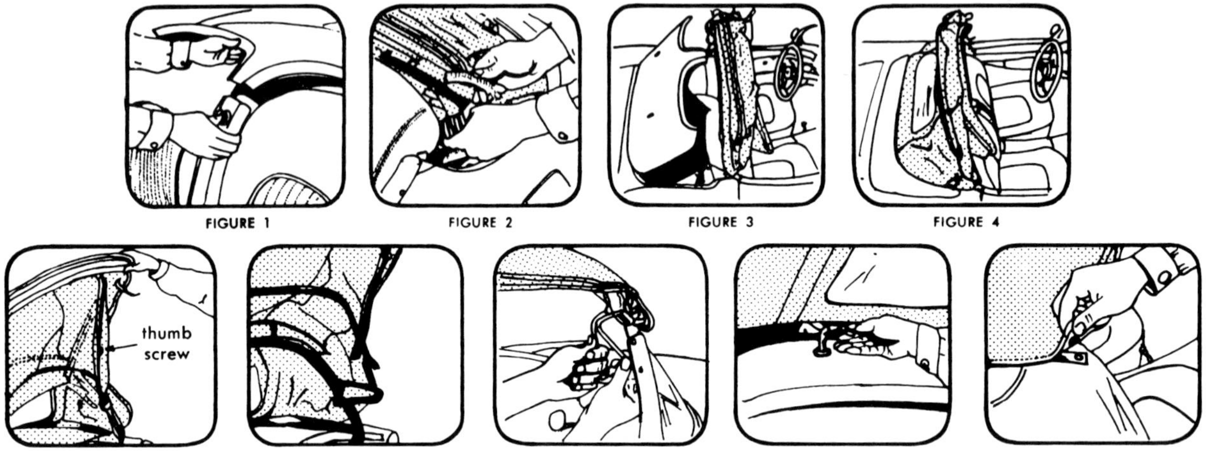

FIGURE 1 FIGURE 2 FIGURE 3 FIGURE 4

FIGURE 5 FIGURE 6 FIGURE 7 FIGURE 8 FIGURE 9

HOW TO RAISE THE FOLDING TOP

1. Push button on the panel between the seats to release the top compartment cover. Figure 1.
2. Insert fingers under the cover and raise it to the open position. Figure 1.
3. Loosen the straps at each end of the top and allow them to lie flat on the bottom of the compartment. Figure 2.
4. Check the cloth top material at each side to be sure it will be out of the way when the top is lifted out of the compartment.
5. With the top material in the clear, slide one hand under the top assembly and lift the complete top out of the compartment. Figure 3.
6. Hold the still folded top all the way forward and close the compartment cover.
7. Allow the rear bow to unfold and rest on the compartment cover. Do not latch the ratchet levers. Figure 4.
8. Lift the header rail and unfold the side irons, locking with the thumb screws. Figure 5.
9. Pull the header forward and rest it on the windshield frame. Figure 6.
10. Insert the header clamps into the holes in the windshield side frames and lock. Figure 7.
11. Hold the rear bow catches in the released position and insert the ratchet levers in the sockets in the compartment cover. Push down tightly. Figure 8.
12. Snap the fastner buttons located just back of the door on each side of the car. Figure 9.

HOW TO LOWER THE FOLDING TOP

Reverse the procedure being careful to pull the top material from between the links as the top is folded.

Arrange the top material in the well to keep the side iron knobs off the plastic backlight.

Bring the hold down straps over the header rail only — **NOT** around the entire top unit. Tighten the straps to protect top from chafing against the compartment cover.

Folding top instructions. Used for 1954 and 1955 Corvettes. Black lettering on white. Shown 70% of actual size.

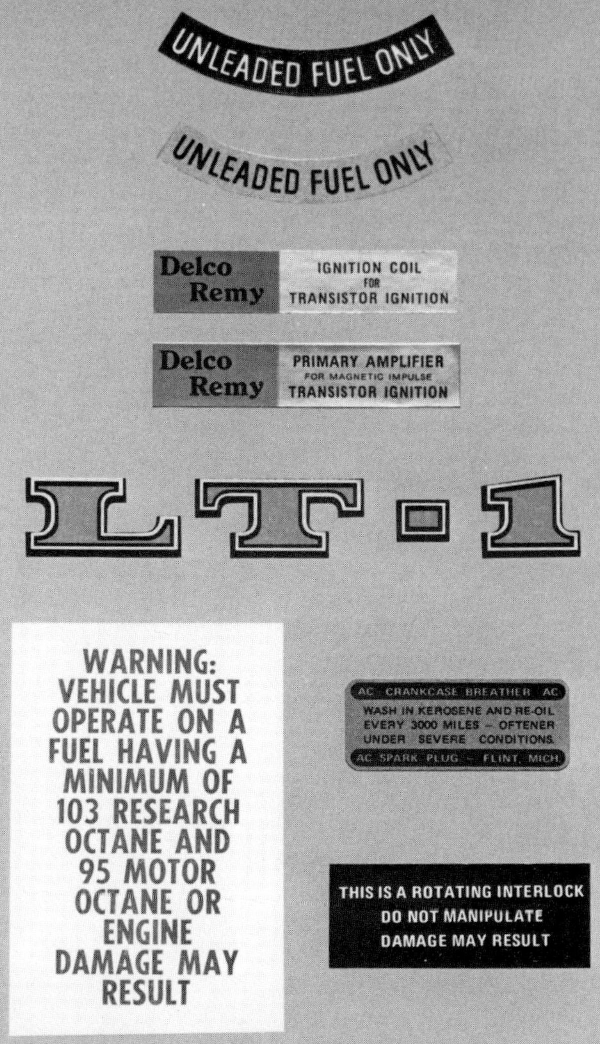

Assorted labels. See text for applications. Top two are white on clear and black on clear. "Delco Remy" are orange and black on silver. "LT-1" is black on clear. "Warning" is red on white. Breather instruction is black on metallic gold. Interlock is white on black. Shown 55% of actual size.

The second steering column label was a dealer-installed tag which was hung from the tilt-wheel lever of Corvettes equipped with cruise control. This was a green tag with black printing and contained the expected instructions. It was used only for the 1977 model, the first Corvette to have cruise control available.

The transistor ignition system available (mandatory with the 396, 425hp/427, 435hp/427, L-88, LT-1, LS-6 and LS-7 engines) in Corvettes was identified from 1964 through 1972 with two foil labels. Each was orange and silver with black lettering. One read, "Delco Remy IGNITION COIL FOR TRANSISTOR IGNITION." It was placed on the coil. The second read, "Delco Remy PRIMARY AMPLIFIER FOR MAGNETIC IMPULSE TRANSITOR IGNITION." It was placed on the amplifier.

If a label should get an award for scarcity, surely it would be the fuel warning label for L-88 equipped Corvettes. This label stated, "WARNING: VEHICLE MUST OPERATE ON A FUEL HAVING A MINIMUM OF 103 RESEARCH OCTANE AND 95 MOTOR OCTANE OR ENGINE DAMAGE MAY RESULT." With a twelve and one-half to one compression ratio, it's no wonder these engines needed the best fuel around. The warning label was nothing exotic, just red printing on white paper. It was placed on the center console for easy spotting. There were twenty L-88 engine Corvettes built in 1967, eighty in 1968, and 116 in 1969, so the total is a mere 216 cars. . . and labels.

The LT-1 engine option available from 1970 through 1972 wasn't as rare as the L-88, but it was surely a favorite. It was treated to a special hood decal consisting of stylized letters in outline. Each hood of an LT-1 Corvette received two sets of letters, one set on each side of the hood bulge.

In 1975, the catalytic converter became a Corvette way of life, and burning unleaded fuel became a must. The magic materials in converters don't get along well at all with lead, and using leaded gasoline renders a converter useless after a tank or two. Owners were warned about the fuel requirements in their owner's manuals and on their fuel gauges. Gas tank filler pipes were made smaller to accept only the narrow unleaded pump snouts. And as a final touch, an "UNLEADED FUEL ONLY" sticker was placed on the filler cap cover starting with the '75. There was a white lettered style for dark body colors, and a black lettered style for light body cars.

★ ★ ★

Well, there you have it. Probably everything you ever wanted to know about Corvette labels. But if you do want to know more, or if you want to purchase virtually any of the labels discussed in this presentation, the man to contact is Murrell F. Dobbins. Reach him at 624 Kelly Lane, Glenside, Pennsylvania. 19038

1980 Corvette

224 As Dave McLellan, Chief Engineer for the Corvette, puts it, "The fuel economy issue figured strongly in the thinking behind the 1980 Corvette." Fortunately for Corvette enthusiasts, the drive for economy hasn't been at the expense of performance. On the contrary, since McLellan believes most improvements in Corvette fuel economy come through weight reduction and better aerodynamics, the 1980 Corvette is an improved model from practically any viewpoint.

The issue of fuel economy was obviously on the minds of McLellan and his staff before the 1979 oil crunch brought it back to the minds of everyone else. The EPA ratings, the CAFE federal standards, and the "gas guzzler" tax on new cars bear review so that their individual and collective influence on the planning and development of the 1980 model Corvette can be understood.

When the Environmental Protection Agency started rating all new cars for fuel economy, a standard laboratory-based test was developed. Actually, the test itself is a spinoff of a procedure developed a decade ago in California to measure emissions. The car being tested doesn't actually move, but its wheels turn a drum linked to sophisticated equipment that simulates actual driving conditions. There is a city and highway "loop" test, each with carefully calculated acceleration, deceleration, and stopping modes.

Auto companies made extensive use of the city and highway EPA mileage ratings in competitive advertising. But time and experience proved that the ratings weren't accurate. Though ads were often cautioned with "Your actual mileage may vary . . .", motorists assumed the estimates could be attained if they drove reasonably and kept the cars in top operating condition. In practice, they found that the highway mileage figure was simply unattainable. Likewise, the city estimates couldn't be reached in all-city driving, though that number did represent a fairly good actual average for combined city and highway driving.

The EPA came to the same conclusion and asked the auto companies to downplay the highway estimates and emphasize the city number. To be even safer, the EPA said the city number should be considered as an estimate only to be compared to other cars. Thus, if a buyer were looking at two

GOODYEAR
EAGLE GT
GOODYEAR

models, one rated at 20 mpg for comparative purposes, and the other at 25 mpg, he should ignore the numbers in regard to actual mileage, but assume that the second model would genuinely get 25% better mileage than the first.

If this is starting to get a bit confusing, hold on. The worst is still coming. Why, for instance, didn't the EPA just change its testing technique when it discovered that it wasn't accurate in actual conditions? Because it is those original EPA estimates on which the maze of legislation concerning fuel standards to be met by auto corporations are based. Not wishing to add more confusion to an already confusing situation, EPA had little choice but to stay with its testing techniques.

Now to the matter of federal mileage requirements and the Corvette. As of 1979, there are two bits of legislation affecting the Corvette. The first is the CAFE (Corporate Average Fuel Economy) standard. The second is the so called "gas guzzler" tax.

The CAFE standard is based on the average of all cars sold by a corporation, so the Corvette doesn't have a direct problem. But there's a lot of misunderstanding about this. Considering just the CAFE standard, GM could sell any car it wanted, no matter how poor its mileage. But they have to sell enough cars that get high mileage so that a corporate average target is met. The target increases each year until 1985, the last year of the current CAFE legislation, which was originally written in 1975. The target mileage for 1980 is 20 mpg. For 1985, it's 27.5 mpg.

But what mileage rating does the target relate to? Is it the actual mileage the car delivers? No. Is it the EPA city rating? No. Surely, it must be the EPA highway estimate? No. It's a combination (45%/55%) of the EPA city and highway estimates, figured in 1975 to be a real world estimate. Of course, it isn't. But let's not get into that again.

The important thing is that the Corvette doesn't **have** to meet this figure, and probably won't. GM certainly will have to take a hard look at some of its high volume big lines, and weed them out as necessary (the penalty for missing the target mileage is a very, very substantial fine, escalating with the amount the target is missed). But the Corvette's volume is miniscule by comparison to usual

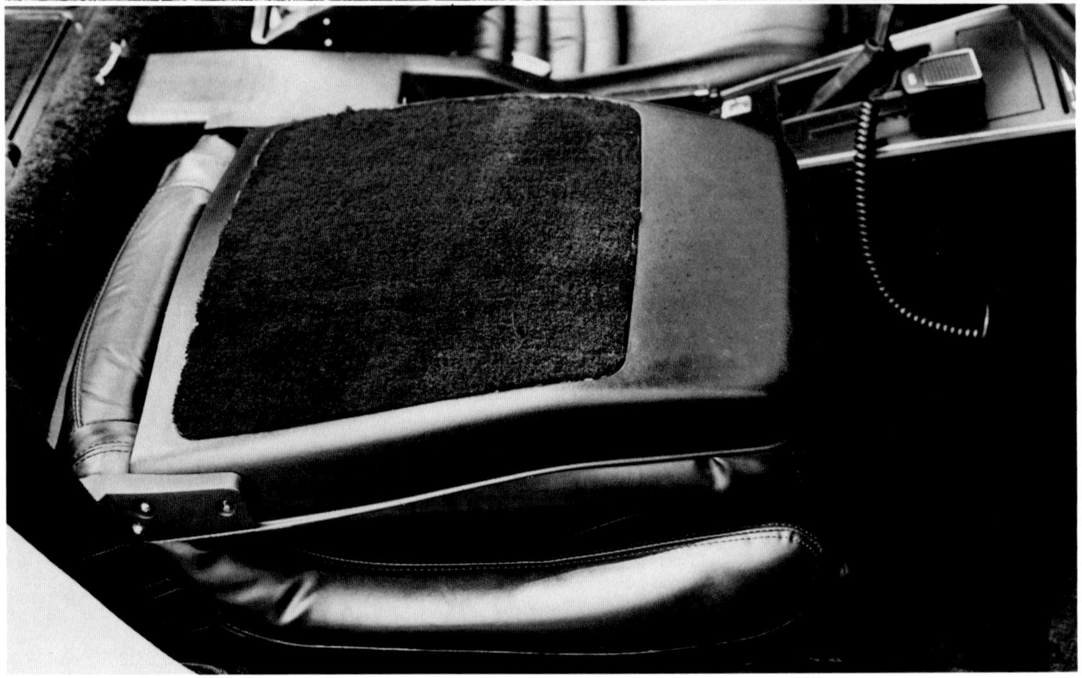

GOODYEAR
GT RADIAL

Left: *For the umteenth time, the side fender vent treatment was restyled for the 1980 Corvette.* **Right:** *New badges for the '80 include L-82 (moved from hood to side fender) and crossed flag emblems.*

GM build quantities. And the Corvette is profitable. If demand is there, GM can support it with respect to the CAFE standard, regardless of its mileage.

The gas guzzler tax is a little different story. This legislation knocked around Congress for a few years, then slipped through during the 1979 oil shortage. This tax is aimed at penalizing sales of low mileage cars by forcing the buyer to pay a tax based on the car's mileage rating. 1980 is the first year of application, and the cutoff is at 15 mpg. Above that, no tax. Below that (but not below 14 mpg) and the tax is $200. Again, this is a stairstepping affair. The mileage numbers get larger each year, as do the fines . . . oops, taxes.

McLellan sensed that the guzzler tax might be coming, and put several weight reduction programs into gear for the Corvette. They've been creeping in year after year, but in 1980, the achievements are substantial. Officially, the curb weight of the Corvette drops from 3620 pounds in 1979, to 3330 in 1980, a 290 pound reduction. Actually, the real reduction is not quite that great since part of the difference owes to the fact that the 1979 model's weight is figured with standard steel wheels, while the 1980's is with the lighter aluminum option wheels. That's not cheating, folks. Henceforth, Chevy's allowed to use the aluminum wheel model for certification, since the majority of Corvettes sold are so equipped. For what it's worth though, the aluminum wheels of the 1980 model are themselves a couple of pounds lighter than last year's aluminum wheels, thanks to some subtle redesign.

Not cheating folks

The rest of the weight savings came from, literally, all over. The thickness of the frame was reduced in some areas for a savings of roughly thirty-five pounds. The rear axle housing and rear crossmember are aluminum in the 1980 model, good for a savings of forty pounds. To improve corrosion resistance, frame components continue to be specially coated as were those of the 1979 model.

The front bumper is a new design and lighter, too. There's a lighter type "A" frame steel structure underneath, plus very light but strong "high performance" fiberglass beams under the facia and at the

L-82

CHEVROLET
USA-1

corners. The rear bumper is also a new design, employing extensive use of aluminum under the skin to kick in its share to the lightness program.

Engine News

The aluminum intake manifold which was a standard item only with the L-82 engine in 1979, has become standard with the L-48 in 1980 as well. More weight savings. Horsepower for the base L-48 engine is rated at 190. The L-82 is 230 horsepower. Interestingly, McLellan points out that both engines are very close in performance at low and mid-range use. The L-82 actually has lower torque, and sacrifices low and mid-range power for more strength at the top. The big difference in the engines is camshaft design.

For the first time, a 305 cubic-inch engine is available in a Corvette. It's available only in California. And it's all that's available in California in the 1980 Corvette. Emission standards tightened in California for 1980 models, so Chevy chose to certify only its 305 engine. But the Corvette engine is rated at 180 horsepower, only ten less than the base L-48 available in the other forty-nine states, and it's a test bed for a new innovation that might make its way into all Corvettes eventually: Tubular stainless steel exhaust manifolds.

As McLellan relates the story of the development of the stainless steel manifolds, Chevy was forced for emissions reasons to design a new exhaust manifold for California use which incorporated an oxygen sensor in a "closed loop." Since it had to be a new manifold, Chevy engineers thought it a nice opportunity to try out a stainless steel tubular design. The relatively low volume, probably somewhere around 5,000 units, is ideal for such a project. The manifolds, which involve a fair amount of hand construction, are manufactured by Walker, a prime supplier to GM of exhaust related equipment.

Optional axle ratios are gone in 1980. Only a 3.07:1 is available. Actually, two axles are used. There is a standard unit for Corvettes equipped with automatic transmissions, and a heavier-duty unit for manual transmission Corvettes. But the ratios are the same, regardless.

Outside And In

Remember those magazine covers a few years back that would always show a futuristic looking version of the Aero Vette and ask, "Is this the 1980 Corvette?" Well, it wasn't. The 1980 isn't the all-new Corvette everyone hoped for, but no one really expected. But it is a much improved Corvette. For several years in the seventies, each model year in the Corvette series got a little heavier, a little slower, and a little less nimble. Starting around 1978, the process was finally reversed, to the joy of enthusiasts everywhere. The 1980 model Corvette actually is lighter than '79, a bit faster, and even better handling.

Shedding the pounds is the key ingredient in these good tidings, but there are other reasons. In their relentless search for an ever-better tire, Chevy engineers have found another winner. Goodyear continues to be the sole source of Corvette tires, but the optional skins for 1980 are new. The new super tire is the "Eagle GT", a steel-belted radial with a side wall design not unlike the open letter "GT Radial." But the "Eagle" has a tread that lays down a track in what appears to be a series of "N" and "H" letters. Reminds you of the old "NON SKID" days. And Chevy engineers claim the Eagle duplicates skid pad performance of the fabulous Pirelli P7 of Porsche Turbo fame.

The outside of the 1980 Corvette has been freshed up with new front and rear treatment, and some new detailing. The changes to the front and rear were much more than casual facelifts, as the incorporation of the front and rear air dams resulted from many hours of experimenting in the Lockheed wind tunnel in Marietta, Georgia, and at the Canadian National Research Council facility in Ottawa. Comparing the 1980 model to a standard '79 without the add-on dams, McLellan says the drag coefficient has been reduced from .5 to .43, which is a whopping reduction considering that the car's basic configuration stayed the same. Chevy engineers figure that the reduction in drag alone is worth between .4 to .5 miles per gallon in increased fuel economy.

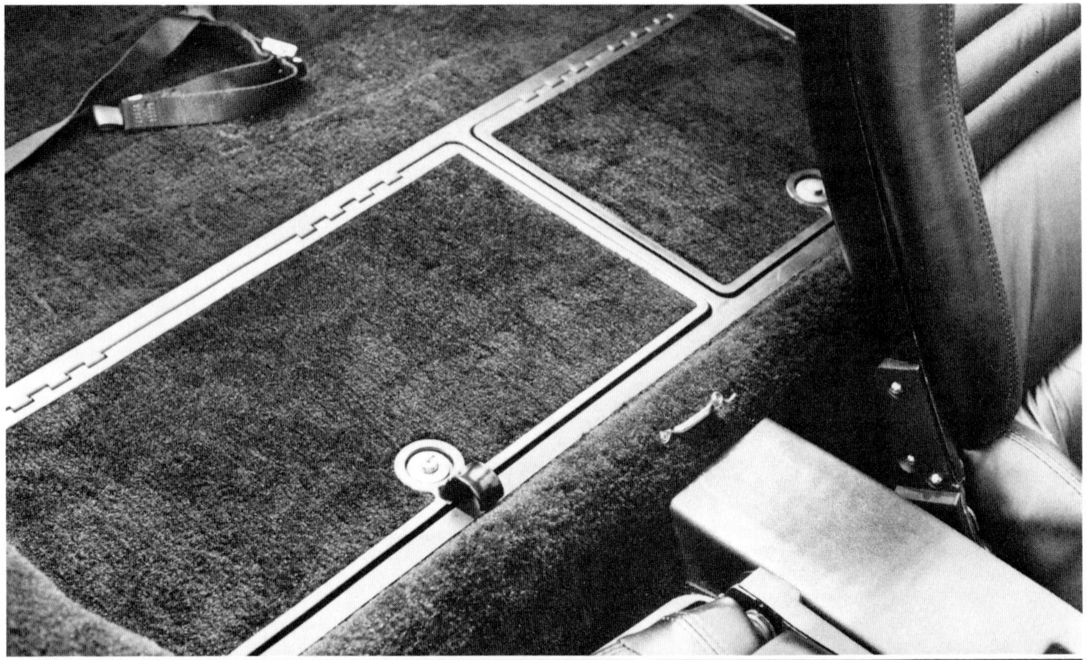

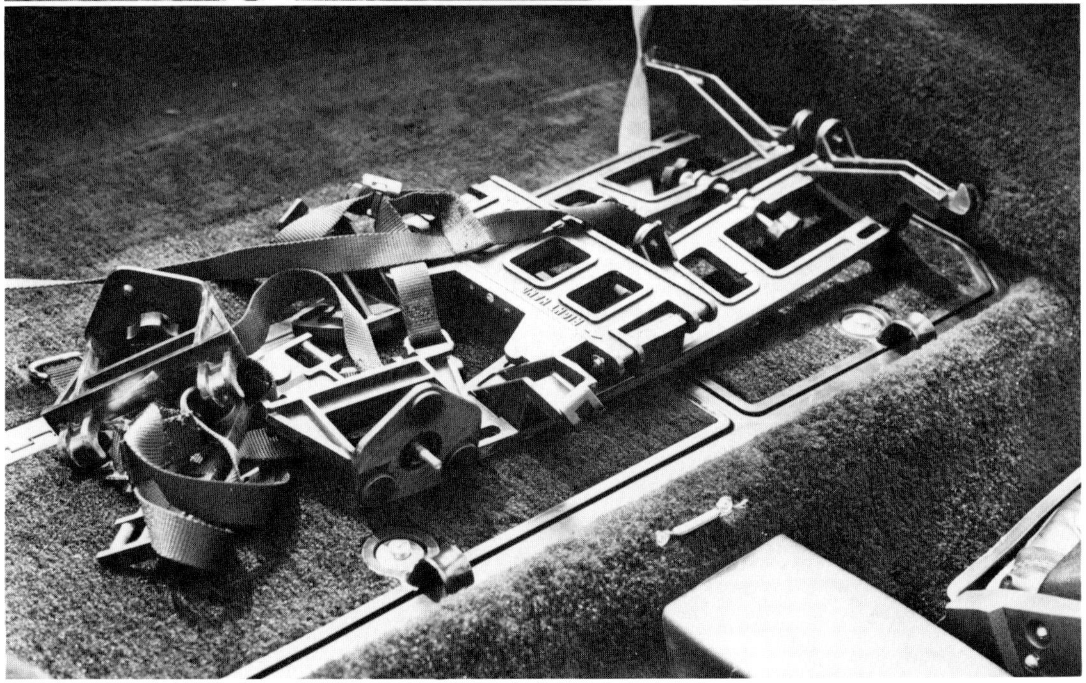

Left: *Top photo shows rear compartment and consolidation of rear storage panel lids from three to two. Bottom photo shows optional apparatus used to mount roof panels on rear deck.* **Right:** *Both front and rear of 1980 Corvette was restyled to incorporate air dams. Note mount holes for roof carrier in rear deck photo.*

1980

A top speed of 85 mph? Not really, but the feds specify that the speedometer can read no more. The government regulations are so specific that they require a detent to stop the needle at 85 mph. Take heart, the '80 Corvette does go just a bit faster.

Numero Uno

The 1980 Corvette has a new side fender vent treatment, perhaps the cleanest design ever. In fact, almost all the panels in the front end are made in a new process, though there's no way to tell that on the finished car. The process involves coating SMC panels with urethane as they are being molded. The urethane coating, usually only four or five mils thick, puts a nice glassy finish on the panel, filling pinholes and preventing later "pop" through. This is all part of Chevy's drive to improve the surface quality of new Corvettes, numero uno on buyers' complaint lists. In addition to the front end panels, the removable roof panels get the urethane treatment in the '80 model. The 1981 model gets it all over.

There isn't too much new and exciting in the Corvette cockpit. The safety march continues and the speedometer now reads a maximum of 85 mph, horror of horrors. It wasn't too long ago that 85 was just past the half-way mark. When asked what he thought of it, McLellan replied, "They didn't ask me." Translated, that means the government says it must be so. Is this really necessary?

For the trivia nuts, note that a few of the last 1979 models built also got the 85 mph speedometer.

The New Plant

The 1980 Corvette is the last to be built exclusively in St. Louis, where production has been since 1954 production began on December 28, 1953. Starting around the middle of the 1981 production Corvette model run, things will start moving to the Corvette's new facility in Bowling Green, Kentucky. Well, not exactly new. The building was formerly a Chrysler Airtemp factory. But it's a beautiful building and, with 800,000 square feet, about double the size of the old Corvette factory. GM plans to build around 8,000 Corvettes in Kentucky in 1981, then move production completely for the 1982 model.

There it is, the story of the first Corvette of the 1980's. How will history look back on this one? A milestone, a classic? Perhaps so. But at the very least, the Corvette that took the first big steps toward the new lightweight generation of Corvettes that loom on the horizon.

Credits

Cover: Letter styling by Dick Yoakam. Photography (dust jacket) by Rich Taylor. Design by Mike Antonick.

XP-819: The XP-819 is owned by Steve Tate. Text by Mike Antonick. Photos appearing on pages 8-9, 11, 16 (top right and bottom), 19, 20, 21, and 22 by Mike Antonick. Photos appearing on pages 12, 13, 16 (top left), and 17 by Paul Siminson. Photos appearing on pages 14 and 15 by Phil Tate.

1975 Convertible: The 1975 Corvette is owned by Marc Erwin. Text by Mike Antonick. Photography by Mike Antonick.

1967 L-88: The L-88 is owned by Dr. William Miller. Text by Mike Antonick. Photos appearing on pages 36, 40-41, 42-43, 44, 45, 48, 49, 51, 52, 53, 54, 55, 56-57, 58, and 60 by Dr. William Miller. Photos appearing on pages 39, 46, and 47 courtesy of General Motors Photographic.

1953-1955 Production: Text by John Amgwert. All photos provided courtesy of John Amgwert, The National Corvette Restorers' Society, and General Motors Photographic.

The Dealer Blitz: Text by Les Curtner. All photos of materials from Mr. Curtner's personal collection. Photos appearing on pages 102-103, 104, 105, 110, 111, 112, 113, 114, 116, 117, 118, 119, 120, 121, 123, 124, and 125 by Mike Antonick. Photo on page 112 by Les Curtner. Photos appearing on pages 106, 107, 108, and 109 by the Jam Handy Corporation, usage courtesy of General Motors Corporation. Use of previously copywritten materials by General Motors Corporation courtesy of General Motors Corporation.

William L. Mitchell: Lead-in text by Mike Antonick. Interview conducted by Mike Antonick. Original art for page 128 by Melbourne Brindle, courtesy of William L. Mitchell. Photography by Richard Clapp Photographic. Photo appearing on page 131 by Mike Antonick. Photos appearing on pages 132, 133, 135, 146, 147, and 162 courtesy of William L. Mitchell. Photos appearing on pages 136-137, 138, 139, 140, 141, 142, 143, 144, 145, 148, 149, 150, 151, 152-153, 155, 156, 157, 159, and 160 courtesy of General Motors Photographic.

John Z. DeLorean: Text by Mike Antonick. Interview questions by Mike Antonick. Photos appearing on pages 164, 167, 172, 176, 177, 180, 182, 188, and 189 by Gerald Williamson, courtesy DeLorean Motor Company. Photos appearing on pages 168-169, and 184-185 by Boulevard Photographic, courtesy DeLorean Motor Company. Photos appearing on page 170 courtesy of William T. Collins. Photos appearing on pages 173, 178, and 179 by Mike Antonick. Photos appearing on page 171 courtesy of General Motors Photographic. Break-away art on page 174, and artist's conception on page 187, courtesy of DeLorean Motor Company.

Corvette Labels: Text by M. F. Dobbins. Labels provided by M. F. Dobbins. Photography by Mike Antonick.

1980 Corvette: Text by Mike Antonick. Photos appearing on pages 224-225, 226, 228, 229, 230, 232, 233, and 235 by Mike Antonick. Photos appearing on pages 227, 231, and 234 courtesy of General Motors Photographic.

Great Corvette Books

from Michael Bruce Associates. Buy from your favorite local book store, Corvette dealer, or order direct from the publisher: Michael Bruce Associates Inc., Post Office Box 396, Powell, Ohio 43065.

Corvette! Sportscar of America

Corvette! Sportscar of America combines a large (10¼″ x 8⅜″) horizontal page format with striking photography and fine layout design to produce a truly beautiful auto publication.

Coverage includes a section on great Corvettes of the past, interviews with personalities who played direct roles in shaping the Corvette's destiny, an incredibly detailed account of Corvette factory production during its first three years (1953-1955), an informative look at the scores of labels used on Corvettes through the years, a chapter devoted to the literature, films and other items used by Chevrolet dealers to promote the Corvette, and much more, all lavishly illustrated in over 250 photos and illustrations, many in full color.

Corvette! Sportscar of America is hardbound in black with silver embossing, and is protected by a coated paper dust jacket. A deluxe package is also available which has the same book but substitutes a hard slip case for the dust jacket, and includes a set of eight 8″ x 10″ selected prints for framing.

PRICE: $34.50 ($44.50 with hard case and framing prints)

Corvette! America's Only

This is the contemporary Corvette book, the book that every Corvette enthusiast can relate to. It has the proper balance of what happened in 1952 when the Corvette dream was first forming, to what happens today. It opens previously closed doors of GM Styling and Engineering, yet includes the exterior world of Corvette concours shows, auctions, and swap meets.

Its 144, 7$^{1}/_{2}$" x 9" pages open horizontally for maximum subject display. There are over 160 photos and styling renderings, many in full color. Chapters are titled The Creators, The Racers, The Stylists, The Mania Explosion, and The Favorites. A special Facts section lists options, option costs, number codes, and numerous other details never before compiled so completely and so clearly. All years from 1953 through 1978 are included.

Corvette! America's Only is written and presented in a manner which informs rather than intimidates, entertains rather than bores.

The standard version is hardbound in silver metallic with blue and red embossing. A deluxe hardbound leather edition is also available. The deluxe book is handbound in black calfskin with gold embossing, and is a strictly limited offering of just 300 copies, each sequentially numbered.

PRICE: $22.50 ($50.00 for leather edition)

The Corvette Black Book

The Corvette Black Book is that little book you've been waiting for. Nothing frustrates the Corvette enthusiast more than not being able to find information when needed. **The Corvette Black Book** jams loads of facts about every Corvette year from 1953 through 1978 into 60 pages that measure just 4" x 6$^{3}/_{4}$". Included are options, option costs, colors, codes, ID numbers, and much more. This isn't just a conglomeration of someone else's charts and figures. We assembled the whole thing. Some of the info you may find elsewhere, much of it you won't. For sure, you'll not find it presented so clearly anywhere else. And its handy size permits it to be carried in pocket, purse, or glove box.

Pains were taken to make this as accurate as possible. Prior to printing, proofs were sent to several of the leading Corvette experts in the country for examination. Change after change resulted in a thing of beauty, factually speaking, to behold. All this, and quality paper and printing too. You need this.

PRICE: $5.00

Notice: This publication is not in any way connected with the "**Black Book**" published by National Auto Research Publications, Inc.